I0568297

MINDSET OF
THE WINNERS

The Big 4 in 1 Book for Unlimited Success in Life:

Changing Habits | Setting Goals | Building
Mental Strength | Stopping Procrastination

by

Patrick Drechsler

© **Copyright 2022 – All rights reserved.**

The content contained in this book may not be reproduced, duplicated or transmitted without the direct written permission of the author or publisher.

Under no circumstances will the publisher or author be blamed or held legally responsible for any damages, recovery or financial loss due directly or indirectly to the information contained in this book.

Legal notice:

This book is copyrighted and intended for personal use only. The reader may not modify, distribute, sell, use, quote, or paraphrase any of the contents of this book without the permission of the author or publisher.

Disclaimer:

Please note that the information contained in this document is for educational and entertainment purposes only. Every effort has been made to provide accurate, current, reliable and complete information. No warranties of any kind are stated or implied.

Readers acknowledge that the author is not providing legal, financial, medical or professional advice. By reading this document, the reader agrees that under no circumstances will the author be liable for any direct or indirect loss arising from the use of the information contained in this document, including but not limited to errors, omissions or inaccuracies

Books

WINNERS' HABITS

3 Steps to Powerful Success Routines

Exercise More, Live Healthier, Work More Productively, and Have Better Relationships

by

Patrick Drechsler

Table of Contents

Introduction

The neighbor again!

He must have gotten up at 5 a.m. for his morning exercise as usual. There's no other way to explain why his music resounds so penetratingly through the walls and reaches you in bed. You pull the covers over your head and just want to sleep on. After your day finally begins at 10 a.m., you meet him outside while taking out the trash and he's bursting with *joie de vivre*. He proudly tells you that he's spending his Sunday working on a dream project, and that he will soon be able to quit his day job and make a living from his hobby instead. He even believes he is on his way to financial freedom.

Is he crazy? Or is he just attracting success with his positive habits, getting closer to a dream that seems almost inconceivable to you because your own, self-destructive habits are getting the better of you? You feel like you are stuck on the hamster wheel in a job you don't like with monotonous free time, because you are not very open to new hobbies and interests.

Why is it that some people create a happy and cohesive family life and do great things together, while others barely talk to each other and watch TV?

I too was trapped on my personal hamster wheel for a long time before I figured out which principles lead to success. I had a well-paid job as a lecturer, but it offered few opportunities for career advancement. The topics I presented were always the same. I didn't really know what to do with my days off as I lacked a positive outlook. I got into the habit of doing things that didn't help the situation. I slept late, and before I knew it the day was half over. During breaks from lectures, I always ate the bad canteen food. When I didn't feel like that anymore, I switched to snacking, and even quit sports. *If I eat an unhealthy diet, I won't be able to do any sport anyway...* I thought to myself, as one negative thing led to another. Eventually, reading numerous books, plus some other experiences, helped me form more positive habits. Sports came back into my life, while healthy eating, and getting up early became easier. Thanks to learning how to cultivate positive habits, I got involved in an environmental protection association, in addition to my career. Even though my futureless job remained at first, life around it changed for the better. In the end, even my profession was positive, as I focused on the good aspects of it, and developed more pleasure in my work.

It is not for nothing that the statement, "we humans are creatures of habit" has been a German proverb for decades. What humans do, they do to a large extent, out of habit. But what is a habit anyway?

A habit can be described as "acquired behaviors that are difficult to resist." But habits aren't just about behavioral patterns, they are acquired ways of thinking too. Because before the action always comes the thought pattern. A person can acquire as many habits that promote success as he wants if he could only just be aware of this.

To this end, a large part of this guide is devoted to the question of how to reprogram your thinking and align it with your goals. Several practical exercises are included that will help you acquire a positive attitude towards life. Scientific evidence, and many interesting theories, will show you how important and powerful, a positive attitude is.

After learning to retrain your thoughts, the book will focus on retraining your habits through exercises laid out in the later chapters. There is plenty of support and guidance to help you find your own unique path to success. After all, every person has his own view of what success actually is.

The exercises will show you how to build useful habits through reward setting, which can be practiced repeatedly until your life starts to transform. When these useful habits are combined with the elimination of negative habits, you get closer to your goal of becoming successful.

A lot of people believe that the way to change your life habits is to consciously resist a bad habit until it is gone, but this can actually be quite challenging because it's so easy to give in as soon as a small negative event occurs in your life, unless you have worked at it with the proper strategies as described in this book.

Here is a list of some of the questions you might be thinking about right now:

- ➢ How do I manage to establish a basic positive attitude?
- ➢ Which habits help me to achieve this?
- ➢ How do I ensure sustainability in my habit changes?
- ➢ How do I find out what success means to me personally?

➤ What are my priorities?

➤ What do I need to motivate myself at the beginning, during, and after the transition to a new me?

➤ Do I need to be disciplined?

➤ How do I determine which actions will lead me to success?

➤ What methods do I use to fight negative habits and establish positive ones?

➤ Can special products help?

➤ Which habits are particularly well-known and recommended?

➤ Which micro habits are universally transferable?

This book will answer all of these questions and put you in an informed position, so that you will be able to choose your path forward to having successful habits that transform your life.

What does success mean to you?

Opinions differ on the definition of success. Some take the easy way out and talk about achievement in the sense of increased assets, fit bodies, and other external factors that can be measured by the opinions of other people, or the standards of society. While others understand that internal success is defined solely by their own criteria.

Those who have inner success as a goal tend prioritize their own desires and choose activities that correspond to their own real interests. While those who aspire towards external success will be guided by the ideas of other people. Keep in mind that you interact with many different people in your life, each with his own idea of what success is. So, you can never succeed in satisfying everyone around you and perpetual external success becomes unrealistic in the long run.

If you prioritize your own interests, desires, and goals, the probability of succeeding is higher because you will have more motivation. Undoubtedly, there will be decisions, here and there in life, where you will also have to follow the interests of other people, like making decisions at the board level of a company, planning a vacation with your partner, and so on. So, we will also focus on that later in the book, but for now the focus is completely on you. Define inner success for yourself!

My wishes, my goals, my interests - my success!

If you want to find out which goals reflect inner success for you, you have to pay attention to your feelings. Feelings, just like habits, come from within and are shaped by our past experiences. Feelings can actually *be* a form of habit. For example, if you are used to being a "couch potato" every night, watching TV on the sofa, and consuming pizza and Coca-Cola, this will make you feel good and safe for now. It can be a way of rewarding a hard day at work. But the feelings in that moment are not everything.

Start listening to your thoughts and feelings when you are away from those moments. It is not uncommon for overweight people to feel good whilst consuming unhealthy foods, because they are giving in to an urge, and getting gratification from it. But this satisfaction is only temporary, as are the feelings. In the many other situations during the course of a day, negative feelings are not uncommon among overweight people because:

➤ Mocking looks in public cause discomfort.
➤ Possible health issues cause anxiety and insecurity.
➤ More barriers to the realization of one's own goals, e.g., cannot wear desired wardrobe or pursue desired activity.
➤ Looking in the mirror causes dissatisfaction.
➤ Lack of mobility as time passes.

The situation is similar in other areas:

➤ Partnership: When you are spending time with your partner, and you watch TV together in the evening as a form of relaxation. But you end up spending every evening together in the same way, because it has become a habit. If you go purely by the moment, you feel happy. But, if you think about it more deeply, you realize that this monotonous evening routine is actually making you unhappy, because you aren't fulfilling your deeper desires. It's time to make a change, but you only realize the need for change when you question yourself on a deeper level.

➢ Occupation: You have been working in your chosen profession for twelve years now; things are automated, and undemanding. Every day you perform your duty and go about your daily routine. At heart you are a varied, articulate, and adventurous person. Generally, you are happy all round, although your job is more of a necessary means to finance your life than anything else. When you take a close look at your feelings, you realize how dissatisfied you really are with your job, and that all you need is a new career for a perfect life. You will come to this realization if you regularly sit down in peace and reflect on the feelings that your job gives you throughout the day.

➢ Education / Study: Your entire family works in the industry in which you are now to train / study. Your family takes your career path for granted, so you choose it according to them despite having many other talents. As a result, your performance leaves a lot to be desired. But because you regularly reflect, you realize early on that the path you have chosen is not the right one for you, which is why your performance is lacking. You then change to another training program or another course of study.

There are many secrets lying dormant in us human beings. And while secrets from other people can have a protective effect, the secrets we keep from ourselves lead to unhappiness, because we run the risk of making decisions that are not in accordance with our real desires. Consequently, our actions will be marked by lower motivation.

Am I really a career person or more of a family person?

Do I want to achieve success only in terms of sports and health because I am already satisfied in all other areas of life?

Is it important for me to include external success, at least in part, because I owe a lot to my parents and want to make them proud?

You should think carefully about the answers to these questions. How to understand your own thoughts and emotions correctly and make the right decisions, will be explained often throughout the book. It is important that you are attentive and open to it. Because lasting inner happiness and success is only possible if you reflect and find for yourself what your heart and mind truly desire.

Find suitable habits for your own success

Every positive habit has its benefits. Some habits can even promote success in multiple ways. At this point we will make a distinction between macro, and micro habits. Macro habits are relatively general, like healthy eating. Micro habits are more specific, like eating fruit twice every night.

If you want to acquire habits that bring success, the best way is usually through micro habits. You select several micro habits that combine into one big macro habit. This macro habit is usually synonymous with your goal or at least a big part of it.

Finding suitable habits for your own success, means nothing other than considering which habits contribute to achieving your goal. The goal is defined beforehand, through comprehensive consideration. To achieve the goal, both types of habits are important, with the small ones coming mostly at the beginning. If you were to use only macro habits to make the changes however, you would find the process more difficult, because you could fall back into old behavioral patterns.

Here, are three examples of useful micro habits, that ensure that this doesn't happen:

1. Your goal is to use your day more effectively and avoid wasting so much time.
   Useful micro habits: Getting up earlier, making small to-do lists, and writing diaries. Bigger habits would be getting up very early (several hours earlier than usual) or keeping a detailed schedule for the day.
2. You set yourself the goal of reducing stress in everyday life and taking more time for yourself.
   Useful micro habits: Set up break times in your daily routine that you strictly adhere to and switch off digital media and chat programs in the evening. Macro habits include meditating regularly every day and doing a regular "digital detox" for several days or hours each week.
3. You feel you are too ungrateful in your life for the privileges you enjoy compared to others from less affluent regions of the world.

Useful micro habits: Start keeping a list of what you are grateful for at the end of each day. The extension of this micro habit are macro habits such as building an environment of positive people around you, and meeting with them regularly. Their positive and grateful attitude toward life can influence you in a purposeful way.

Note: This guidebook wants to support you on your individual path. Accordingly, there will be no rigid guidelines on what you have to do to succeed. Rather, you can expect a customizable collection of ideas and methods. Among them are habits that have great potential to promote success. One of these habits is to keep your thoughts and feelings optimistic. You will learn how to do this, and why it is important, in the third chapter. But first, we will focus on the findings and theories about the properties of habits, in order to understand why negative habits tend to be so ingrained, despite the fact that positive habits lead you to success more easily.

The nature of habits

How do habits develop?

Even though the research on habits has few really robust theses, at least several similarly insightful, smaller approaches exist.

All of the types of habits presented in this guidebook recognize certain triggers as their cause. These triggers reflect our attitude towards life and are the motivation to perform certain actions. Triggers that start with our own negative emotions (e.g., doubts, fears, laziness etc.) lead to the development, and consolidation of negative habits. These habits carry over to other areas of life, so they partially shape our character. As an old Chinese proverb says, "Watch your thoughts, for they become words. Watch your words, for they become actions. Watch your actions, for they become habits. Watch your habits, for they become your character. Watch your character, for it becomes your destiny."

Negative habits highlight certain basic negative attitudes that should be changed in order to get closer to personal success. The more of these negative triggers are present, the more strongly habits become anchored, until at some point they become automated. These automations are success killers. While positive habits on the other hand, make success much more likely.

Four processes that establish habits

In his work *The 1% Method* (2020), James Clear, who is now considered an expert on habits, describes the processes that foster them. He identifies triggers, cravings, routines, and rewards as the driving forces of habits, precisely in that order. While the first process made a habit arise, the further processes would gradually contribute to its consolidation, according to the author.

The processes can apply to both positive and negative habits as we will highlight by comparing the habit of going out partying every weekend and being regularly involved in an association.

Trigger

Attending a party, and consuming alcohol brings people together on the one hand, and lifts barriers on the other. The mood becomes more relaxed, the sense of shame decreases, and everyone is on the same level.

Registering in a non-profit association gets you involved with other people, while contributing to a cause that is close to your heart. The common interest also removes barriers to socializing.

Request

The second process in Clear's model, occurs when a thing appears desirable. This happens precisely when value is added by the trigger. A person who takes it a little too easy at their first party and embarrasses themselves to the bone (possibly even ending up in the hospital with alcohol poisoning and having to meekly explain themselves to mom and dad), will not develop a great desire for parties, at least for a while. The risk of getting used to parties every weekend and maintaining one's circle of friends only when drunk, decreases. On the other hand, the feeling of increased self-confidence and exuberance, due to drinking at parties, can lead to drinking regularly or in larger amounts. A "consolidated circle of friends" can develop in this environment which pre-programs a negative habit.

In contrast, a positive habit can develop in the case of charitable activities in an association, if the mood is good and the club's objectives are achieved. Such activities are often perceived positively by the public, which creates additional value and can strengthen the desire to make a habit out of it.

Routine

Routine ensures that the respective habit can be practiced more easily so the process becomes automated. In the context of our examples: Through acquired friends at parties, networking increases and on the way to the party there are agreements in the group on a different driver who does not drink alcohol. The same applies to associations, where carpooling is used on excursions or out-of-town commitments, private appointments etc.

Reward

Reward, the 4th and final process, provides even more incentive to repeat a habit. In the case of parties, being known as gregarious, or even the king of the party, can be perceived as a reward. In the association, rewards depend on the particular field of activity. For example, if you are in a group for nature lovers, and you have participated in the creation of new green areas in the city, you will have a visual reward every time you pass the area. In a sports club, the trophies and medals would be satisfying evidence of your success. Perhaps, in addition, you will meet a person with whom you develop a special friendship, and you will benefit from a social contact and more support in your life.

What you can take away from Clear's model

Clear's model breaks our habits down into processes to help us understand the nature of the habit, identify how strong it is engrained in us and how it got there. It also shows us how to replace negative habits with more positive ones. After all, if you can make something attractive and reward yourself for it, you can also make something else unattractive and punish yourself for it.

Lewin model of change

Kurt Lewin's model of change explains how to develop new behavioral patterns through the displacement of old ones:

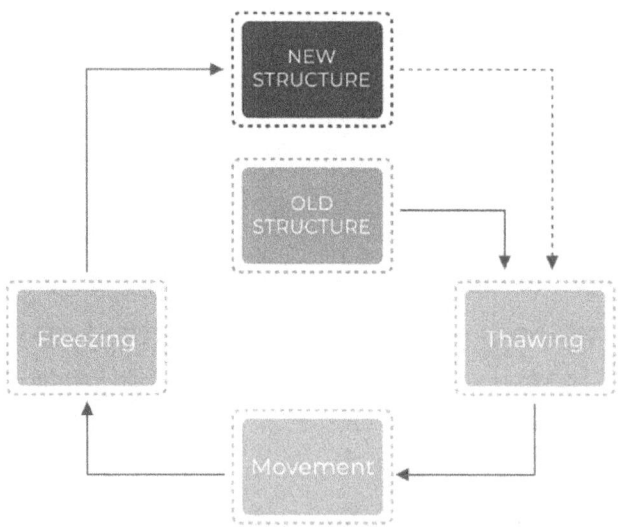

Figure 1: Lewin model of change

Starting point difficult to overcome

Old structures that prevail in a person serve as the basis and starting point of this model. You may consider the old structures as your current habits which you wish to replace by new structures or better habits.

According to Lewin, the individuals concerned are often aware that a behavior needs to be changed. However, he said, emotions are an obstacle, because of the deep-seated predisposition to habit. Since everyday processes would need to change, insecurities would arise. These are unwarranted, according to Lewin, because the goal is never to make complete changes. Instead, the goal is to change part of one's habits step by step, in order to adapt to the environment, expand one's own behavioral repertoire and, in the long term, master the complete change of habits.

1st phase: thawing

If one equates negative habits with a block of ice, in order to enable a change in behavior, thawing would be the appropriate means. Thawing is the process of gaining the motivation to change the behavior. You may assume that you are already, at least partially, in this phase, because if you hadn't identified a problem, you probably wouldn't be reading this guidebook.

Thawing encourages people to confront their negative habits. The process is set in motion by recognizing that their previous habits are not purposeful. Failures, dissatisfaction, loneliness and similar negative states or regularly recurring events, and serve as the motivation for a change of behavior, once highlighted.

Phase 2: Movement

As soon as something is in motion, something is happening; actions lead to change. Lewin's approach is about trial and error, until the best approach can be found for each person.

Phase 3: Freezing

Lewin's model describes freezing as a phase of change. Should a change increasingly become habitual, it would be frozen and become a new structure. Freezing he says, requires a change that has been successfully accomplished. It is tantamount to the acquisition of a new habit. Lewin argues, that looking back at the old structures and making clear the added values of the new structures, promotes the sustainability of the change. This leads to a stabilization of the new state.

What you can take away from Lewin's model

Lewin's model primarily addresses the process of habituation, which is a useful extension to Clear's model that highlights the formation of habits. Parallels between the 2 models exist in that habits are considered deeply embedded in the person in both cases. Lewin refers incidentally to the role of emotions in change, whereas Clear goes into particular depth here, providing an explanation of how the emotional significance of habit occurs. A change in the affected person's view of the old, or existing structures, is necessary in both models, to establish new and more beneficial structures. Although the 2 authors did not work together, both models complement each other extremely well.

In the following chapters of this book, the insights from Lewin's model will help you to make the transition process more effective. By means of practical exercises, you will be given sustainable concepts for making the transition successful over the long term. If everything works out, you won't just be riding the wave of success for a short time, but as often, and for as long, as you want.

Habit loop: Scientifically based

Very briefly, we will now discuss the habit loop model, as it is largely similar to that of Clear. What differentiates the habit loop is that it triggers rewards and cravings that are increasingly related to each other:

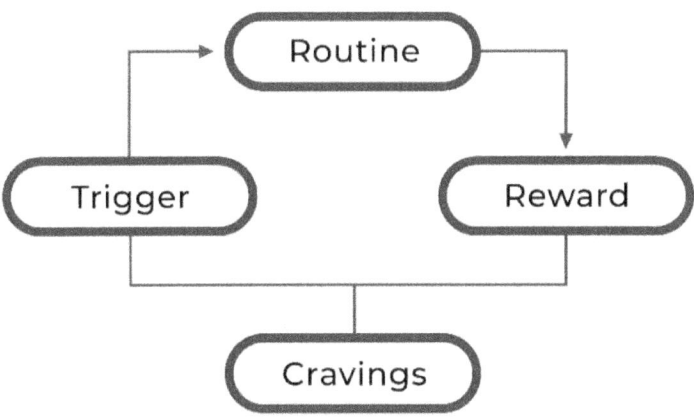

Figure 2: Habit loop model

In contrast to Clear, who sees craving as a second process in the habit loop, craving as a trigger, and longing for the reward, are given more emphasis. This underscores the powerful impact of human emotions in the context of habits; after all, craving, as a combination of the words "crave" and "addiction," is a deeply rooted emotion. To feel longing is to be addicted to something. So, the habit loop emphasizes the intensity of craving, which is why Chapter 3 places a high priority on controlling your emotions. Appropriate exercises will help you to become master of your emotions and to use this purposefully for changes of habit.

How much time does it take to get used to the new system?

You may have heard, through your own research on the Internet, in books, or in conversations, that changes of habit generally take 21 days. A negative habit would have to be replaced by a positive one, and this positive habit would have to be practiced for 21 days in order to get used to it. Where this time estimate comes from and what it is based on is not known. One possible origin could be the best-selling book *Psycho-Cybernetics* (1960) by Dr. Maxwell Maltz. The author, a plastic surgeon, performed cosmetic surgery on patients who still disliked their appearance immediately afterwards. About 21 days after surgery, however, they were happier with their appearance, he said. The doctor attributed this to the patients getting used to a certain self-image they had of themselves. They had been used to being dissatisfied with their visual appearance. In addition to this "habit" (Dr. Maxwell Maltz never uses the word "habit" in his book; note), he observed how patients suffered from phantom limb pain for up to 21 days after amputations too.

The reasoning is that Dr. Maltz's practical experiences may have been picked up by habit theorists and applied to habit research. This seems plausible. It could be that after 21 days, for certain types of habits, a change of habit is successfully accomplished but there is no guarantee of this. Instead, it would be better to assume that a change of habit will take more time.

The extent of the habit, the type of habit, and your individual character, all affect how quickly you change from a negative to a positive behavioral pattern.

- ➤ **Extent of habit**: Habits that you have already cultivated for several years, or decades are more difficult to displace than fresh habits. Especially habits that brought you positive things in earlier times have a nostalgic or emotionally high value that is difficult to dislodge.

- ➤ **Type of habit**: A habit may be closely linked to worldview. Such habits of cultural, religious, or experiential value are persistent. They require a partial adjustment of one's character. In contrast, there are habits that are hardly linked to beliefs, but which you already know are disadvantageous. Here, readjustment is easier.

- ➤ **Your character**: You will have a very unique attitude, especially toward the practical tasks that begin in the second chapter of this book. One person will think the exercises are silly, while another will get down to business with fervor. This much can be said: The person who is the most willing at the beginning, and who cooperates the most, will make the fastest progress.

At best, you're looking at an adjustment period of several months. A recent British study conducted by Lally, Cornelia et al. (2009), which included 96 participants, and was about getting used to morning exercise and healthy food and drink, found: that the subjects needed between 18 and 254 days, until they had reached a stable level of habituation. Only then could there be talk of a new habit. The mean value for the habit was a duration of 66 days. Since then, some other sources have also reported 66 days as an average timespan for the formation of new habits.

Step 1: Conversion begins in the mind

Our actions lead to success. If you look at all the movers and shakers who are attracting attention these days, you won't be able to avoid the conclusion that their reputation is due to actions.

Elon Musk is admired by some people, not because he talks about revolutionary business ideas, but because he puts them into practice against all odds. In China, they are partially changing the laws for Musk, and in the USA, the Corona regulations for his factories were relaxed. When things get tight for one of his companies, he is the first to work night shifts at the factory and treat his stress-related sleep problems with pills. None of this is sustainable or healthy, but it *is* success at first glance.

Greta Thunberg's success can be traced back to her habit of sitting in front of the Parliament building every Friday. Her persistence, and unwillingness to compromise even in front of the world's greatest politicians and personalities, paved the way for the visible results her movement for environmental protection is achieving.

Even if you look further back and take a closer look at the origin of Germany, you will see in Charlemagne a man who entered the history books through his actions. He proselytized the Saxons and expanded his Frankish empire. Driven by the mission to expand Christianity, his career took him to the gates of Rome, where he had himself crowned emperor, as a German king. This was the beginning of the Holy Roman Empire, which only came to an end after almost 1,000 years at the hands of Napoleon Bonaparte.

You can think what you want about these people. However, they were or are, undoubtedly successful in their own way. Actions led them to success. But human actions are preceded by something: thoughts. These are accompanied by another large and difficult to control component, namely feelings. Successful actions do not come out of nowhere. They come from a combination of thoughts and feelings.

In order to establish habits in the long term and in a goal-oriented manner, you should work your way through, step by step to the actions. This approach requires that you first deal with the upstream system, the thoughts and feelings. This system must be trimmed to success by habit, so that you can also make the actions successful with full conviction.

This is also illustrated by the three personal examples given above: Elon Musk became aware of inequalities during his childhood at the time of apartheid – he was born in South Africa – whereupon he made it his goal to want to change the world. His deeply held beliefs led to thoughts and feelings that made him stick to his goals and take action. Greta Thunberg's unwillingness to compromise and persistence are due in part to her illness, which has a considerable influence on her thoughts, and makes it almost impossible for her to weigh up differentiated arguments. Greta Thunberg will probably always pursue her goals with everything that makes her tick. Charlemagne, on the other hand, according to historical lore, met the Pope in early childhood. His vow to proselytize the pagans into Christians and to spread the Christian faith, as well as his irrepressible faith in God, led him to have the fixed conviction that he had to extend Christianity by all means in his power. And so it came to pass.

Feelings and thoughts come at the beginning. To retrain them and make them successful is the key to a simplified practice. Exercises exist for retraining thoughts, but the brain is too complex to be reprogrammed as desired by a few simple exercises alone. Therefore, let's first take a look at how the brain works.

Feeling, thinking, sensing, acting

In his work *Fühlen, Denken, Handeln: How the Brain Controls Our Behavior* (2001), Professor Gerhard Roth describes how the human brain functions, leading to action via emotions and thoughts. In an article published by *Deutschlandfunk*, the author, Matthias Eckoldt remarks that Roth's work should actually be called "Fühlen, Denken, Fühlen, Handeln" (Feeling, Thinking, Sensing, Acting). He justifies his suggestion with Roth's statements that the limbic system of the human brain, which is responsible for emotions, has the first and the last word in decisions related to the execution of actions.

To illustrate this with an example: A dangerous animal sprints towards a human being. The latter first reacts on the basis of his experiences, which make it clear to him that it is a dangerous situation. The first thing that comes up, is not the thought of what animal it is and whether it is white with orange stripes, or orange with white stripes. Instead, fear immediately shoots into his consciousness, from which the first reactions of the human body occur; the pulse and breathing accelerate to increase the oxygen supply and prepare for escape. In this extreme situation, the feelings are so dominant that thoughts – that is, reason and the use of one's knowledge – do not come into play at all. Instead, the feeling of fear dominates, and flight is chosen. This confirms Roth's assertion that feelings have the last word.

On the other hand, let's take another situation that is less extreme: The alarm clock rings at 5 a.m. Anke L. has no desire to get up. The desire for comfort, contentment, a sense of well-being and other pleasant feelings would be responsible for turning off the alarm clock and continuing to sleep. But Anke L. has, if she is not too sleepy, the opportunity and time to use her reason. She decides to defy her feelings based on valid arguments (e.g., going to work, taking children to school). However, she cannot help but notice, that while she is defying these feelings, they are still present and want to persuade her to go back to bed and continue sleeping. Again, Roth's assertion is confirmed: although the person makes a decision contrary to her feelings, the feelings are present both before and after the decision.

In every situation in which you fight your feelings with reason, try to observe how strong the power of your feelings is. It is different for each person. Some people are even able to put their feelings aside completely. These people are usually called disciplined. Other people have to fight harder against what is popularly called the "inner pig dog".

Did you know?

The cerebrum accounts for 85% of the total brain mass. It is surrounded by the cerebral cortex. This is also referred to as the cortex. The neocortex has the highest share of the cortex, at 90%.

It has developed during the course of the evolution of the human sensory organs. Among other things, the limbic system is located here, which controls the development of emotions, and drives behavior, as well as the release of some hormones. It has been proven that signals from the outside world are first processed in the limbic system. Only further processing in the upstream brain regions, which are decisive for the formation of the human mind, leads to a balancing of the emotional and rational aspects. This is how humans arrive at their actions – first via emotions and then via thoughts.

Knowledge about the physiological processes in the brain explains why thoughts and feelings play such an important role in determining actions. But why the feelings with certain persons in certain situation, come to bear and gives way to reason, isn't answered. Here other components must be included, which are revealed with a deeper look at the human consciousness.

Subconscious: Deep anchoring of beliefs

Placebos. Placebo. Deception. When a placebo works, it achieves a desired effect without administering a drug that would normally be necessary. It is a placebo without any efficacy. And yet it works: If a patient is in pain and is administered a placebo without knowing that it is one, the patient's expectation of efficacy sometimes produces the intended effect. It relieves pain or otherwise contributes to improvement in some patients, even though it is not supposed to do so. The medical reason for this is that the patient's expectations and accompanying beliefs cause them to release hormones that reduce pain.

Research has found that the body already releases dopamine and endogenous opioids at the level of the spinal cord to relieve pain. In research done in the 1970s, it was recognized that after the placebo effect had occurred, the administration of an opioid antagonist (an agent that inhibits the release of opioids; note) inhibited the placebo effect.

Man is able to initiate corresponding processes in the body just by believing in an effect. This impression is reinforced by the fact that, in addition to placebos, there are also nocebos. Nocebos are medications that contain an active ingredient but do not produce the intended effect.

Why do things sometimes go one way, sometimes another? Why does one body respond to medication, but not the other? In some cases, there are medical reasons. They can be non-responders for various reasons: The body simply does not respond to the respective active ingredient because, for example, it lacks enzymes, or because a (further) disease prevents it. But nocebos would not be called nocebos if they could be explained by the facts just described. One speaks of nocebos only if the drug should work on the respective person but does not. Science is in the habit of giving a name to phenomena. The cause of these phenomena probably lies in the place where you also develop positive habits in your thoughts: the subconscious.

What is the subconscious mind? Does it even exist?

There are few scientifically reliable statements about the human subconscious. In contrast to the limbic system, which can be measured by hormone release, the subconscious is a kind of mystery. The question arises whether the subconscious even exists.

Modern cognitive psychology and brain research describes the subconscious, in short, as an accumulation of processes in the brain that take place so quickly that only the results of thoughts become conscious, but not the individual steps that led to the results, such as a certain action or the pronunciation of certain words. According to the theory, the background of the subconscious is automation processes within the human brain, which serve to reduce energy consumption and simplify thought processes. There is also the theory of Sigmund Freud, who connects the subconscious with repressed drive representations.

This book follows the thesis of modern cognitive psychology and brain research, which describes the subconscious mind as rapidly running processes. This thesis is now contrasted with the theories of scientists who believe that there is no subconscious. The facts are as follows: No, there is no subconscious that can be clearly located in the brain and proven by means of measurements; at least not according to the current state of research. There is no clear proof that subconscious processes take place, which is widely criticized by researchers. Professor Nick Chater of the British Warwick Business School, for example, points to the lack of evidence for an existing subconscious. There is no evidence that, while we are thinking about one thing, other thought processes are going on somewhere inside us, Chater says. This is the radical view of a science that dwells only on solid evidence.

Now please think about the following situations and judge for yourself whether there might be some form of subconsciousness after all:

➢ Have you ever made your way to school, university, work, a friend's house, or another frequently visited place without having to think about the route?

➢ Have you ever succeeded in instinctively giving a correct answer to a question even though you were mentally absent?

➢ Have you succeeded in movements or workflows without thinking about them in more detail?

One of these cases has certainly occurred before in your life. We call them automatisms: The human being performs something frequently; knows it off the top of his head. Which is why he masters the correct execution right away, regardless of whether he is currently mentally present or not.

Now the bow is drawn to the pessimists and optimists of the world, who steer their thoughts in a negative or positive direction by force of habit. It is noticeable that some people are gifted in seeing disadvantages in all things. They almost automatically have a negative basic attitude no matter how desirable a positive attitude could be. Observe this best with yourself or in your circle of acquaintances. How many people maintain a positive approach and in which circumstances, and how many tend to be more negative?

There is no subconscious that can be anatomically or physiologically located in the brain as functionally demonstrated. But the subconscious exists as a term for processes and basic attitudes that are deeply rooted in us. Nocebos, placebos, optimistically and pessimistically attuned people, automated flawless actions with simultaneous mental absence and many other occurrences are proof to the existence of a kind of consciousness that lies hidden deep within us and that controls us to some extent. Therefore, the subconscious also controls success somehow too.

Did you know?

Few scientists dare to look for scientifically tenable explanations as to how the subconscious could contribute to an improvement in external circumstances through a positive basic attitude. The idea that one can influence the environment through positive thoughts seems too romantic. One, at least interesting effort, is that of Dr. Ulrich Warnke, who assesses the influencing of the immediate environment with physical forces. Allegedly, the nerves and muscles responsible for speech and action contribute to the creation of action potentials. It is known that through the brain – and the thoughts and mind that control it – signals are sent through the body to cause movements of the mouth when talking, or other parts of the body during other activities. Molecules have an elementary function in this process, he said. Molecules are composed of protein compounds that are influenced and changed by the mind. Besides, it is certain that the molecule connections are influenced by electrons which have a certain rotation – called "spin". Just like the molecular compounds, spin would be influenced by consciousness and thoughts. Because the energy of the human being could work outward, it is a certainty for Warnke that the human being influences matter outside of his body through the mind.

Scientific theses such as those of Dr. Ulrich Warnke venture into a field that attempts to fathom the effect of a possibly existing subconscious, by means of logical and known physical processes. First of all, there is the realization that there is something slumbering in man that influences his thoughts and actions. It works conspicuously fast and far away from our control; automated if you will. It was given the name subconscious. The existence of numerous best-sellers and the methodologies of respected psychologists speak for the fact that the subconscious exists. They are the key to learning how to trim the subconscious for success.

Rearrange the subconscious mind: Why? How? With what?

Assuming the thesis that the conversion of the subconscious mind is synonymous with the creation of a certain basic attitude towards life – how can this thesis be consolidated? The answer, because the subconscious mind refers to a set of automated processes in the brain, it can be called the place where basic human attitudes are hidden. A person who thinks exclusively and automatically negatively is characterized by a negative basic attitude. If in one's own subconscious mind, which is obviously negatively attuned, a positive mindset were to lie dormant, the result would be that the person would have a positive basic attitude and would increase the probability of achieving success.

Too complicated? Then here it is again in the simple version:

➢ If we increasingly think negatively and look for something negative in every circumstance or "paint the devil on the wall" so to speak, then we automate the brain to always take a negative viewpoint.

➢ Since we are talking about automated thought processes, we can assume a deep rooting of negative views, which leads us to the subconscious.

➢ Switching the subconscious mind would result in automated positive thought patterns.

➢ Since thoughts and feelings lead to actions, and a positive automation of them directs actions in a positive, safe, and successful direction, a conversion of the subconscious mind is purposeful.

Thus, by changing the subconscious mind, one replaces, step by step, the negative, or non-target beliefs with positive or target ones. This is how you get closer to success. Success habit "positive thoughts" is the first step in the formation of positive habits in the aim of becoming a successful person. The challenge with this first step is that what is programmed in the subconscious mind is deeply rooted.

Accordingly, the question is how and with what, can you change your subconscious mind? The solution to this riddle is: forming positive habits in relation to thoughts. For this purpose, there are several beliefs and exercises, with which the thoughts are reprogrammed. Anyway: enough of theory, and into practice!

Positive basic attitude through a positive subconscious: The practice phase

In connection with a positive conversion of the subconscious, one model is better known than almost any other: the law of attraction. It is said that this law is a principle known for thousands of years. Rhonda Byrne writes in her world-famous bestseller *The Secret* even before the table of contents:

> *"As above, so below.*
> *As inside, so outside."*

She locates this quotation on an emerald tablet dating to the third millennium BC. If you are looking for further evidence, you will find it in the Bible:

> *"Therefore, I say to you: Whatever you pray for and ask, believe that you have received it, and it will be given to you."* – Mark 11:24

In addition, there are the many works by successful people and other doers, who cite the law of attraction as the key to personal success. For example, T. Harv Ecker formulates in his successful work *So denken Millionäre* (2006) that the "subconscious financial behavior pattern" is the core factor that determines whether all learning, knowledge and all activities produce change. According to this, the occurrence of success is dependent on the correct programming of the subconscious mind.

These examples should make it clear that nothing is taken out of the air, but that the model is rather world-famous – apparently since several millennia! But what does this model, demand from you at all? What must be done so that it works in your favor?

The Law of Attraction requires you to think positively in every way: in terms of money, your dreams, family, career, and everything else in your life, you are to think in such a way that you steer success in your direction. Whenever a task or challenge comes up, you are not to think about the obstacles and adversities. The focus should be on your personal abilities and belief in success. Getting into the habit of this automated positive mindset – this is exactly what the Law of Attraction requires. The fact that this habit is anything but simple is already revealed to you by the previous contents in this book about the functioning of the brain and the subconscious. New automatisms must be developed, which requires exercises. These exact exercises are presented below to help you magnetically attract success, happiness and all other important objectives.

The following examples provide an impression of what is possible:

➢ **Occupation:** You are in sales. Product-selling is hard at the moment. The reasons lie in the market, in the target group and in certain features of the product that are difficult to market. But you are an optimist! You are used to always thinking and acting as if you sold the product to the last customer and had a remarkable run. Even if you were not successful with a hundred customers before, you only think about success anyway. Because in your world of thought you have already sold umpteen products and are a doer!

Is that unrealistic? Is this way of thinking unwise? If you are in product development, yes. But if you have no influence on product improvements and are only responsible for sales, then you have to make the best out of what you currently have at this point. In this case, the best way to act is to approach each customer with optimism, friendliness, and the confidence of having made many sales. At some point you will really sell the products because your attraction will not allow you to do otherwise.

➤ **Love life:** There she / he walks by. The woman / man of your dreams. Love at first sight is only a few steps away. But you yourself have always been shy. Now you happen to have the right topic ready to start a conversation. But there are doubts because you have never approached the opposite sex with confidence. Fortunately, your recent reading has taught you what's important: that you don't think about your past history at all in this situation. You create for yourself the thoughts of a person who can approach others and seize opportunities. That's how you do it, and before you know it you've already made a sympathetic start to the conversation with that confident smile and a bright, calm, yet fun-loving "hello." The rest will take care of itself...

Is this scenario unrealistic? A person who was completely despondent now proactively approaches another; the opposite sex at that? In fact, a positive approach ensures that the positivity will be reciprocated. If you approach the apparent love of your life confidently and sympathetically, you can expect a similar response, whereupon you gain even more confidence. If, on the other hand, you yell at the person to get over your subconscious dominant insecurity, then of course many things might go wrong. In this example, there is no guarantee of you

immediately following in Casanova's footsteps and succeeding at eve-
rything interpersonally. But you will increase your probability of suc-
cess and the probability of a string of positive experiences with a
positive mindset.

➤ **Exams / Competitions:** Negative thoughts are distracting because they worry you. Calculating, reasoning, or
completing the exam task under pressure requires a clear
and focused mind. A subconsciously programmed mind
that says, "I can do it!" Will leave you hungry for exam
tasks so that you will continue to put in an excellent performance. The same is true for competitions: if you know
you will make it because there is no alternative in your
mind, you will hit the golf ball with greater conviction and
get significantly closer to the hole than if you hit it tenta-
tively and with uncertainty.

Now sports, too! Does the law not stop at any area of life? No,
because the way one approaches any matter shapes the way one per-
forms. Success is more likely to occur with a convinced approach,
because full attention without worries and negative thoughts serves
the purpose of contributing one's own competences and abilities in the
best possible way.

Lesson 1: Avoid negations

This first lesson will lead you to become aware of your goals,
to record them, and to record them *correctly.* For now, it doesn't
matter whether you have big or small goals: write down everything
you can think of about them. These can be vague statements like,
"I want to take more time for certain things." or concrete statements like, "I want to be a millionaire by the time I'm 35." In the

beginning, you just collect what's on your mind; long-term as well as short-term goals are welcome. If you are unsure of what you want, sit down and think about where you are in your life. Set realistic goals that are achievable using the resources available to you at the desired time. Keep your goals in small steps or stages so that you can see your progress more quickly.

Up to this point, it is usually still quite simple. If all of your goals are not yet clear, at least some already are. Some classics among the goals are a successful diet, a higher income, a life partner, living out hobbies and regular travel. Where it gets significantly harder, however, is in the formulation of goals, wishes and dreams. The mistake that most people make is based on the subconscious negative attitude that they have become accustomed to in part or in full. It manifests itself in thinking in negations:

> ➤ "I don't want to get a bad grade."
> ➤ "I don't want to embarrass myself."
> ➤ "I don't want to fail."
> ➤ "I'm not afraid."

Task 1

Read through each of the sentences in the list and let each one sink in for a while. Try to notice what images are created in your mind by each sentence. Select other sentences in which the words "not" or "none" are used. What images do these sentences evoke in your mind?

If you couldn't find a concrete solution to the problem, it doesn't matter. However, thinking about it is the first important step in understanding the problem. The fact that you may not have had a concrete thought from the sentences or that no image appeared, is because many such sentences do not actively encourage a concrete image. They merely deny one thing, while leaving millions of other things still conceivable. To derive a concrete and purposeful, positive message from them is almost impossible in these cases. But it is much more likely that the negative message gets through to the brain because the brain cannot process negations. In formulations such as "no fear," "don't fail," or "don't get a bad grade," the negation is prefixed, but what is the brain more likely to perceive – the negating addendum – or the particular cue (e.g., fear, failure) that is associated with emotions based on previous experiences in life? The answer is – more likely the latter.

Did you know?

Despite a lack of scientifically robust evidence on the effect of negative wording, various professional and personal groups assume that it should be avoided in order to achieve a goal. In sales psychology it is taught not to use words like "problem" at all, even if it is "no problem". These are alarm words that immediately leave a negative impact in the subconscious. Doctors who want to be a support for their patients in serious illnesses often speak of the survival rates of certain treatments instead of mortality rates.

An important point was already revealed in the box: There is little to no scientifically reliable evidence for the effect or non-effect of negative formulations. The observations from several decades of psychology, behavioral research, marketing and other disciplines are almost the only resilient theses. The amount of advocates to build on positive formulations instead of negative formulations is meanwhile overwhelming; so overwhelming that even in science a little bit is happening. Andrea Birchler writes in her thesis on the role of positive and negative suggestions in anesthesia induction (2018), citing several scientific sources, that positive suggestions may well lead to a reduction in numerous complaints in patients after surgical procedures. A logical explanation for the "non-effect" of negations can certainly be discerned in the functions of the brain, putting the whole thesis on a more solid footing: While the left hemisphere of the brain processes logical connections, the right hemisphere is responsible for processing life events. The right hemisphere of the brain works faster. Thus, when the negation "do not fail" is thought or uttered, the image of failure is first generated because it is associated with events that one has experienced oneself. The later connection with the "negation" subsequently plays only a subordinate role.

Task 2

Focus on positive phrases. Replace all goals, wishes, and other desires on your list, if phrased negatively, with positive phrases. For example, "I don't want to live alone," becomes "I'll find a partner." Let's go!

It is not easy to switch from the negative to the positive if you have been used to "painting the devil on the wall" for several years or decades. If it is difficult for you, then at the end of this first lesson there is still a realization that should give you great courage: Everything negative has a positive antithesis. This positive contrast is not as far away as you might think. Because it is on the same scale.

Fear --

Doubt --------------------------------

Lack of Self Confidence ------------------------

Lack of Optimism -----------------------------------

Failure -------------------------------- *Success*

Task 3

Are you still looking for the appropriate positive keyword for your goal to replace the negation? Then start writing down the negative cues, and on the same line with some space in between, write down the positive opposites. In the space between, mark on a scale how far you are from the positive aspect. Then continue reading the book. After lesson 3 in the next but one section (after having done all the exercises) go back to the scale and assess whether anything has changed. Feel free to keep your personal scale for the long term to document how your beliefs evolve – ideally a little bit to the right each week; from fear to courage, from doubt to confidence, from pessimism to optimism, and so on for the many other scales you have found for yourself.

Lesson 2: Positive affirmations!

In principle, the word combination "positive affirmations" is doubled, because affirmations are positive by nature. They are doubled for stylistic reasons to emphasize the importance of this topic. Affirmations are used to describe a state or situation – always as good, always as positive. With affirmations, there is no longer any talk of set goals or formulated wishes. If one applies affirmations, one imagines having already achieved something:

> ➢ "I'm wealthy."
> ➢ "I have an attractive body."

> ➢ "I got a very good grade."
> ➢ "I landed the deal."

While the first two example sentences refer to general and longer states, the last two apply to individual events (a grade from an exam, a result from a negotiation). In affirmations, these events are in the future. One wants to feel confident and courageous for a future event by suggesting to one's subconscious that it has already taken place with success. Accordingly, affirmations refer to both actual and target states. However, one always speaks and thinks as if one had already achieved one's goal or dream.

Task 1

Think about the advantages and disadvantages of telling your subconscious mind that you have already reached your goal, even though this is not (yet) the case. After all, this is what affirmations demand. From this, deduce in which situations it would make the most sense to make use of affirmations, and when it would be better to proceed with caution. Write down your thoughts on a piece of paper.

Affirmations like the belief that you have already achieved something, increase the danger of carelessness (perhaps you have already noted this). After all, when something is achieved, you can rest on your laurels – can't you? It's a bit of a character issue, but the general risk is there. Interestingly, there are several robust studies on the effect of affirmations, that say the risk is outweighed by the added value. Emily Falk of the *University of Pennsylvania* in Philadelphia conducted one such study with 46 subjects. The results were measured with functional magnetic resonance imaging (fMRI). One particular part of the study focused on self-affirmation. It found that when a person tells himself several times that he is helpful, self-confident, disciplined or ascribes other such positive character traits, it changes his attitude and shapes his character. Applying the findings of this study, it may not be advisable to ascribe to yourself that you have already landed a deal, won a competition or achieved some other goal straight away, because this could still lead to carelessness in preparation for the event. But ascribing general positive qualities or characteristics to yourself can be a sustainable way to enhance your self-image.

Task 2

You could go far enough out on a limb as to say then, that positive affirmations about yourself are definitely beneficial. Therefore, I recommend using them to steer your character in a direction that is conducive to your goals. For example, if you have the goal of getting rid of your closed-mindedness to new experiences (e.g., trying different recreational activities, foods, and / or styles of clothing), set goal-directed affirmations: "I like to try X." If you want to give this a stronger foundation, make further use of a rationale: "I like trying X because I recently had Y [insert positive experience]." Write down any affirmations you want to use.

This guidebook would be only half as helpful if it dealt exclusively with the positive sides of each theory. Therefore, it must be admitted, that there is also scientific counter evidence regarding the added value of affirmations. A study by Wood, Perunovic et al. (2009) showed that, among test subjects, those most in need of the effects of affirmations could benefit the least from them. The affirmations could possibly even do harm because the subjects naturally looked for counter evidence, and easily found it. There-fore, the researchers involved in the study recommended that af-firmations be used "moderately." So instead of using overly comprehensive and euphoric phrases such as "I have a fantastic body," moderating it to "I have made good progress with my body" should be preferred.

Because the benefits of affirmations are there, but the critical voices also have their justification, it is recommended that you find your own golden mean. You should not make yourself be-lieve that you have already successfully overcome upcoming events. This distorts reality. Also, you should not put yourself in a euphoric light within the framework of general affirmations. Make sure that you encourage yourself and tell yourself that you are getting closer to your goals. But leave the affirmations open to the fact that you still see room for improvement and will continue to work towards the goals.

Task 3

Consider the affirmations you formulated in Task 2 and revise them so that they are more moderate. Everything that follows is pure practice: Take 3 to 5 minutes at a time, several times a day, to talk positively to yourself. Say the affirmations out loud. You could stand in front of a mirror and make an optimistic facial ex-pression. Alternatively, you could sit down and think the affirma-tions with a high level of concentration. Do not jump from one affirmation to another but do use every break in the day for an-other affirmation. The more often you do these affirmation exer-cises, the more the positive beliefs will anchor themselves into your subconscious mind.

Lesson 3: Visualizations with strength!

To visualize something means to see it – regardless of whether it is there or not. If you remember your school days or have had experience with lectures in your job, you will surely know how important visualizations are: A lecture where only speaking is done is less interesting than a lecture where additional pictures, graphics, videos and more are shown. Nowadays in marketing, the importance of visualization is also enormous. Influencers on social media increasingly work with infographics, and even top companies make use of animated films or other media. Visualization has the important property of communicating complex issues in a simple way. Consequently, the conveyed content remains better in the memory, consciousness and even subconscious. It is exactly these advantages of visualization that you can make use of to penetrate your subconscious mind more concisely with positive beliefs.

Task 1

Consider what types of visualizations might apply to the beliefs you wrote down in the first 2 lessons. Imagine both mental and physical visualization possibilities, using various objects and materials.

Successful people are said to be gifted in the field of visualization. An ideal example of this, which Rhonda Byrne also cites in her work *The Secret* (2007), is inventors. The Wright brothers with the airplane, Thomas Edison with the light bulb, Alexander Graham Bell with the telephone – according to the author, all these inventions could not have been created if the inventors had not had a picture in front of their eyes. Even nowadays at major corporations, such as Apple and Microsoft, designs are first recorded and visualized using graphics programs before they are physically implemented in the products.

Did you know?

83% of information is absorbed through the eye. For some time now, companies have been making use of this insight in brand psychology. According to Florack, Scarabis et al. (2012), the eye is the most dominant sensory organ in human perception. Contexts are answered faster because more brain regions are involved. The effect of images on the brain becomes even stronger if they convey emotions. As findings by Müller, Andersen et al. (2011) show: Measuring brain waves in subjects showed that an emotional stimulus intensified the effect of the images to such an extent that patients were distracted even when they had previously been highly concentrated.

Visualizations are a decisive factor on the road to success. Without visualizations, a considerable amount of innovations and successes would not exist. However, based on scientific research, it is becoming apparent that the goal should be to stimulate emotions in the course of visualizations. This is apparently how the greatest effectiveness on the human brain is achieved, leading to penetration deep into the subconscious. All this evidence raises the question of the appropriate methods of visualization: *How do you manage to create visualizations in relation to your goals and desires that leave a lasting impression on the subconscious due to the emotional impact?*

> ➢ Bringing movement into the performances.
> ➢ Encourage imagination through music.

- ➢ Design images.
- ➢ Create vision boards.
- ➢ Use software.

Because not every person has the desire, time or skill to tinker, we will first describe a simple method of visualization that is feasible for you in any case: your own imagination. Take the goals and desires that you want to visualize and imagine how you will achieve them. This is how simple this first method is. Practice makes perfect, so in the long run you will be able to visualize without much preparation. In the short term, however – especially if you're doing it for the first time – you should create an appropriate backdrop for visualization. Ideally, this setting should be quiet, comfortable, and free from disturbance for at least 5 to 10 minutes; for example, any room in your home: You can visualize in the bathtub, in bed after waking up (this is a good morning ritual as long as you don't fall asleep right away), in the living room, in an armchair or in other similar places. It is also good to visualize outside on a park bench. If it suits you, you can encourage relaxation by lighting a candle or something. Most importantly, take your time and clear your mind of negative thoughts. Get yourself to the destination of your dreams and feel your success!

My experience

I was helped enormously by visualizations before my contracts. Before I started with visualizations, I always had a strong aversion to a lecture. I projected negative experience onto new listeners I didn't even know yet, and I went into the lecture with a negative basic attitude. Inspired by the fact that I had kept order in other areas of my life, been disciplined on my days off, and had cultivated a general zest for life, I decided to approach the lectures positively too. For this, I created images in my mind of the best lectures I had ever given. I closed my eyes for 5 minutes before each lecture, and imagined the people's laughter, the high-level conversations, the interest of the audience, and the pleasant breaks we spent together loosely. Then, I went into the lectures in a more positive mood and was able to cope relatively well, even with the lectures that normally would have gone completely wrong.

Just the thought of success can help you. To promote effective visualization in your mind, here are two tools from a previous list: exercise and music. Rhonda Byrne in her cited work, referring to the experiences of Dr. John Demartini, points out the problems associated with static visualization: It can easily collapse in on itself. Bringing movement into a visualization can help you to avoid this, as it creates a dynamic that makes it easier for you to break away from negative beliefs that may still be present. For example, you could visualize the entire process from the present moment until you reach your goal. In this way you would see a small movie with intermediate stages, and ups and downs, as well as the deserved reward at the end. The second method that will help you to visualize, is choosing appropriate music. Music can accompany both static visualizations, and inner movies. Despite the specificity of music tastes, some artists, bands or certain tracks are considered to be more optimal motivational music in helping you achieve your goals. Here is a small track list for inspiration with 5 instrumentals and 5 (more exotic) songs:

> Two Steps from Hell – Heart of Courage

- ➢ Hans zimmer – time
- ➢ Emancipator – minor cause
- ➢ Steve Jablonsky – My Name is Lincoln
- ➢ Brad fiedel – terminator 2 main theme
- ➢ Eminem – Lose yourself
- ➢ Survivor – Eye of the Tiger
- ➢ Queen – We are the Champions
- ➢ T. I. – live your life
- ➢ College feat. Electric Youth – A real Hero

With time you will probably find your own tracks or maybe learn to love these ones too. In general, it has been shown that motivational songs usually develop their best effect sonically and in "epic" versions. Thus, visualizations become maximally convincing through moving images, movies in front of the inner eye, dynamics and music in your own imagination.

Task 2

It's time to activate your imagination. On the one hand, you have learned about visualization through imagination in an appropriate environment. On the other hand, you know how to underline the visualization with dynamic scenarios in your thought processes, as well as with the right music. Practice makes perfect, so try yourself out in a one-week practice phase: Take time at a preferred moment each day to do the visualization on your own terms. Whenever and however, you do it: do it right and don't underestimate the power of small details! You are welcome to continue reading the contents of this book during the week of practice and complete the next exercises in parallel.

The inner, mental visualization can be supported or replaced with external tools: The creation and use of images and vision boards, as well as special software, are good options for this. It sounds like sophisticated art, but in a way it is banal. Cut a photo of your role model from a magazine and replace its head with yours. Take a pinboard to which you pin pictures of your intended success and milestones. Use special software to create your own movies and insert pictures of yourself. Strictly speaking, you don't even have to pin your pictures anywhere. If you really appreciate a person as your role model, even photos of this person on a pinboard are enough to achieve the visualization effect. The advantage of this external visualization, which does not only take place in your own imagination, is that you are regularly confronted with your goals by simply looking at the pinboard or watching the movie.

Task 3

Choose at least one method of physical visualization and design it. It is enough to pin 2 or 3 pictures of yourself reaching the goal on a wall. For visualization software, you are welcome to check out *Mind Movies*. Add at least one physical visualization method to the mental visualization from Task 2. Keep the physical visualization for the long term. The advantage being that, once created, you can look at pictures, boards and movies at any time thereafter. Take the opportunity to look at your visualization regularly during the day or week.

Lesson 4: Rethinking your own views

So far, work has been done on the emotional side; the habits of not thinking in negations, repeating affirmations moderately and consciously, and making use of visualizations serve the emotional side. If you think automatically about positive things because you have learned this through habits, the positive emotions are activated directly along with it. But the brain doesn't only work according to emotions and automated thought processes. As you have already learned, after the emotional part, further brain regions switch on, which are classified in the vernacular as reason, understanding, the rational side, intelligence etc.

It's about you being able to exert thought processes that no longer just follow emotions. These thought processes are not automated but are actually controlled by yourself. If you are a person who is generally less controlled by emotions, lessons 1 to 3 will possibly help you only a little. For what is the use of an automated positive thought, if you then only have eyes for the negative arguments in your mind and – driven by these – decide to approach a matter pessimistically or without confidence anyway?

An example of what has been described up to this point: A very good friend who has had a lot of success in his life comes back to the city where you live after several years. Both of you are happy to see each other again. The friend, who is very wealthy, wants to start a business with you. Your first thoughts are automatically positive – after all the hours of visualizations and affirmations, that's probably the least you can do. But as soon as your friend says goodbye, you begin to brood in the evening. The shadows of moonlight settle over the enthusiastic initial thought processes. You weigh argumentatively how many people have already been betrayed by friends, that you haven't seen your friend for a long time and that he might want to harm you... Whether these thoughts are right or not doesn't matter at this point. The point of the example was only to show that automated thoughts or feelings focused on success are not everything. It is also important to direct your rational arguments, your mind, and your other mental competences in a positive direction. Please don't misunderstand: It's not about turning off critical thinking and having eyes only for the positive aspects. This would be fatal under certain circumstances. You would miss valid arguments that speak against something. The aim of the following paragraph is merely to banish unnecessary and all-overshadowing blackness from your thoughts. In lesson 4 you should get used to reconsidering your own views. Away from the always negative, towards the: *Maybe I am overdoing it with my negative view and should start to take other perspectives as well?*

Notice

Taking on board other points of view, which is explored in more detail in Lesson 5 (and can be deepened for challenging issues), is also a trump card that goes beyond getting used to positive thinking. As soon as you get used to taking on board other people's points of view, you will find that you can direct the conversation much better and make it more successful. This will give you new opportunities in professional, personal and other conversations. Being able to have nuanced conversations defines interpersonal success and thus, in part, overall success.

What helps in order to consider other points of view is the so-called NLP (Neurolinguistic Programming). You will encounter it in several places in this book. Because what evergreens are for the music scene, NLP is for lay psychology in recent years. It is in demand in several industries, for example management. The article from WirtschaftsWoche *Marketing or Method? The dispute about neurological remote control* (2019) tries to evaluate the current importance of NLP. The NLP seminar market is flourishing; companies, managers and private individuals are booking seminars in rows to better analyze customers, applicants and fellow human beings. Nevertheless, the magazine, citing the views of scientists, emphasizes that NLP has several shortcomings. It presumes to make human behavior predictable and people manipulable.

Did you know?

NLP was developed by Richard Bandler and John Grinder in the 1970s. Both observed and analyzed the work of the most successful psychologists of the time in order to derive laws from it. NLP is based on certain assumptions, which are used to analyze communication processes. By means of instructions and advice, NLP helps to successfully shape communication processes. With the further development of NLP – over several generations – additional areas of application have been opened up. These include the development of positive habits, anxiety therapy, self-motivation and more.

Several theses of NLP have been refuted. The critics, however, demonize the entire model because of individual weaknesses, which is not fair. This is because NLP consists of a large number of assumptions, methods and mechanisms, not all of which are useful in life, but many of which are. Some of the more useful assumptions are:

> "The map is not the territory."
> "The best option available is always (unconsciously) chosen."
> "If one person can learn to do something, then in principle other people can too."

These three assumptions can be beneficial for your further path. You could get off to a good start with the first assumption, which means nothing other than that each person perceives the world differently. Politics, for example, is a popular topic of argument. What seems correct to you may seem completely wrong to another person. You and the other person have grown up under different conditions. This is one of the reasons for the different views. Mostly, the topic of politics is therefore avoided before it degenerates into an argument. But a discussion with openness for the opinion of others and a rational consideration without including personal emotions, can actually be purposeful for both parties. Perhaps both would learn something? So, it is important in human relationships to develop openness to other points of view, insofar as it enriches you with new and differentiated knowledge.

The second basic assumption leads you to the statement that man always chooses the method which subjectively seems to be the most meaningful to him. Exactly here a problem arises: What is subjectively best is not automatically actually so. These objective considerations are of great importance, and NLP helps you to get used to developing several choices in your mind, which do not only follow subjective, emotional and subconscious criteria.

The third basic assumption from the list serves as motivation. It says that if others can learn something, you can learn it too. It is not meant to say that every person finds it equally easy or difficult to learn a certain thing. It is only pointing out the fact that, in principle, every person can learn a specific thing.

Task 1

Sit down quietly and take at least half an hour. Think back to the last 5 to 10 conflicts you had; whether they were internal conflicts with yourself or conflicts with other people doesn't matter. Show yourself to be open to other points of view by considering whether you really went about it the right way. Should you have been more open to an argument? With time, you will notice that it is easier for you to judge less emotionally.

There is nothing wrong with reacting instinctively, as long as you don't let it blind you. The goal in this fourth lesson is to reduce your emotions. If you learned to think positive automatically in the first 3 lessons, it was still beneficial. This is because a positive initial reaction will make you more willing to deal with an issue and approach it with maximum confidence. So, since you'll never be able to completely suppress emotions, you've done an important job. Now the goal is for you to get used to turning on your mind more quickly in order to weigh arguments clearly and make the objectively right decisions.

Task 2

Begin this task by conditioning yourself to control your emotions. Several mechanisms exist to help you do this, including affirmations again: Try to convince yourself that you are in control of your emotions. Eventually this will enter your subconscious mind. Possible affirmations are "I am absolutely in control," and "I am a very calm person."

Supplement these affirmations with regular breathing exercises and meditations. Even if this is not your thing; just do it. Do it for a few minutes a day for 1 or 2 weeks. Because even if you don't like the exercise, it has already helped many people achieve their goals. Success-proven exercises should always be done consistently if you are serious about your goal.

Also, expose yourself more often to situations in which it is difficult for you to control your emotions. These situations can be acted out with other people. The confrontation will toughen you up. Alternatively, you can determine an inconspicuous finger gesture that you make whenever you are overcome by emotions. This gesture serves as a signal for you to calm down. With regular practice, you get used to holding back emotions. This is beneficial for negative emotions, but also for exuberant positive emotions.

Now the only thing left to do is to let the withheld emotions be followed by rational arguments. NLP comes into play at this point. It helps you to take a different perspective. This applies to conversations with other people as well as to your own thought processes in order to master inner conflicts. For this purpose, three methods of NLP will now be presented to you.

> **Dissociation**: Inner conflict with yourself? Then imagine that you are not affected by it, but that another person is in your place. Sit down, close your eyes, and imagine a movie playing before you. See yourself in this movie as if you were watching another person. What would you say

about this person's thoughts and actions? Good or bad? Through dissociation, the problem is no longer bound to you, but becomes unbound from you. So, you illuminate the problems as an outsider and gather more objective arguments.

➢ **Filter change**: When you talk to another person, take their perspective. Use different filters: What culture is the person from? How did the person grow up? How does the person feel today? What challenges has the person had to overcome in his life? Gather as much information as you can about a person and look at each topic of conversation from their point of view. You don't have to go off the deep end the first time you talk and make bold statements that might hurt the person. Get into the habit of being confident in your conversations but avoiding sensitive topics or remaining neutral, so that you can get their perspective first. In this way, you will be able to talk to them without hurting their feelings or questioning their view of the world.

➢ **Meta-model**: The meta-model of language states that people represent certain facts contrary to reality through language. The same happens in thoughts. That is why NLP encourages us to question these facts with regard to the following three aspects: erasure, generalization, distortion. Erasure is the representation of a fact with the omission of important clues. Generalization means a generalization of the facts. And distortion means formulating things differently than they really are. All three mechanisms can be used by people in thoughts against themselves, to deny a truth they do not want. Likewise, it is possible for a person to use this against another person in conversation. Therefore, arguments should be questioned: Are any of these three patterns of behavior present? Get into the habit of questioning your actions when making important personal decisions if you are not absolutely sure you are doing the right thing.

The application of these 3 methods from NLP is a long-term task for you. It is not about questioning yourself in every little thing or illuminating every little issue. But because thoughts in interaction with emotions lead to successful action and are characterized by sustainable and well-considered decisions, you should get used to using the ability of objective consideration. These methods of NLP and all the other lessons of the chapter so far will help you to do that.

Lesson 5: Pro and Con Lists for Challenging Issues

Decision trees, Benjamin Franklin lists, decision mind maps – the world is now full of visualization methods designed to simplify decisions and make them as correct as possible. No visualization method is simpler than the pros and cons list. Get into the habit of choosing it as a decision-making tool when:

1. You have the time to think about one thing for at least an hour.
2. You find a decision particularly difficult.
3. Multiple parties, and their perspectives, are involved in your decision.
4. The issue you have to decide on is complicated in different respects.

Pro and con lists are used for visualization. Advantages and disadvantages of a decision are compared with each other. This is done by means of a design element that every person is familiar with: a table. One column contains the advantages, the other the disadvantages. Line by line from top to bottom, one advantage and one disadvantage is listed. By writing down your thoughts, you make sure that no important aspect is forgotten. This risk would be present if you were to think about a decision without writing it down. Writing down your thoughts collects the arguments. It is advisable to extend the creation of a pros and cons list over several hours or days and to do something else in between. As you go about your daily life, new arguments will come to mind over time, so your pros and cons list will become more and more detailed.

Notice

In addition to simply listing the advantages and disadvantages, it is also helpful to weigh them. If you want to be especially accurate and maximize the likelihood of optimal decisions, then you should determine some categories with which you give a weighting to each argument. This way, arguments that are more influential will receive the necessary attention. In issues where only you are concerned, it is important to take into account the emotional aspect. After all, we humans are not robots...

You have learned to think in a differentiated way. This competence will benefit you especially in lists of pros and cons. You will increase the probability of proceeding correctly when making decisions about difficult issues. You will find a wealth of arguments and thus no longer disregard any aspect. Emotions will play less of a role, instead you will decide according to objective criteria in a way that is best for you and other people involved. This will bring you closer to your success – pro and con lists as a habit of success when making decisions.

However, challenges can arise with these acquired competencies. Because when you compile a large number of arguments, by considering a wide variety of viewpoints, you will end up with very long lists of pros and cons. Now the question arises how to bring clarity into all the arguments and make a decision.

The solution is to delete all pros and cons that are mutually exclusive and equally weighted. Example: You have noted a higher salary on the advantage side of a decision, and a higher expenditure of time on the disadvantage side. If available free time is as important to you as earnings, then these are two aspects that are equally weighted. Since the two aspects are mutually exclusive – you can only earn more in this example if you spend more time on it, so you cross out these advantages and disadvantages. In turn, you highlight the other arguments that are not mutually exclusive, to see if there is a preponderance on the side of advantages or disadvantages. The more advantages come up in the decision, the more likely you are to go for it.

Step 2: Change the habit of acting - identify meaning and determine correct habits

After the conversion of thoughts in the first step; in this chapter, it is time to act. Success is achieved through action. Whether possible actions are right or not, it will be dealt with in the third step.

This chapter is purely concerned with making sense of the new habitual action. The insights gained so far in this book, which include taking different perspectives from lesson 4 in the last chapter, will help you to do this. The goal is for you to be completely convinced that you will live better as a result of the changes in habit. Then you will develop what is essential for success: motivation and discipline.

Motivation and discipline - differences, role, connection

"Motivation refers to processes in which certain motives are activated and translated into actions. This gives behavior a direction toward a goal, a level of intensity, and a sequence of events. A person's motivation to pursue a particular goal depends on situational incentives, personal preferences, and their interaction." (Stangl, 2020).

If you understand change of habit as a process, you need motives to learn the new habit purposefully, intensively with consistency, and in a certain sequence. Without motives there is no motivation. To make motives as attractive as possible, there must be incentives that give you advantages in the situation and that are related to your desires.

"Discipline comes from Latin and stands for instruction, discipline and order. Discipline is the act of following rules or regulations. Self-control is referred to as self-discipline." (cf. Brockhaus 1988, p. 553; Stangl, 2020).

You want to develop new, positive habits that bring you success in some form of order. You create your personal idea of order. If you follow the accompanying rules for order and success, you will be self-disciplined and achieve your goals.

Motivation and discipline are two factors that help you make the transition. Motivation makes the change attractive for you, so that you *want to* change. Discipline, on the other hand, does not start with your desires or attractiveness. It is the strength to follow a certain goal, in a sense, *willpower*.

The following assertions can be made:

➢ You can still make a successful transition without discipline. In this case, it can be assumed that the motivation is so great that it surpasses the weakness of will.

➢ Without motivation, it is also possible to master the change. The assumption here is that your willpower is so great that you have a high level of resilience and still perform actions that do not suit you.

➢ *Without* motivation and discipline, you'll give up on a change after just a few days or even hours. You need at least one of the two components to persevere.

> ➤ With motivation *and* discipline together, it is easier to make the transition successfully.
> ➤ Discipline – or willpower – cannot be trained overnight. Mostly, a change of habit is about motivating yourself. Willpower is either present, absent, or occurs over time.

According to these explanations, the most important thing is that you first filter out the motives for the desired changes. You either have the discipline or you don't. To dwell on this point would be time-consuming. In the further course of this chapter, you will dedicate yourself to the motivation that arises from the fact that you recognize a sense or a motive in the change – at best even several motives.

Did you know?

As you get used to it, you may notice something fascinating that explains the connection between motivation, discipline, and habits. Namely, over time, routine replaces motivation and discipline. The more often you practice the new habit, the more likely it is to take root in your brain. You gain routine and have to exert less effort to comply with the habit you are striving for. Thus, the importance of motivation as well as discipline, to follow something, gradually decreases, until its importance is almost completely gone, and the routine drives the new habit so that you follow the actions automatically.

The motivation you need is temporary. There could hardly be more positive news for you because it follows that you will have to make less and less effort, during the transition, as time goes on. Although the need for motivation and discipline will increase in the first few days or weeks, this is only an initial phenomenon.

After overcoming a critical phase in which the changeover seems more difficult than at the beginning, the routine sets in, and it becomes constantly easier.

Lesson 1: Define success attractively and realistically for yourself

You are motivated when you set a desirable goal. You need, as you know since chapter 1, something that radiates attractiveness to you and awakens a desire in you. Then the emotions and thought processes play in your favor. Given the fact that you are reading this book, which relates habits and success, it is assumed that you want to become successful by changing your habits. Accordingly, your roughly formulated goal is success for now. In such a rough formulation, success sounds good, but nowhere near the level that you would find it attractive and strive for it with every fiber of your body. Yet that is exactly what you want to achieve; you must pine for what you define as a goal.

The destination can't be dictated to you, but the path by which you find a highly attractive destination can at least be shown to you. So, let's go: Practice says hello again!

A goal is more than just a word – paraphrase it!

When you formulate your goal, first make it precise with one word or one phrase. "Wealth" would be a phrase that is absolutely appropriate. Likewise, "family happiness" would be appropriate. "Graduated with an average grade of 1.0" also fits. One or the other goal may possibly leave more room for interpretation. This issue will be addressed later. First, exercise your senses to look at the respective goal from as multi-layered a perspective as possible – "multi-layered attractive" of course.

Task 1

You may remember your school lessons and the role of the 3 parts of speech: adjectives, verbs, and nouns. Adjectives describe what something is like – this is a good place to start! What the particular goal is may be formulated in one word. But what it is like to get there, to feel it, to enjoy it, to savor it, etc. is something else again. Therefore, write down all the adjectives that come to mind in connection with the goal you want to reach. If you don't have many ideas, feel free to use the wordassociations.net website, which will give you suggestions for adjectives that go with the word. For "wealth," some results would be "blessed," "intoxicating," and "influential," for example. It's also sometimes worth looking at similar verbs like "enjoy" and "marvel" in place of "wealth". Use this website, other websites, and your own imagination to paraphrase the goal attractively.

You may become rapt as you perform this task because you begin to feel your goal and enjoy its description. If you have ever felt an "exhilarating" state or have been "marveled at" by others, you will understand how desirable these states are. This will motivate you to realize your goal.

The goal, your success, is much more than just a word. You can look at the goal in so many ways that it becomes a shining image. And now comes a link with the first chapter: If you have already visualized the goal, you may now enrich the visualizations and other exercises with the images and ideas that this first task has generated in your mind. Make the goal as creative and appealing as possible!

Make fast progress real!

If you were assured that you would achieve your long-awaited goal in just one day, but in order to do so you would have to get up at 4 a.m. on that day, work for 12 hours, do 3 hours of sports, and study for 4 hours, you would not turn down the offer despite the high demand. Motivation is particularly high when big goals are achievable in an extraordinarily short time, or when the way to get there is easy.

This book cannot guarantee, that you will reach your big goal of success at lightning speed. It is also impossible to guarantee that it will be easy for you to reach the goal. But you probably already knew that. Nevertheless, this subchapter holds an important motivation for you, how to increase motivation by making use of a trick with which you "fool" your brain: the division of the goal into stages.

Several scientists believe that it makes sense to divide goals into stages. One of these scientists is psychology professor Wilhelm Hofmann from the University of Cologne. You will get to know him better in the next chapter as part of an experiment conducted in the documentary film *The Power of Habit*. The experiment from the film will provide you with several methods and tricks to help you with habits in the next chapter. Hofmann believes that changes of habit should be carried out using a clear strategy. Part of this strategy should be smaller stage goals.

The explanation for the benefit of stage goals is provided by an article in the ZEIT newspaper, which quotes the words of renowned brain researcher Gerhard Roth: "Instead of chasing after a big goal, you agree with yourself on small steps for which you think up equally small self-rewards." Increasing the intervals between the stage goals and lengthening the periods until the reward would additionally contribute to the changeover process, would eventually become automatic, and a new habit would develop.

So, the previous recommendations as targets for remapping are summarized step by step:

1. Define your big goal, and paraphrase it with adjectives, as well as other types of words, to make it attractive and linked with emotions.
2. Make goals even more attractive, through visualization methods and other means.
3. Make progress more visible and accelerate it through milestones.
4. Come up with rewards for individual stages, to increase motivation.
5. As the duration increases, increase the distance between the stages and the duration to the next reward.

Task 2

Proceed exactly as described in this sequence of steps with the major goals you have written down. For example, divide the goal "wealth" into several stages. You may assume that such a general word requires a particularly large number of stages. You can use account balances as stages. Alternatively, you are free to divide, according to the number of planned promotions, and the accompanying salary increase. Find your meaningful division in stages. Take plenty of time to do this. Set a reward for each stage. Make sure that the reward does not destroy the progress you have made so far. For example, after a week of successful dieting, having a fast-food day that resembles a "calorie escalation" would be counterproductive.

In particular, brain researcher Roth's recommendation to increase the distance between stages, and the duration until the next reward seems plausible, and is in line with the previous findings in this book. As motivation and discipline are increasingly replaced by the manifesting routine as the change progresses, rewards and the achievement of stage goals become less important. Eventually, the action gets into your blood and requires less incentive to implement.

Lesson 2: Find habits that bring success

Some habits exist that are universally conducive to success. "Universal" in this case means that they are beneficial regardless of your definition of success. To prove it, here is an example that was used several times in the first chapter, that is extremely understandable: a positive basic attitude towards life. The habit of thinking positively and optimistically is helpful when you:

> ➢ Want to lose weight.
> ➢ Are going into an exam.
> ➢ Plan your future.
> ➢ Enter a new environment.
> ➢ Are interacting with new people.

Positive thinking is universally good. Having it as a habit is success-bringing. Because thoughts and feelings come before actions, positive thinking is even more important. You've learned that and confirmed the Law of Attraction as a universal principle.

But these are only the thoughts and feelings. What are the right habits of action?

Everything that brings you closer to your personal goal is correct. Habits that are directly or indirectly related to your goal are good choices. A bad example would be a weight loss goal where you choose getting up early as a habit. Getting up early is beneficial but is not directly related to diet. So, the good habit of getting up early would in all likelihood not have the desired effect.

Identify suitable micro habits

For now, we are concerned with spotting the appropriate micro habits. "micro habits" is a newly introduced term, appropriate to the subject matter of this book, that refers to specific habits. These habits differ from larger habits in that they are superficially easier to get into and contribute to the larger habits:

Micro habits	Macro Habits
Are special and denote exactly one action.	Are general and describe character as well as other properties.
Contribute to a macro habit.	Are composed of several small habits.
Examples: ➤ Get up early. ➤ Eat more fruit. ➤ Meet more often with friends.	Examples: ➤ Be disciplined. ➤ Healthy living. ➤ Maintain social cohesion.
Require less time to get used to.	Take more time to get used to.
Can be equated with milestones.	Can be equated with a superordinate goal.

Small habits, then, are a contribution to the big picture you desire. The macro habit, in its entirety, contributes significantly to the achievement of your goal. Professional success comes to people who are disciplined or skilled – or both. One big habit, that of discipline, for example, requires several smaller habits that, taken as a whole, contribute to the achievement of the goal.

When you look for the micro habits below that are important to your goal, don't have any doubts just because they seem to be small things. Each habit by itself seems insignificant and weak. But in their totality, micro habits bring you closer to your goal.

Task 1

Look at your big goals – not the stage goals (!) – and think about what general character traits and qualities you need to achieve them. The character traits and qualities you write down will lead you to the macro and micro habits. Write down all the macro and micro habits that are possible for your goal. Write down all possible habits first, even if some of them seem unworkable to you. Maybe they will be at a later time. So, write everything down first.

To make it easier for you to carry out the tasks in this lesson, the entire chapter will be laid out using an example. The example is a deficit that you have identified in yourself: You are overweight and generally not living a healthy life. This is problematic in that it shortens your life expectancy in the long run. In the short term, lower well-being and worsened social participation are some consequences. You recognize the problem and want to live healthier. This macro habit of living healthy is your overall goal. This you have paraphrased with adjectives, verbs and other words to make it attractive: Recognition, feel good, pretty, muscular, confident, etc. In order to better achieve the goal and increase motivation, you have also set milestones. These stage goals include integrating exercise into your daily routine and replacing fast-food with vegetables. It is useful to derive micro habits from the stage goals. To integrate exercise into everyday life, the following micro habits are worthwhile, for example:

➢ Go jogging in the evening
➢ Accompany the children to the playground
➢ Take stairs instead of elevator
➢ Prefer bicycle to car
➢ Walk to shopping instead of driving
➢ Get up earlier in the morning and do crunches

This is how micro habits are formed. Of course, other macro habits are also related to healthy living, such as being disciplined. In this sense, you could regularly expose yourself to temptations and resist them to promote your discipline. Thus, numerous macro habits and micro habits come into question for each goal. You are called upon to independently compose your path. In doing so, it will be necessary for you to think around the corner at one point or another in order to find creative solutions. This book cannot take the task off your hands.

Task 2

After you have discovered, and written down, the possible macro and micro habits for you based on your goals and milestones, you select the habits that seem feasible to you at the present time, or that will be in the near future. In this way, you narrow down your choices to what is realistic for you. However, do not cross out the habits that cannot be implemented at the moment, just save them for later.

Continuing with the example, Task 2 would entail, subjecting each of the habits, from the small example list, to an examination for current feasibility:

Habit	Feasibility currently available?	Perspective
Go jogging in the evening.	No.	You always have to take care of your children in the evening. Even on the weekend, this doesn't change.so this habit is not realistic now or in the near future.
Accompany the children to the playground.	Yes.	This is possible. Suddenly you get a flash of inspiration: You can also implement the previous habit through this one. Because if you have to take care of your children in the evening, you can also accompany them to the playground in the evening – especially in summer, when it is still light at 6 or 7 p.m. Maybe jog with your kids to the playground.

Habit	Feasibility currently available?	Perspective
Take stairs instead of elevator.	Yes.	Since you don't suffer from any physical limitations, this habit can be implemented anywhere there are stairs.
Walk to shopping instead of driving.	Yes.	You don't live in a wasteland, you can carry the bags, and you're generally able-bodied, so this habit is also implementable.
Get up earlier in the morning and do crunches.	Yes.	Now you're overcome by your inner critic: You could get up earlier, but you don't trust yourself with this habit because you like to sleep late. One thing is clear: If you have other habits to choose from, you're welcome to postpone this change for a while.

The last habit on the list should tell you that the goal is not to establish habits that overwhelm you "come hell or high water." Proceed in a way that seems feasible for you personally. The lower the demands on motivation and discipline are in the beginning, the easier it is to stick with the change. Over time, the level of difficulty will increase.

Align habits with goals

Speaking of stage goals: Now it's time to match your individual micro habits to your stage goals.

Task 3

Start with the first stage of your big goal and see which micro habits promote the achievement of that stage. Then go to the second stage and add to these micro habits so that the level of difficulty constantly increases.

Applied to the example, a small graphic illustrates roughly in which direction it should go.

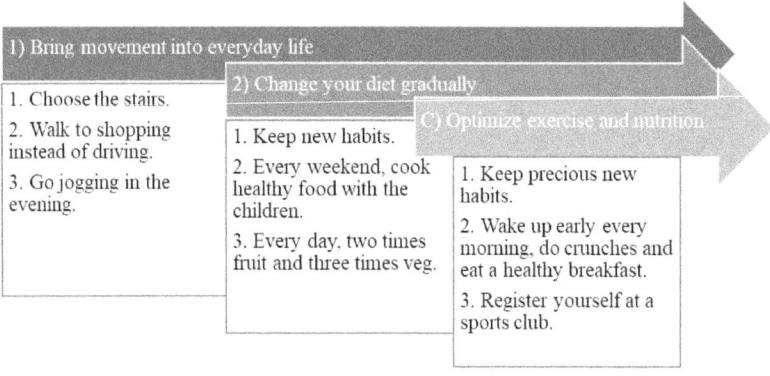

Figure 3: Overarching goal: Healthy living

Gradually building habits brings you several benefits: The added values grow. The challenge behind larger habits is reduced. Synergies between micro habits and the larger macro habits emerge.

If you proceed in the same way as described so far in the first two lessons of this chapter, you will align your habits with your goals. Stage goals and micro habits promote each other, so that they grow together into larger constructs, that promote the onset of a routine, and new larger habits. Do it right! Do it with these strategies!

Lesson 3: Consolidate habits and new structures

The yo-yo effect, the relapse into old behavior patterns – how does this phenomena occur? Something hard-earned does not last. It is replaced again by what we were used to before. At least this is how it happens in some, possibly even in many cases. The frequency of relapses into old habits should not even be debated. Your goal is simply to counteract relapses. The reason for relapse is not that you don't like the new habit or that the added values are not clear. Relapses are due to the simple fact that residuals of the old structures are still present. They are so strongly present that they have the ability to overtake the new habits. Three measures in exactly the order mentioned should be taken to heart in order to reduce the risk of relapse:

1. Be honest with yourself about progress!
2. Allow yourself a generous time frame to complete the transition!
3. Keep the new habits without compromise!

Honesty

Most of the time you notice it yourself when you are being led around by the nose. If at some point you skip a few steps in the retraining process or loosen the leash, you'll notice in your sub-conscious that something is wrong. Don't lie to yourself. Deviations from the planned stage goals have a reason, which is usually to be found in the fact that you do not implement the change as planned. If it happens that you can't keep to something because, for example, you have to visit someone in the hospital or work overtime at work, then there is no question that these are exceptions. However, if there are no valid external arguments and you still deviate from your plan, the reasons for this are to be found within yourself. This is where you need to make adjustments.

Hint!

Exceptions from the targeted goal are not automatically negative. Sometimes exceptions can even have less serious backgrounds (not hospital visits or work related) but be due to a nice evening with friends. If you haven't met in a certain circle of friends for months or years, and only this one evening represents a chance to meet again for the next few years, make the exception! You only live once. Enjoy it. The important thing is that this exception doesn't move you to make more exceptions. You ensure this by letting exceptions really be exceptions; that is, they should happen rarely to very rarely. In addition, Step 1, retraining your thoughts, has helped reprogram your thoughts and feelings so that exceptions are less likely to throw you off balance.

If you notice that you are deviating from the plan, it is useful to take several points of view with the help of the first chapter:

- ➤ Is there a lack of motivation?
- ➤ Are the stage goals too far apart?
- ➤ Are the rewards not enough?

Take these and other questions at hand. Weigh them as objectively as possible. Making minor modifications should help your goals settle back in and keep you from lying to yourself about progress. This will help you recognize when new habits have formed. Once new habits are in place, you will be better able to maintain them by being honest with yourself.

My experience

I never deviated from my positive habits because I was always honest with myself. If I slacked off without a reasonable justification, it was usually due to motivation. For example, when my snacking between lectures increased again and I felt uncomfortable during exercise afterwards, I realized from these clear body-signals that I was on the wrong track. For example, to motivate myself, I decided to reward myself for each week I went without snacking during lectures with a sinfully unhealthy dinner on Sunday. It was always a new dinner to keep things interesting. Another point where motivation was often lacking was when the lectures went worse than I had hoped for with the positive approach. For this case, I had a ritual scheduled for after work: I would pamper myself with a wellness program for the rest of the day once I had mastered the hard day. From then on, whenever the audience made me despair, I almost immediately had a smile on my face. Because I knew: Today, wellness is on the agenda again as a reward!

Patience

You may be longing to have finally acquired the habit you are striving for. Therefore, you might skip certain milestones and proclaim, "I've changed my habit."

The deceptive thing about this approach, is that the euphoria about the supposedly successful change of habit, can hide the fact that you have not yet changed. But as soon as the euphoria has faded away, the previous automatisms tempt you again to follow the old habit. Therefore, always allow yourself enough time, before declaring habits as eliminated and new habits as acquired. For micro habits, you can calculate with the scientific 66 days of adaptation time. For macro habits – depending on age and the strength of the previous habits – several months and up to years are to be expected as a period of adaptation. If it takes years, you will still feel a significant simplification after just a few months. This will be the welcome routine.

Resistance

Both during the adjustment phase and after the adjustment has taken place, it is best if you maintain a certain lack of compromise. If exceptions are appropriate or even necessary, then they are allowed. Otherwise, however, you should concentrate fully on the positive new habits and their retention. The easiest way to ensure consistency is to use specific measures.

> ➤ **Keeping a diary**: By keeping a diary regularly, you can look back on the path you have already taken. This is especially helpful if you've been on the wagon for a while and your motivation is waning, because it will help you to feel proud of a long, successful journey. It would be a shame if you fell off the wagon, wouldn't it? Walked the whole way for nothing? Absolutely not!

➢ **Backward visualization**: You've learned to visualize goals before they are achieved, to make them more attractive. Backward visualization highlights existing successes by comparing them to the previous you. You may even have photos of your previous self to strengthen your memory. Backward visualization is authentic because it brings back to light what has already happened, showing you clearly how far you have already come.

➢ **Clarify added values**: If you regularly remind yourself of the benefits of what you are doing, it will increase your stamina. All that you've learned so far in this book will help you to achieve this. To enhance backward visualization, we can use the principle of deterrence: If you have recordings, or photos of yourself during your former negative habits, or you can observe other people in the same bad circumstances you used to be in, you can use these things to deter yourself from falling back into old patterns.

Step 3: Methods for acclimatization

To change our habits we need a strategy, and a method. A practical example of how it can work is provided in the documentary, *Macht der Gewohnheit,* by *W wie Wissen,* broadcast on ARD. In addition to expert information, and informative sequences on the subject of habit, the documentary includes an interesting experiment featuring a couple, the Webers, as well as the tattoo artist, Jens. Accompanied by the television crew, the Webers and Jens receive help from psychology professor Wilhelm Hofmann from the University of Cologne, in taking the first steps towards eliminating their negative habits. The fact is it's not easy, because habits are deeply rooted in the brain. Fittingly, Professor Hofmann speaks of a necessary reprogramming.

The first step is to make people aware of the unattractiveness of their habits. They are filmed acting them out (a tool you can also make use of). When you see yourself from the outside for a change, you get a completely different perspective of your situation. The footage of the Webers and Jens reveals the following scenarios:

The Webers are sitting quite far away from each other on the couch. Jennifer Weber is busy with her smartphone, sitting on one corner of the couch, and Bilian Weber is playing with his console in the middle of the couch. This is how they both spend their evening. Both hardly interact. When they see the footage of themselves, their "teeth fall out of their mouths," to use Bilian Weber's words. Jennifer is also not very taken with it: "It's not a nice picture to see yourself like that," she said. Both of them even speak for the first time about it actually threatening their relationship over the long term. Shock at the extent of the negative habit is evident in both of them. In addition, for the first time they do not look at their relationship through rose-colored glasses, but see the danger clearly: relationship breakup, due to lack of interaction. Their ideal is to sit together, talk, and take the occasional evening outing.

Jens passes the time every evening with sweets, potato chips, beer and whisky-cola – not necessarily all in one evening, but at least some of it every evening. In the past, he says, he had his dog as motivation to exercise more. But it has passed away. When he sees himself, his statement is, "Oh, man! When you see it like that from the outside, you think to yourself, somebody ought to step in and stop that." His ideal is to not indulge in his habits on a daily basis, but occasionally he would like to allow them to be his personal kind of indulgence.

The expert, Hofmann is supposed to help. The people are asked to think of strategies to replace the negative habits with positive ones. According to the expert, strong will alone is not enough. As soon as a stressful situation comes, the change of habit wouldn't last if it were built solely on strong will. To make it work we need to substitute the habits with big changes, and stable triggers. Jens quickly comes up with solutions: fruit platters and chewing gum should replace the sweets. The whiskey supplies are too precious for him to give away. Instead, he takes them to the wine cellar. He also gets a new dog. The psychologist is optimistic, because both the replacement habit, and a stable trigger in the form of the dog are in place. The Webers find it more difficult to find solutions. The expert identifies the lack of a positive vision as the cause. Finally, they decide to go out to dinner and watch movies together. At least there are some rapprochements they can make, even if only slightly different from the old habit.

What will happen to the participants after the experiment is still up in the air. According to the psychologist, it's important to get into a rhythm and maintain it consistently. Jens treats himself to another beer after just three days, but otherwise remains consistent. His children enjoy eating with him when he eats fruit and provide him with additional motivation. Jens admits that the habit is not out of his head, the matter is not over for him; that would be too easy. Bilian and Jennifer Weber say they are taking more time off from their smartphones and resolve to see new activities as positive steps forward.

These experiment examples illustrate that positive visions are needed, as well as strategies, because will alone is not enough.

You have already learned these components for successful change.

Chapter 1 highlighted the basic positive attitude needed in thoughts, chapter 2 the motivation, the "attraction", of the change of habits and the will.

Now it's time to look at strategies, the third important component of a transition. This chapter focuses on methods and related tasks, that will help you find and maintain suitable strategies.

Apart from that, interesting insights into science and product creation are given, for you to find useful further assistance in your own transition.

Methods for exercise: weaning and acclimatization

There is no shortage of methods. The trick is to find methods that are universally applicable for retraining. An example of a useful, but less universally applicable method, is anchoring, which is found in Neurolinguistic Programming (NLP).

With anchoring, you choose a gesture, an object, or another similar resource to use, whenever you want to replace the old habit with a new one. In this example, the anchor is a small object that you always carry with you. You take the anchor in your hand, during the practice phase and think of the positive habit you are striving for. The brain is conditioned by this trigger to pursue the positive habit whenever the anchor is touched or held. The more often and consistently you practice, the stronger your brain's programming becomes. If at any time you find yourself in a position where you feel tempted to practice the negative habit, you pick up the anchor, and switch to the positive one instead. If the anchor is strong enough, then with its help, you replace the negative habit with the positive one every time.

The problem with this method of re-conditioning is that it is not applicable to all habits. If you find it difficult to get up early in the morning for example, then this anchor is of no use, because you would have to get up early to condition yourself with the anchor in the first place. If you can't manage to get up early, you can't anchor getting up early either.

Therefore, the following methods are presented as solutions with universal applicability that will show you how to:

➢ Put hurdles in the way of negative habits.
➢ Reduce barriers to positive habits.
➢ Keep the quality of positive habit triggers high.
➢ Benefit from other people.

These methods are transferrable to any habit with a degree of creativity.

Lesson 1: Hurdles for bad habits

Hurdles make it harder to pursue an activity. The more hurdles, and the stronger the hurdles are, the less likely you are to pursue the activity. Hurdles are a useful tool for breaking bad habits.

The most practical hurdle is one that makes the habit impossible, or nearly impossible, to practice. If, for example, you tend to consume too much beer or wine in the evening, and are worried that alcoholism could develop from this, then ideally, you'd make it more difficult for yourself to consume alcohol, by not having any at home. This does not make consumption impossible, because the gas station may be nearby. But if you were to buy it at a gas station, there would be further hurdles – like having to go to the gas station, which would mean a lot of effort, and the high gas station price for the bottle of alcohol, which serves as a deterrent. Now creative people might come up with more ideas, like ringing the neighbor's doorbell to ask for a bottle of alcohol or calling a cab driver to drop it off. But this would be either embarrassing or even more expensive. So, the conclusion is: when alcohol is hard to come by in the evening after the store closes, several hurdles arise to pursuing alcohol consumption. The hurdles are high, so not storing alcohol at home is a good measure. Of course, for addicted people, it is quite different from a mere habit, but the principle is the same. Increasing hurdles make the practice of habits more difficult.

My experience

I was helped a lot by the formation of hurdles. It was the first measure I chose on my way to creating positive habits. Right from the start, I knew that getting up early would be the most important thing for me to accomplish. If I could manage it, then I would gain 4 to 5 hours each day. My hurdle was setting 10 alarm clocks and spreading them throughout my apartment. The alarm clocks were time-shifted: First the alarm clock by the bed, so that I really heard it and woke up, a minute later it was the alarm clock a little further away on the closet, then those in the other rooms and so on. After I had switched off all 10 alarms, I was so unnerved that I wouldn't have fallen asleep even if I tried. Over time, I reduced the number of alarms because I was managing to get up by myself at 6 a.m. without an alarm. I gained important and productive hours of life every day with this newly acquired habit.

Ideally, you make sure that hurdles are placed in the way of your bad habits. You can do this by means of a sequence diagram or a mind map, taking your bad habit as a starting point. The following example is of watching TV in the evening. It makes a graphic representation of your choice that illustrates how one hurdle leads to another and gets in the way of your habit:

Figure 4: Mind map bad habit

Task 1

The hurdles in the example are creative; perhaps even too creative. Do with your negative habits as you see fit. Write down every negative habit you find, on a piece of paper, and think about realistic hurdles. For the beginning, these should be small hurdles. If they don't work, feel free to move on to bigger, and more radical hurdles. The fact is that it must be feasible and realistic for you. Afterwards, try out the hurdles to see if they help you with the transition.

Lesson 2: Reducing barriers to good habits

If the erection of barriers makes the practice of habits difficult, or even impossible, the reduction of barriers logically ensures the opposite. The fewer barriers that stand in the way of good habits, the easier they become to practice. The biggest barrier that makes good habits difficult is one's own motivation. Work has been done to overcome this barrier. You made the goal attractive for this purpose and divided it into stages. Besides motivation, however, there are other barriers to practicing good habits that you may not notice.

Lesson 1, which you have just read and will hopefully put into practice with all the means at your disposal, already contributes to a reduction of the barriers to good habits. Thus, it is also a part of the second lesson. In which way? Imagine that you force yourself through various hurdles to get up early in the morning instead of sleeping until 10 or even 12 a.m. Since these hurdles automatically make you achieve your goal of getting up early, the barriers to the good habit are automatically gone.

In simpler terms:

When you set hurdles for bad habits, choose, if possible, hurdles that make the practice of bad habits **impossible.** *This will, at the same time, remove all the barriers that stand in the way of good habits.*

When this approach is not possible, you should think about what specific barriers to positive habits might be standing in your way. Physical barriers are particularly obvious. The more preparations you have to make, or errands you have to run, in order to practice a positive habit, the more detrimental it is. Again, healthy eating serves as an example: What are the possible barriers here?

> ➤ Elaborate recipes: Healthy eating is often associated with elaborate recipes. In fact, a healthy diet can already be covered by high-quality, ready-made food. There is also a large selection of simple recipes available on the Internet. Time estimates, difficulty levels and the scope of the ingredients list, allow conclusions to be drawn about the effort behind a recipe.

> ➤ Availability: If fruits and vegetables are not purchased, they are not available. Thus, the healthy diet becomes impossible. General availability must be distinguished from immediate availability. "Immediate" means that you have the plate of fruit at your fingertips 24/7. "General," on the other hand, can mean that the fruit is hanging on your trees in the plot 50 kilometers away – not very practical. With immediate availability, you're more likely to consume healthy food.

> ➤ Lack of knowledge: Those who are poorly informed, not only do things wrong, but even tend to put mistakes on a pedestal. The tasks are thus judged to be more difficult than they really are. Being broadly informed about a topic actually reduces psychological barriers. Because if you are aware of the simplicity of something, you will develop a greater motivation.

Task 2

Now it's your turn to reduce the barriers to your envisioned new habits. Think about how you can remove mental and physical barriers. "Mental", means acquiring new knowledge, or taking steps to strengthen your motivation. "Physical" provides for actions, using things or objects that entice the practice of the new habit. In the course of these tasks, reconsider your hurdles to the bad habits from Lesson 1. Can these hurdles be transformed, or intensified so that they make the practice of bad habits impossible, and the new habits the only alternative?

The important thing to remember with lessons 1 and 2 overall, is not to overly trust any of the measures. Hurdles to bad habits, for example, may be effective, but setting those hurdles requires a certain amount of self-discipline. People are often gifted at lying to themselves when they need to fight old habits. So, at some point, there may come a time when you'll think you don't need the hurdle anymore. It may be as early as the 3rd or 4th day that you already think, "I'm so sick of having to dig the remote out of the garden bed. I'll stop this nonsense now. For sure, I'm not going to use the remote and the TV anymore." Be sure right now that this is a lie. It's a lie from your inner critic, your second voice, your old habit – your unwanted self. Call it what you will, but no habit is stably eliminated on the 3rd or 4th day.

Did you know?

"Just one more time, just one more time," is often said by drug addicts, alcoholics, and otherwise addicted individuals when they promise to get better. While some individuals compare addictions to habits, science is a bit further along. The difference is that with a habit, the reward signal eventually goes out. Because the person in question has become accustomed to a thing, so a reward is no longer necessary. Drugs, on the other hand, are addictive because they artificially maintain the reward signal through hormonal intervention in processes of the brain. Consequently, you will be spared the extreme struggle, in which every fiber of your being is consumed by just one more time of exercising the habit. But still it is to be assumed that your brain will try to play tricks on you.

So, you must not rely too heavily on your own thoughts, on your way to withdrawal, because they have a high potential for deception. That's why it is important that you plan a firm schedule, during your transition. Up to this point you have the big goal, the important small stages, and the macro and micro habits together. Now it's time to set a fixed schedule for eliminating the negative habits and replacing them with positive habits.

Task 3

Start with your first stage goal, where you determine the time you need, to implement your micro habits: Should the stage goal be achieved within two weeks? Is this realistic? In what order and time frame do you want to set hurdles for each negative habit? In what order and time frame do you want to reduce barriers for the positive habits? When do you set a higher hurdle, if you find that the first hurdle is not enough to defy the negative habit? Define a set of goals, habits, actions, countermeasures, timing, and any other details you can think of.

With respect: Life is not a to-do list. But neither is it a pony farm; especially when it comes to the desire for success, a strict approach is necessary. Of course, some people have an easier time achieving success in their lives. The inequalities are undeniable. That is why some people just have to put in more effort than others. Are you ready to plan accurately and leave nothing to chance? You *will* succeed if you put together a surefire plan. This second lesson, combined with everything you've learned so far, will help you do that.

Lesson 3: Maintain or increase quality of triggers

Positive habits can be initiated by means of triggers. The mere thought of a habit is a trigger. With negative habits that are internalized, the quality of the triggers are high because routines and automatisms have developed. Thoughts of positive habits are a good start, which must be followed by reinforcement of the thoughts. Visualizations and affirmations contribute to reinforcement. So does the reduction of hurdles.

Button up all your triggers and make sure their quality stays high. Increase the quality if necessary. Affirmations have the disadvantage that they are purely mental triggers of positive habits. With visualizations you can do much more. For example, it is possible to regularly add new pictures of yourself, and the path to success, to a pinboard you have made. Before-and-after pictures for physical goals, grades from semesters when studying, pictures of new friends or groups for social goals – these are all possible quality enhancements, for the use of visualizations as triggers. If you reduce barriers to positive habits by acquiring knowledge or picking simple recipes – as was noted in the example – you expand your knowledge base, which is also an increase in the quality of the trigger.

As you can see, it's not just having the triggers that counts, as has been the theme of this book so far. It is important, at least in the long run, to update and optimize the triggers. Not perfection, but progress is necessary.

Lesson 4: Benefit from others

Don't worry it's not about taking advantage of people. This lesson shows you in a moral way how to take advantage of relationships with acquaintances, friends and family to achieve your goals. The greatest benefit you can get is through sharing your goals with other people. Tell as many people as you can about what you plan to accomplish. Even though you may think:

> ➤ "But that's nobody's business!"
> ➤ "Ha! And then when i don't make it, everyone laughs their heads off at me. Certainly not with me!"
> ➤ "I don't know how to do it, though."

On the first point, of course you don't have to share extremely private goals. However, it is good to talk about it, at least with those closest to you. You will thus get your worries and doubts off your chest, which will make you feel better. A few words of encouragement from these people will also help. You don't have to talk to anyone about your complete goal, or the new macro habits you are aiming for. You might as well tell them about micro habits that you want to develop. This way, the overall goal remains secret because you are only telling them about a small fraction of it.

There will be more about the second point on the list shortly. This point has a special place, because in it lies hidden the great secret recipe of lesson 4.

For the 3rd point on the list, it is true that, in conversations with some people, it is difficult to address certain things. There isn't necessarily a natural compulsion to do so. So perhaps, only talk openly with your closest confidants about your plans to develop a successful habit. There are rarely any inhibitions here. Talk to other people about your plans when it arises, for example, because a suitable topic is being discussed.

Task 4

Make a list of people with whom you can easily talk about your plans and intentions, without having to worry about whether your concerns are in the right hands. On another list, write down all the people with whom you have a good relationship. In a third list, write down all the acquaintances you could tell about your plans if the opportunity arises. Even if you think you will never have the courage to talk to some of the people on these lists about your plans, make the lists anyway. After all, no one knows what you will decide to do later...

Now, to the second argument on the list; on which a lot rides:

Telling other people about the plans exposes the risk of being ridiculed by those people once the plans fail.

Advice on the Internet, in books, and from famous personalities, literally overflows with praise for the strategy of first keeping plans to oneself. The pluses for this strategy are plausible. No question about it. Besides the fact that you don't run the risk of being distracted from your goal by negative talk around you, and you don't embarrass yourself in case of failure, you have another advantage – if you succeed, you surprise everyone. When people suddenly see you 30 kilograms slimmer, learn that you have become a millionaire, or hear about your professorship – what a success, they will say!

But think back to what was on the syllabus in chapter 2. You internalized how important positive thinking is. Now, what does it say about your lessons when you hide your plans? Not necessarily something negative, but it certainly can't be said that it's a completely positive basic attitude. Why don't you just assume that other people will speak well of you when they hear about your goals? Do it, tell them about your goals and plans! People will help you. And if not, use the amused comments as a visualization measure. How stupid they will look when you achieve your goal! Visualize your satisfaction to develop even greater motivation.

Besides these facts, the risk of embarrassment if the goal is not achieved is not necessarily negative. After all, motivation and discipline are undoubtedly increased by the fear of embarrassment. In addition, there is the fact that it is basically the same for everyone; we all have dreams, desires and goals. Those who are upfront about their dreams exude *joie de vivre*. They are not afraid of embarrassment; they feel gratitude for life and accept failure easily. In contrast, there are people who talk little about their desires and goals. However, this does not mean that they successfully implement everything they plan. On the outside, these individuals look like doers, but on the inside, they may feel weak. A numerical example provides more clarity: Nicholas formulates 2 goals and achieves both. Cindy formulates 20 goals and achieves

5 of them. To the outside world, Nicholas looks like the doer because he achieves everything. But viewed soberly, the enthusiastic Cindy is the winner in the comparison.

My experience

I am absolutely on fire for talking to other people about the goals I set. In my formation of new habits, I have told many people about what I plan to do. A few declared me crazy for setting 10 alarm clocks in the morning. Others thought it was creative. The important thing for me in the initial conversations, was to spot the people who were sympathetic to my ideas about changing habits. When I realized that certain people were labeling my involvement in the environmental protection association as "brain-cracked" (that was the exact wording) and were almost attacking me personally, I gratefully accepted this, because when a person flares up so negatively, I know I should reduce contact with them. I have learned through conversations with other people, that the objective critics and supporters who can justify their opinions are important. So, I got good insights for the implementation of my change of habits and shared my successes with the supporters. A few people even joined in with some of the remapping, such as my brother, who visited me for 2 weeks and got up with me at 6 a.m. every morning. This motivated me. His laughter at the 10 alarm clocks right in the morning was refreshing for both of us, and heralded the beginning of absolutely outstanding days – positive mornings have a breakthrough effect on the entire day!

The above example is not meant to say that Cindy is better than Nicholas, or that either of them is doing anything wrong. I'm not reinforcing the idea, that it is better to tell everyone about your goals than to keep them to yourself. I'm merely aiming to show, that concerns and fears about other people's reactions, should not be the deciding factor in whether to tell people about your goals. Motivation requires, among other things, enthusiasm, and positive thinking. So, let's bring enthusiasm and positive thinking to the fore! Show both, openly and just *try* to tell other people about your plans in the beginning. No matter how these people react. You provide yourself with additional resources to change by involving other people. Use these resources by seeing the positive in them. You have already learned this. People may even agree to help with the transition, providing additional motivation. Everything is possible – most likely when you act offensively in every respect!

News from the bag of tricks: How science and business make change easier

The impetus to integrate this subchapter into the book was given by the documentary *The Power of Habit,* which has been mentioned several times. In it, researchers from the University of Siegen were presented, who produce small devices to help with negative habits. These devices work by either annoying you, so that the practice of the habit is omitted, or animating you to reflect on whether it is reasonable to pursue the respective habit. Dr. Matthias Laschke and Prof. Marc Hassenzahl, a mathematician and a designer respectively, combined their expertise, and that of their respective teams, to develop the inventions.

The Key Moment – food for thought

Their invention "Key Moment" is designed to make you think. It has a system in which, when you try to grab one of the keys, the other one slips down. The meaning unfolds, precisely when the key associated with the bad habit, is placed on the side where it does not slide down.

To clarify: In the documentary, the classic example of "car vs bicycle" is used. The bicycle should be preferred to the car, as a good habit, in terms of environment, health and exercise. So, the car key is placed in such a way, that when the person tries to grab it, the bike key slips off. Of course, it is up to the person concerned to decide against the bicycle key and take the car key instead. But either way the person cannot avoid thinking about it.

With a little creativity, Key Moment can be used for many other purposes. Imagine you have an allotment for example. The plot gives you company, through the other members of the garden association, as well as exercise and creativity, in the fresh air. On the other hand, there is temptation in one of your rooms at home, namely a PC, where you could "waste" your time, day after day, playing games. You can't manage to give up your bad habit, so you take a key to the room, and you lock it. You attach this key and the key to your plot to Key Moment. Then, whenever you grab the key to the "game room", the key to the plot tumbles down first, and you end up wondering about mowing the lawn today or having a barbecue with other members at the allotment club instead.

You can adapt such Key Moment scenarios with little effort. The scientists from the University of Siegen show that it primarily requires creativity.

Stairs instead of elevator – individual product

An invention that encourages people to take the stairs instead of the elevator has not yet been specifically named and launched. However, it has already been demonstrated. It is a kind of stem that is mounted in, or just outside of the elevator. The stem, when the desired floor is clicked on, talks to the occupant, emitting words recommending they choose the stairs.

The interactive shower curtain – mastering low water consumption

Because the majority of the population in Germany has less to worry about than in other corners of the world with regard to an adequate water supply, there is an increasing tendency for un- necessarily high, water consumption to occur. In some house- holds, water consumption is wastefully high, while in others it is at least higher than it should be. Surprisingly, one's showering and bathing habits are an area where there is less judgment about it than in other areas of life. When, in fact, there are habits in show- ering and bathing that could also do with being analyzed. People who turn off the water while soaping up in the shower use less water for example. Whereas those who leave the water running continuously, and even shave or brush their teeth in the shower, will tend to waste water.

The scientists at the University of Siegen have also thought about these problems in their interdisciplinary teams. The result is an invention that has been christened the "interactive shower curtain". This shower curtain costs more than a regular one, but it has the bonus of an integrated feature that displays your water consumption, in the form of an animation. Easy to understand, this animation motivates you to use water resources more carefully. In multi-person households it is even conceivable to organize competitions. Different peoples' information can be programmed into the shower curtains' memory and their showering behavior compared with others. Who will soon take the crown as champion of the lowest water consumption?

The power-saving caterpillar – switch off the TV, otherwise it's annoying!

With the power-saving caterpillar, the scientists presented, what is probably the most annoying invention in the documentary. It makes annoying noises if the TV is not turned off completely, or if it is left on for a long time without being watched. It alerts you to turn off the TV after use, so that the power consumption is less than it would be if the TV were left on standby.

Products in free trade

As indicated, you don't have to be a scientist to create products that help kick bad habits.

The "Good Habit Bracelet," which is available to buy at trnd.com, works as a universally applicable aid. Whenever the negative habit is pursued, the bracelet emits light electric shocks. These are not harmful to health, of course, but they are unpleasant. Users can program when the bracelet should emit the shocks. It offers plenty of customization potential, for example, to stop disregarding alarm clocks and get up earlier, or to stop postponing sports activities and follow them immediately. The manufacturer recommends pressing the bracelet itself for non-programmable habits to trigger the electric shock.

In addition to physical products, a range of digital products exist for kicking habits. This doesn't necessarily mean the typical advertised courses from online marketers that cost several hundred euros. Instead, many free, or low-cost apps are available for download from on-line stores. One app –*Streaks* – makes it possible to create up to 12 tasks. Each task corresponds to a negative or positive habit that you want to either eliminate or establish, and success graphs are displayed. Other apps have different approaches. For example, if you follow the method of involving other people in your habit, *Habit Share* proves handy. This application clearly lists your progress to other users. You may be able to find like-minded people through *Habit Share* and gain additional supporters for your transition.

Top 10 unusual habits

In this last chapter, things get more specific, and at the same time, slightly extravagant. Up until now you've been given instructions on how to find meaningful habits that will lead you to success. Here and there you also read examples of popular habits to try out for yourself. But generally speaking, specific advice was used sparingly, because it is highly individualized and doesn't necessarily advance every reader. In this chapter, the top 10 most unusual habits are waiting for you! You will get to know special and partly exotic habits, which do not suit every person, but will definitely be an additional support on your way to success. And I will also share my experiences, with some of the habits that worked for me, and give you tips on how to implement them, to maximize the benefit this last chapter can offer you.

#1 Reduce stress with the same wardrobe

Making decisions is a challenge. You have to weigh between different alternatives, which demands mental resources. For some people, much of this decision-making effort goes into choosing what to wear that day. Especially people who are often in the public eye. After all, they are also under a lot of pressure when it comes to clothing. An amusing example of this is coach Julian Nagelsmann during RB Leipzig's first two games in the 2020/2021 UEFA Champions League. In his first appearance, social media reactions described him as having been dressed like a confirmation boy. While his second appearance earned him comparisons to a senior citizen, with some of the press even questioning him more about his outfit than the game, after the match was over. Perhaps something similar has happened to you with your fashion, being ridiculed by friends or colleagues at work?

Some successful people make it look easy, with former Apple CEO Steve Jobs and current Facebook CEO Mark Zuckerberg being popular examples. Steve Jobs almost always dressed the same, with his trademark classic black sweater. Mark Zuckerberg usually chooses fairly similar clothing and varies only minimally. By having a fixed wardrobe, two main benefits already alluded to occur: First, the amount of choice is reduced – especially in the morning, you want a relaxed and stress-free day, which is where a fixed wardrobe helps. Second, after a few trial runs, a wardrobe crystallizes that does not give rise to any approaches to criticism in public. Thus, fashionable *faux pas* are avoided.

Something that is rarely thought of with a monotonous clothing style, but which nevertheless arises as a potential further advantage, is unmistakability. Over time, it becomes your unique selling point to be spotted in exactly this clothing combination every day. That's how you'll most likely earn yourself a bit of a reputation.

#2 Use cold showers to improve your immune system and mental state

Taking cold showers is a habit that should be familiar from military movies. Often this habit is dismissed as "over-hard" military programming. You would not want to miss the pleasant warm shower or the warm bath after a strenuous day after all! Or would you?

Studies have produced several interesting findings in this regard. In a Dutch study, for example, it was found that, among test subjects, those who took cold showers had 30% less sick leave than those who took warm showers. One plausible medical reason for this is the mobilization of leukocytes by the cold stimulus. Leukocytes are the white blood cells found in blood, tissue, mucous membranes and lymph nodes. They contribute to defense against pathogens and are an essential component of the immune system.

It is possible to strengthen your immune system, and reduce your susceptibility to minor infections, as well as major illnesses by taking cold showers. This gives you more time in full health, which you can use as planned. Infections, on the other hand, will throw a spanner in the works of your plans due to the recovery time.

Furthermore, cold showers can improve your mental state. In a study, scientist Sevchuk determined that cold showers can help with depression or depressed mood patterns. According to the scientist, because of the high density of cold receptors in the skin, it is conceivable that cold showers send multiple electrical impulses from the peripheral nervous system to the brain. This could lead to an anti-depressive effect. His investigation confirmed this assumption, although he admits that further investigations are needed to make scientifically reliable statements.

There must be some truth behind the invigorating power of cold showers for the mind, because there is no other way to explain the many positive experiences that people have in self-tests. Better blood circulation, alertness and increased oxygen intake are among the other benefits highlighted, which is why a cold shower is recommended, especially in the morning before starting the day. Whenever you do it, it's hard to imagine that cold showers won't bring you benefits as a habit!

#3 Drink lukewarm water in the morning as a basis for well-being

Drinking lukewarm water in the morning is an approach that has its roots in the far East, possibly in Japan. How much to drink, sources, and even the Japanese, disagree on. Anything from 1, to 4 glasses seems reasonable. The lukewarm water should be drunk on an empty stomach and before coffee. So, it's the first thing you feed your body after getting up. But why? It is clear that water is essential for survival. But why lukewarm?

First of all, the consumption of water generally sends a digestive impulse to the gastrointestinal tract. But the lukewarm temperature has another effect also: boosting the metabolism. In the morning, when the metabolism is still sluggish, this can be worth its weight in gold. You may be able to digest breakfast better and prevent morning sickness. It is not uncommon for people to complain that they cannot eat in the morning because they get stomach aches. A glass of lukewarm water can solve this problem. Even for people who have had no problems with digestion in the morning so far, there is nothing wrong with starting it already.

There are a number of other benefits that lukewarm water is supposed to give immediately after getting up, they are not proven, although many people do report these improvements. For example, it is said that the intake of lukewarm water in the morning can alleviate complaints or diseases such as high blood pressure, stomach problems, diabetes and constipation. Weight gain can also be prevented, and weight loss in turn can be promoted, because warm water supposedly dissolves the fat components in the digestive tract better.

My experience

I myself am on fire for the glass of lukewarm water. I first learned about the ritual at a project weekend with my team. A colleague, who had spent around 4 years of his life in Asia, had been performing this custom for 10 years. From the very first day, I found it pleasant to drink lukewarm water in the morning. I felt positive effects with my digestion only after several days. All in all, the ritual still works for me today. Another positive side effect, as I see it, is that it encourages an abundant consumption of water. I personally find it easier to reach the recommended 3 liters of water consumption per day in the morning with the lukewarm water, because after about a quarter of an hour I have already drunk more than half a liter.

#4 Eat foods you don't like on a regular basis

An absolutely underestimated habit! It is normal that certain foods do not appeal to you and others even more so. Surely you have noticed that there are people who eat almost everything. Even if they are served something they don't like, they eat it without disgust or grumbling. These people are not even necessarily overweight or not "moderate" in their food habits. They simply have open tastes and a high tolerance level. Those who want to accept things as they are will simply say, "Tastes differ." But those who want to work on themselves and take advantage of a more tolerant sense of taste will say, "Taste can be trained, and so can tolerance."

What advantages does this actually have?

➤ The higher tolerance means that you as a guest no longer have to refuse food that you don't like. In this way, you will presumably make a better impression on your hosts, and you will be spared having to give the unpleasant explanation of why you don't eat something.

➤ You become more open to different foods and test more, which expands your taste horizons. As a result, you can even become a gifted amateur chef.

➤ In emergency situations, where there is less or hardly any food, you are less likely to be picky. Therefore, you are likely to get through the situation better.

This habit is not about giving up your preferences to certain foods. The goal is for you to condition yourself to try all foods, to be open to them, and over time to increase your tolerance to the foods you don't like. There are several ways to do this. One of these ways is the varied preparation or use of foods. For example, there are many people who do not like raw cheese. To them, cheese stinks and nothing will change that. This view is fine. But if you put a pizza topped with cheese on the table for the same people, they wouldn't be so averse. You realize you can approach the taste of your "food dislikes" by processing them differently. For example, you don't have to eat raw ginger right away, but you can use it as a spice and make a warm ginger tea later. In this way, you can slowly feel your way to the taste.

The other way you can change your tastes is the hard way: by planning to eat one or more foods you don't like at certain meals each week. That way, you'll get used to the foods more quickly over time.

My experience

I used to dislike foods like cheese, milk and numerous vegetables. Due to a stay abroad for several months, during which I had hardly any choice in meals due to a strictly timed program, I was regularly forced to eat exactly these foods. Especially the vegetables were always on the program as it was oriental cuisine, and these vegetables could hardly have been more exotic. With the milk I was confronted with goat's milk, which was completely unknown to me – Imagine my doubts! For the first few days with this menu, I was only conditionally enthusiastic. But with time, everything improved. Today I have much more tolerant tastes and even enjoy eating foods that I used to reject! For health, of course, this is also an advantage, because more healthy foods are on the menu.

#5 Let your favorite song wake you up to start the day optimistically

One thing I made use of to help me get up better was multiple alarm clocks at first. When getting up early with a single alarm clock was no longer a problem, I still thought about what I could do to maintain my discipline and get up early while adding a good mood factor. I decided, since I had read it on numerous websites, to use my favorite song as a signal when waking up. Several websites had suggested that my favorite song would help start the day on an optimistic note. So, it was for me as well. I listened and still listen to the song *A real Hero* by the band Electric Youth every morning as a wake-up signal.

Hint: It isn't always your favorite song that is the best choice. An <u>article in the Süddeutsche Zeitung magazine</u> drew my attention to the fact that some songs just don't evoke optimism. In the article, the author reports that during his childhood he used to wake up to Bon Jovi's song *Always*. This schmaltzy rock song may motivate you to get up if it is your favorite song. But at the same time, it has a serious background. This is exactly what the author mentions in the article – people tell him today that he was a serious child.

Accordingly, it would be important for you to choose a song that you like a lot, but at the same time has a positive melody and content. For example, *Happy* by Pharrell Williams would be a selection that could contribute to an optimistic day.

#6 Be proactive early in the day to make it the way you like it to be

This is a habit that Mark Zuckerberg particularly emphasizes in his own case. In his eyes, it is important to be proactive in your daily routine from the beginning of the day.

By this he means:

1. Having concrete ideas of your own about the course of the day ahead.
2. Actively pursuing these ideas right away.

Otherwise, Zuckerberg says, you end up having to spend a large part of the day reacting.

A simple example will help you to understand this: Imagine that you have not planned your day and have no tasks ahead of you, except for perhaps a few obligations. Then someone calls you and asks you for support. You don't want to provide this support because you actually feel like relaxing. But you have no choice because you have no fixed appointments as genuine excuses. Contrast this with a case where you've planned the day exactly and have firmly integrated relaxation into your schedule. You turn off the smartphone and relax in a warm bath or even go for a booked massage. There is no possibility of anyone stopping you from your plans because no one can reach you. In this case, you have proactively designed and implemented your day.

So, plan your day in a binding way so that nothing can get in your way, and eliminate as many disruptive factors as possible for the activity at hand.

#7 Allow the child in you space to feel the joy of being alive

There are some situations when you are overcome with the urge to do something that only children actually do. Maybe it's the leaves lining the streets in the fall that you want to kick away. Maybe you want to balance on the curbs near pedestrian walkways. Or maybe you just feel like acting completely silly and making weird faces in public. Basically, there is nothing wrong with giving in to all of these temptations because they are not negative impulses. For example, you wouldn't want to make weird faces if you were sad or worried. Balancing on curbs near pedestrian walkways can be a sign of lightness and a desire to be active.

Since you are not a child, you should be careful with some things. This is the case with grimaces, for example, as other people might feel offended. But as long as you do it thoughtfully, the appeal is there for you to get into the habit of leaving plenty of room for the child in you. Even build regular phases into your daily or weekly routine, where you pursue childlike activities for 15 minutes. Try out what suits you – often it can even be difficult just to categorize something as strictly childlike, let alone do it.

Warren Buffet, the US multi-billionaire, has developed a childlike eating habit. If you believe his statements, he eats ice cream and drinks cola every day. His reasoning: he has found that children have the lowest mortality rates. Since they prefer to eat ice cream and cola, he has incorporated these foods into his diet. How much truth there is behind this abstruse comparison remains to be seen. In any case, he is now 90 years old and healthy.

It is best to choose kid-friendly activities that are beneficial to your health though and that increase your activity levels at the same time. Then you will benefit in more ways than just one. It's quite possible that after you have been childlike a few times, you will develop a greater zest for activity and life, as well as looseness.

#8 Double check everything to bring security into your life

The line between ensuring security, and the less desirable need for control can be fine. Therefore, you should not overdo it with this habit and only double-check everything, while not excessively checking 5 or 10 times. According to relatives, rap icon Eminem from the USA only goes to sleep once he has personally double-checked all windows and doors. If they are closed, then he can fall asleep in peace and safety. This is not unreasonable, because 1) what's wrong with a little check, during which you might notice other important things, and 2) hasn't it happened to you that you forgot to close a door or a window? This is not only about burglary protection, but also about well-being. After all, if you come into your office room in the morning during winter after the window has been open all night, then your motivation to work will quickly vanish.

Checking that the stove is off before you go out saves potential hazards. Making sure that everything that doesn't need to be on is really turned off before you leave work, saves electricity and possibly less hassle with your boss too. Double-checking makes sense in many ways, including the supplies in the fridge; Is there really enough milk left, or am I confusing the current situation with a picture from last week that I still have in my head? Double check everything, but not unnecessarily often. Also important is to check first and foremost what you are responsible for. Just don't start messing with other people's business without good reason. Otherwise, you will quickly lose sympathy or gain a reputation as a control freak.

#9 Play through important conversations and situations in your head to be prepared for anything

This is an unconscious habit that many people have. They imagine an event that is yet to come, and go over the associated conversations, and processes in their head. Sometimes they imagine themselves succeeding. This is a helpful visualization method. Pessimists do it the other way around and sometimes upset themselves by imagining someone telling them off in conversation, or otherwise imagining bad processes.

Make this a controlled conscious habit that you use as preparation for important conversations and moments in your life. By imagining the various progressions, objections, challenges, and more, you can at the same time better influence the flow of the conversation in reality. As life repeats certain patterns in conversations, you will benefit from being prepared for more situations in your life through regularly practicing this.

My experience

For a while, I wasn't necessarily imaginative when talking to women and I couldn't handle small provocative remarks well. These and other difficulties made dating conceivably difficult for me. At some point, I started imagining dates and different conversation processes. In the process, I came up with various counters, compliments, anecdotes, and similar ideas. At some point, I started dating women again and prepared specifically for them: name origin, nationality, or culture, and much more. The goal was never to manipulate people, but to be able to contribute more to conversations. After some time, I realized that my training, which was geared towards dating, helped me in all kinds of conversations – even professional ones! I had, and still have, almost always the right words ready to act and react.

#10 Walk barefoot more often for greater well-being

Steve Jobs liked to do it in the office: Barefoot running. In fact, if you look at people in parks, schools, universities, gyms and numerous other places in recent years, a small trend has developed around this practice. Opponents say it's unsanitary. So, the advice is that you don't walk barefoot in restrooms and other spaces where high numbers of germs are likely to be. But there is almost nothing against walking barefoot on grassy areas, even on pedestrian walkways and, if it is allowed, in offices. In fact, there may be several advantages.

Feet consist of numerous small muscles, tendons and receptors. A shoe that promotes the foot's natural posture when walking is rare, which often leads to a regression in foot health in the long run. Barefoot walking prevents this. The likelihood of foot and nail fungus can be reduced, and better mobility, as well as a greater sense of well-being – especially in the warm months – can be enhanced.

Closing words

"But it's a habit, you can't get rid of it that easily." As you've probably already noticed, this phrase, which is often used as an excuse, is completely true. There are 2 main approaches to you remain consistently on the ball. One is to keep problems and difficulties a secret. The other approach is to be open about what the challenges are. The latter is probably the better approach. It might be difficult to remain motivated in the face of the many challenges that lie ahead. But having walked the walk, you are much more crisis resistant and capable of dealing with problems as they arise. Hopefully, the openness of this guidebook will encourage you to be just as open with yourself.

You have learned how deceptive the human brain can be. Don't fool yourself into thinking that everything is going to be easier than this guidebook says. This is the last, and perhaps most important lesson you can learn. Go carefully through every detail, and every step of the transition – including the pitfalls. And prepare yourself for the possible obstacles. Take all the hints and tasks seriously because your success depends on it. Don't feel too tired, or too silly to perform the tasks that challenge you. Through practice, you can ensure the achievement of plans, antidotes to problems, and ultimately, a sustainable transition.

Readjustment is not an easy undertaking. In addiction therapy and in other therapeutic branches, it is often recommended not to set long-term goals. This has been covered in the section on stage goals but get into the habit of thinking in even smaller stages every day. You don't have to avoid a habit for several months at first, but only for the next day. At best, you can develop this thought anew every day. Because although you are only talking about the next day, the regularity of this sentence covers a long time period in the end. You have the chance, through these types of thought processes, to use the self-deception mechanisms of the brain, to your advantage. Only creativity stands between you and further resources for success.

Creativity is a source of success anyway; the more creatively you think, the more options you will find, to put up barriers to bad habits, and reduce those to good habits. The more creatively you think, the more ways you will find to make your visualizations appealing. The more creatively you think, the better you will be, at using adjectives to describe your goals, and the more motivation you will develop. Therefore, use techniques such as mind-mapping or tabular representations where recommended. Enrich the recommendations of this book with further creative techniques. In this way –and only in this way – you will be able to exploit it to its full potential.

Meanwhile, never underestimate the effectiveness of a measure. This applies to the positive as well as the negative. You have registered how effective micro habits are. Never doubt that an action will have some effect. Nothing positive is too little to not to be effective. Likewise, nothing negative is too little to be a risk. All the more important, is adherence to the clear plans and structures that you have been given, and have developed for yourself, also. Do not, under any circumstances, allow relapses to occur in your transition. If you feel the tendency to relapse, you should always loosen the leash first by establishing the positive habits at a slower pace. "Better to take an extra month to get accustomed, than to break down after a long road because you overestimated yourself," should be your motto. And in reference to the opening words of the entire book – humans are not machines, of course! You have your own strengths and weaknesses at a core level. Negative habits are the expression of those weaknesses. Denying them, or not taking them seriously enough, and going too fast in the process of retraining, would automatically backfire.

Openness towards yourself, consistency in following the advice in this book, creativity and appreciation towards any success or danger, no matter how small – these are the last words that should remain in your mind. Everything else is a matter of practice. New habits are a matter of practice. Practice makes you a master. Become the master of your success and not of your failure!

And what if it does turn out to be failure? Then remember that every failure can be followed by a success that outshines everything that has gone before. Great movers and shakers on the world stage, VIPs, and talents, have become successful only after several failures. But they never stopped believing in success. If things don't work out, feel free to put the book aside for a few weeks or months to think about potential improvements. Then start your way again, because that's the main principle: keep going, keep going! Isn't that the best habit of all you can develop?

References and further reading

Literature:

A. Florack, M. Scarabis, E. Primosch: Psychologie der Markenführung. München: Verlag Franz Vahlen, 2007.

Byrne, R.: *The Secret – Das Geheimnis*. München: Random House GmbH, 2007.

Clear, J.: *Die 1%-Methode – Minimale Veränderung, maximale Wirkung*. München: Wilhelm Goldmann Verlag, 2020.

Cabane, O. Fox: *Das Charisma-Geheimnis – Wie jeder die Kunst erlernen kann, andere Menschen in seinen Bann zu ziehen*. München: Münchner Verlagsgruppe GmbH, 2020. 3. Auflage.

Ganseforth, H.: *NLP - Neurolinguistisches Programmieren. Wissenschaft, Magie oder Methode?* Studienarbeit: 2004.

Eker, T. Harv: So denken Millionäre – Die Beziehung zwischen Ihrem Kopf und Ihrem Kontostand. Kulmbach: Börsenmedien AG, 2006. 6. Auflage.

Ready, Romilla; Burton, Kate: *Neuro-Linguistisches Programmieren für Dummies*. 2. Nachdruck, Wiley-VCH Verlag GmbH & Co. KGaA (2014)

Online:

http://paedpsych.jku.at/cicero/LERNEN/AllgemeinesLernmod
ell.pdf

https://www.marathonfitness.de/gute-gewohnheiten/

https://onlinelibrary.wiley.com/doi/abs/10.1002/ejsp.674

https://www.deutschlandfunk.de/denken-fuehlen-handeln-wie-
das-gehirn-unser-
verhalten.700.de.html?dram:article_id=80426

https://medlexi.de/Gro%C3%9Fhirnrinde

https://www.pharmazeutische-zeitung.de/ausgabe-
462017/placebo-effekt-wirkung-ohne-wirkstoff/

https://www.spektrum.de/lexikon/biologie/unterbewusstsein/
68591

https://www.geo.de/wissen/gesundheit/22098-rtkl-
psychologie-es-gibt-keinen-hinweis-dass-ein-
unterbewusstsein-existiert

https://www.youtube.com/watch?v=1VhFhR_1Sdw&feature=yo
utu.be

https://siga-
fsia.ch/files/Ausbildung/Abschlussarbeiten/XUND_Lu
zern/2018_Diplomarbeit_Andrea_Birchler.pdf

https://www.wissenschaft.de/umwelt-natur/was-das-gehirn-
empfaenglich-fuer-ratschlaege-macht/

https://www.psychologie.uzh.ch/de/bereiche/dev/lifespan/erle
ben/berichte/mehr-berichte-1/selbstwertgefuehl.html

http://www.report-psychologie.de/nc/news/artikel/der-
einfluss-emotionaler-bilder-auf-das-gehirn-2011-12-22/

https://www.wiwo.de/erfolg/management/coaching-und-
motivation-marketing-oder-methode-der-streit-ueber-
die-neurologische-fernsteuerung/24674220.html

https://wordassociations.net/de/

https://www.zeit.de/zeit-wissen/2013/02/Psychologie-
Gewohnheiten/seite-4

Stangl, W. (2020). Stichwort: „Motivation". Online Lexikon für
Psychologie und Pädagogik.

WWW: https://lexikon.stangl.eu/337/motivation/

Stangl, W. (2020). Stichwort: „Disziplin". Online Lexikon für
Psychologie und Pädagogik.

WWW: https://lexikon.stangl.eu/5158/disziplin/

https://www.spektrum.de/news/sucht-und-gewohnheit-im-
gehirn/1399787

https://www.trnd.com/de/toptrnd/ein-armband-gegen-
schlechte-gewohnheiten

https://futurezone.at/apps/5-apps-mit-denen-man-schlechte-
gewohnheiten-los-wird/400945208

https://www.aerztezeitung.de/Medizin/Wer-sechs-bis-acht-
    Stunden-pro-Nacht-schlaeft-lebt-am-laengsten-
    232317.html

https://www.rki.de/DE/Content/Gesundheitsmonitoring/Stud
    ien/Adipositas_Monitoring/Verhalten/PDF_Themenbl
    att_Schlaf.pdf?__blob=publicationFile

https://www.medicalnewstoday.com/articles/323145

https://www.aerzteblatt.de/nachrichten/105181/Soziale-
    Kontakte-im-mittleren-und-spaeten-Lebensalter-
    koennten-Demenzrisiko-senken

https://www.focus.de/gesundheit/gesundleben/fitness/studie-
    zeigt-wer-soziale-kontakte-pflegt-lebt-
    gesuender_id_10851369.html

https://www.tagesspiegel.de/wissen/studie-ueber-einsamkeit-
    soziale-kontakte-verlaengern-das-leben/1892120.html

CLEAR GOALS

What Do You Really Want to Achieve in Life?

Ultimate Success Through Personal Goal Planning in 4 Steps

by

Patrick Drechsler

Table of Contents

Introduction

Imagine this: You've just resolved to earn money on top of your low-paying job. It is supposed to be your way off the hamster wheel that you are currently trapped on doing a job every day that pays poorly, and that you can't stand. So, you take on a weekend job working on the black in a restaurant to increase your income. But after only 3 weeks you are physically and mentally drained because the workload is simply too much for you. You start showing up irregularly for your side job, get fired, and you're back to square one again. Only this time you feel much worse, because in addition to disliking your main job, you're physically and mentally exhausted. This is a classic case of ***setting too many or too high goals for yourself.***

Another scenario: You are about to embark on a new phase of your life. You've got your high school diploma in the bag with a fabulous average of 1.0. Your teachers predict an outstanding future for you. You are feeling happy enjoying your free time after graduation, but you know that important decisions have to be made soon: Study/training, or a relaxing year abroad? The latter appeals to you because you want to explore the world and don't know which course of study is right for you at the moment anyway. Your parents however urge you to study Medicine right away. They are proud of you and just decide what is best for you from their point of view. You're not even remotely convinced, because being a doctor doesn't match your actual desires for the future, but you decide to go for it anyway. The result: dropping out of college, angry parents, and you as a disillusioned and indecisive dropout who spent 2 years of his life doing something that didn't live up to expectations. Even though you knew beforehand that it would be the wrong path, you did it anyway and messed up a promising future. This is a classic case of *setting the wrong goals or letting other people influence your goals too much.*

Goal setting is an art in itself. Those who master it increase their likelihood of succeeding many times over. The opposite is true when your goals are not set correctly: too high goals, too many goals, not following one's actual interests and dreams, being influenced too much by other people, showing little motivation and discipline as a result of setting the wrong goals ... these cases are very likely to lead to failure. Although it is obvious, unfortunately a surprising number of people make these mistakes over and over again. Have you noticed people in your circle of acquaintances doing things they don't really want to do? Have you observed how some people pursue such a large number of goals that they can't manage it and fail? Do you often hear people around you complain that they don't like what they do? And most importantly, are similar things happening in your *own* life?

It's time you started setting your goals properly with the highest probability of success; I say *with the highest probability* because there are no guarantees that you will achieve your goals. But here comes a fascinating message for you: as long as you pursue goals that are truly in line with your dreams, it is not always necessary to actually achieve them. Because by simply pursuing them, you fill your life with motivation, purpose, enthusiasm, and fascination anyway. Even with the most successful people goals are sometimes dropped because life develops and evolves in equally interesting different directions.

But whatever your goals in life, and whatever is closest to your heart's desires – this guidebook will give you valuable, authentic assistance and suggestions based on my extensive experience in the matter. Goal setting is an important area of personal development and I want to make sure you get it right. Through a unique fusion of personal development and business management techniques that came about one day when I noticed, during a review of my business studies, that a significant part of business administration is devoted to the question of the ideal objective. When I took a closer look at the content, I was thrilled. *Surely this high level of precision and fine subdivision of goals can also apply to people in their everyday lives!* was my thought at the time. When I combined areas of goal setting and planning from my business studies, with my life experiences, I was thrilled with the benefits I achieved, from my personal life to my family to my hobbies and career. Do you want to set and achieve your goals in a clear step-by-step sequence, with really precise methods? Then you've come to the right place! This guide offers you completely original methods that work, as my own life experience demonstrates.

When it comes to goal setting, there are 2 factors that really matter: first, there are the things you have to do – the **obligations**. Then there is the space you have free for planning, in which you set your **desired goals**. After the introductory first chapter, chapters 2 and 3 will teach you how to correctly plan your commitments and desired goals, step by step, with the help of 2 lists which you refine following the tips on filtering, laid out in Chapter 4, and long-term planning in Chapter 5. It's kind of like your own personal life guide. In between the main sections, there are plenty of hints on how to find suitable goals, what you should pay attention to in your environment and other important elements to help you perfect your goal setting skills. The tasks in the chapters and the big final task at the end of each chapter will help you to put the theory into practice.

Planning your goals lets you live every dream precisely!

This guidebook is unique because the inspiration for it came in an unusual way. But equally unusual – at least at first glance – was the path I took to optimize my own goal setting achievements.

The foundation for my success with various goals and plans was my business studies. Then I poured through numerous guidebooks and listened to courses from many coaches, but for a long time nothing could help me to properly formulate my ideas. Then one day I held a book from my former business studies in my hand, and it came to me. This idea led me to the perfect way of dealing with goals. Now I pass this idea, that runs like a thread through the entire book, on to you. I hope it will help you, as it has helped me.

So, what is this idea? If you look at business administration and study company objectives as an essential part of entrepreneurial activity, you will find that companies are **systems**. From this realization follows important insights for goal setting. While reading about the subject, it dawned on me that exactly the same applies to people. You and your environment – you are a system! If you internalize this and all the consequences that follow from it, you will have the ability to set goals optimally and keep the probability of achieving them at its highest.

Don't worry: You won't be dehumanized in this book, when being treated like a business. You'll just learn how to harness the enormous precision of successful corporations in goal setting – for your job, for your personal life, for your social contacts, for your hobbies, for your dreams, and so much more! The most powerful and famous corporations achieve most of their goals because they plan everything meticulously. Now imagine if you did the same as a human being: accurate planning, high precision, yet plenty of room for spontaneity and unforeseen events – you would be living your dreams. Let's start today!

Man, and his environment as systems

By definition, a system is a whole composed of several parts. These parts connect with each other so that there are constant interactions. It follows that when you act, it affects multiple parts of the system, from which you expect a certain improvement to occur.

Now imagine that you achieve your intended improvement. Perhaps it has the desired effect, but at the same time affects another area of life in a way that is not desired? Besides this, it could be that an action doesn't only produce that one expected improvement. Instead, 2 or 3 additional improvements occur in other areas of life that you would not have expected. All the greater would then be the joy. So, in a nutshell, *many of the goals you achieve have multiple effects, not just the one you planned.*

What parts are present in the "life" system? Of which parts is your personal system composed? On the one hand it is you, on the other hand it is your environment. Imagine how much these

2 parts make up already – just you yourself consist of hundreds, maybe thousands of other parts. You see what I mean? Sometimes your inner critic wants to bring your system out of balance. But if you overcome your inner critic, you are happy to have fulfilled a duty and not to have postponed it. In the evening, after a hard day you are tired, but your wife and children are waiting for you in top form. Wife and children – other parts of the system you have to consider. With every little decision or act you perform certain parts of the system start moving. How are you supposed to keep track of it?

Example

You have ambitious professional goals. These start with a degree, then move into your first few years of work, and finally culminate in a doctorate. The result is even more appointments, duties and opportunities that you don't want to miss. You already know during your studies that the most salient features of your daily life will be a full schedule. What makes it tough is the family life on top of your professional activities: How can a person with so many work commitments have a happy family life? It is possible, no question! But it is difficult; more difficult, at least, than for a person who doesn't have a 12-hour workday followed by appointments. This is probably the most common way in which the system characteristics of a person's life show up: Work or family? Sometimes it's hard to balance both. If both are your goal, early planning is required to successfully manage a life with both career and family.

Any person who sets more than one goal in their life faces the challenge of balancing between mutually influencing factors. This also influences your daily routines. Let's assume that a person doesn't want to prioritize between work and family: something like this can go well for a while until, before an important professional lecture, a call comes that their child is seriously ill in hospital. What decision is made now? The person decides to take care of the child and the next day has to hand in his or her notice because a deal has fallen through due to the missed lecture, resulting in high sales losses for the company.

So, for you a central factor in goal setting is prioritization. Which goal is more important in general terms? Which goal is more important depending on the reality at this particular moment? A person who works with tunnel vision towards only one thing has a much easier time of it. They don't have to weigh up different goals. A balancing act between family and work is avoided because she has already committed herself to one thing. This person strictly follows her path and disregards side effects. While she also lives in a system, she doesn't care about the interactions. Perhaps she is even willing to go over dead bodies, although that would be an extreme case.

People who pursue a single goal with tunnel vision can be very successful; temporarily. In the long run, however, this lifestyle produces negative side effects. For example, tunnel vision leads to overlooking opportunities for synergy between different goals. Few new things are tried. Possibly, the physical and psychological strain is so strong that burnout occurs at some point as well.

Tunnel vision is not the rule. Most of the time, people have multiple dreams. Or they have dreams *and* obligations, which require the pursuit of several goals at the same time. This results in the elementary challenge for you, which this guidebook would like to help you with. You live in a system. One part of this system is you with everything that belongs to you. The other part of this system is your environment; likewise, with everything that belongs to *it*. Your goal is to bring transparency into your system, or to get clarity about it in the first place, i.e., to find goals that are important for you, that can realistically be fulfilled according to the current circumstances. After that, the trick will be to pursue these goals in coordination with everything that surrounds you. Only in this way can the entire system, i.e., your life, function according to your dreams.

There are no simple *if-then* principles in life. In most cases, a decision not only results in the desired effect, but also in additional (side) effects. Big players in companies are aware of this. Therefore, no decisions are ever made on a whim. There are no ill-considered actions. There is less risk of negative surprises afterwards. Of course, companies have certain advantages because decisions are usually made in consultation with several people. Emotional decisions are highly unlikely in teams of several people and are not found at all in the largest companies.

You can acquire these qualities yourself as well. A key factor in avoiding decisions that are too spontaneous, emotionally driven, or based purely on luck, is controlling emotional impulses. If you have read my book *Stop Procrastination Immediately*, it offers plenty of methods to help you do this very effectively.

My experience

How much we humans are part of a system of interactions, I got to experience first-hand when I joined a new circle of friends via a work colleague. It was completely different from what I had been used to. The looseness of my new "friends" fascinated me. However, the same looseness had the disadvantage of exposure to a constant use of clichés, outdated role models, and other unwise expressions. Why these people had such a strong attraction to me, I still can't answer to this day. But they did. Over time, I adapted their ways of thinking to some extent. My interpersonal skills and previous discipline faded. Today, I am fortunately out of that environment, which did not suit me. But I would never have thought that my character would change so much in the meantime due to a different environment. It had an impact on everything I did and thought.

First: Find the right goals

Basically, this whole book and each of the 4 steps presented is about this one thing: finding the right goals. Once you have the right goals, you will have ...

> ➤ analyzed your system and identified the interactions.
> ➤ Knowledge of how you react to the potential interactions.
> ➤ Prioritized the most important goals over the less important ones.
> ➤ Followed what is close to your heart.
> ➤ Developed motivation, discipline and consistency as you follow your dreams and create the best conditions for achieving them.

These aspects and more will be ensured once you have found the right goals. Because "right" means nothing other than that: you will know what corresponds to your dreams while at the same time taking your system into account. For example, if you have a spouse, it's important to agree on certain goals together so that there's a common thread. The same applies to circles of friends. Setting goals is therefore not always a matter for one person but is sometimes linked to the interests of others too.

This guide also teaches you how to involve other people in goal setting where necessary. In order to be able to formulate and pursue goals adequately, you need to understand the word "goal" as precisely as possible. A few words about this ...

The waiter of life: What do you really want?

Welcome to the life restaurant! Here you really get everything you want, as long as it comes from this world and is formulated correctly. So, let's go! You hang up your coat and are glad to be in the warm. The fireplace gives you comfort, and the piano player provides the appropriate background music on this fantastic evening. Today you get what you want from life!

You sit down. After a short while the waiter approaches you. "Can I help you?" he asks you, his notepad and pen ready in hand.

You reply, "I'm hungry. I want to eat."

The waiter repeats his question, "Can I help you?"

You repeat, more forcefully this time, "I want to eat!"

In response, the waiter slowly shakes his head and says he'll give you some more time to think about it until you really know what you want. To help you, he gives you the menu, although it's actually unnecessary. After all, in the life restaurant you get everything you want! Then the waiter leaves and turns his attention to the other guests.

You watch him and the other guests as they exchange. They actually get everything they want. On top of that, the waiter is friendlier to them than to you. Has the whole world conspired against you? What's going on here? You look at the menu and you are shocked: In this restaurant, anything really is possible! It's almost like it's an impertinence that you can't decide.

Sooner than you would like, the waiter comes back to you. He inquires again about your wish. What now? You go by the process of elimination and answer hesitantly, "Well ... I don't want all the meat dishes. I eat vegetarian."

The waiter makes a note of this and is already gone. Before you know it, not only does the waiter return, but a whole entourage comes with him. Both the waiter and his entourage are carrying plates. You wonder why there are so many plates. Have they prepared everything for you that is vegetarian? That would be too much!

In fact, it becomes more paradoxical ... "Here you go," the waiter speaks as he and his entourage place all the plates on your table, "here you have all the meat dishes that are on our menu. And our menu is big because we are the restaurant of life." He smiles.

While the smell of pork knuckles and chicken legs, rises to your nose and the waiter smiles provocatively at you, you lose your nerve: "Why do I get exactly what I didn't want?!?" you ask loudly and excitedly.

The waiter is not aware of his mistake: "I'm sorry, but my time is precious. I don't work on the exclusion principle. What you think about and what you say, that's what you get. I don't pay attention to individual unimportant words."

You understand and then just want a Diet Coke because you're sick of everything. The Diet Coke is served to you a little later. While you are content with it, the people around you are already devoting themselves to the 3rd and

4ᵗʰ courses of their menu. They help each other with their orders and sometimes even with emptying the plate.

Author: Fabian Ries (https://www.fabianries.de/)

Life is just like this restaurant. You have an incredible number of choices. If it seems absurd to you that a person would sit down in a restaurant and just say that they want to eat, realize that this is exactly what happens in real life. Haven't you ever said you wanted something, but weren't specific enough about it? Be honest with yourself:

➢ I want to be rich.
➢ I want to be successful.
➢ I want to be attractive / pretty.
➢ I want to have more friends.
➢ I want to have more career prospects.

Here's the problem: Where is it formulated what wealth, success, etc. mean and what exactly has to be done to achieve it? If you define wealth in terms of money or assets, then you should specify what sum you are aiming for. This already makes it more concrete. Next, the challenge arises that such large and general goals cannot be achieved in the first go. Of course, it is possible to achieve them over the course of several years. But why then burden yourself with a single large goal instead of setting smaller intermediate goals? A division into intermediate goals favors greater motivation. After all, achieving intermediate goals shows progress.

Precision in formulation. Subdivision of major goals into smaller goals. Determination to want to implement the respective goal. These are some of the things that there is hardly any way around when it comes to precise goal formulation. Life is the biggest restaurant in the world with the biggest menu imaginable from which every person has to choose. You are probably aware that every restaurant that does well expands over time. Or at least it expands its offer. So, it is with the life restaurant. This brings us to a typical problem of today's age in setting goals: oversupply.

Today's challenges in setting goals

Developments in recent decades and years have created a wealth of opportunities. These opportunities are expanding prospects for many people. The Internet has created new opportunities for earning money. Becoming self-employed with your own business or as a freelancer is no longer necessarily associated with a high financial outlay. Rent for stores and thus high running costs can be omitted. At this point many councilors are advising you to make money on the Internet. But as much expertise as these guides may contain, they are also very specific: not every person defines success in terms of higher earnings. Even if this were the case, it would not necessarily follow that the models presented in the guidebooks would appeal to the respective reader.

In addition to opportunities for self-employment or in the professional field, a plethora of opportunities have arisen for young people to shape their lives after leaving school. Taking over a parent's business or job as in the past, is no longer the norm. Young people can choose between a lot of training and study programs. As well as study abroad programs so they can explore the world. Hiking through New Zealand for 6 months or rather working with professional rangers at a wildlife park in South Africa?

It's all within the realm of possibility. These things are not only available to young adults from the wealthy class of society. Because Germany is a welfare state, there are numerous support programs that young people from other countries can only dream of in a global comparison: State sponsorship for studies and training, State sponsorship abroad, scholarships, organized work & travel and much more!

There is even a wide range of political opinions. Numerous political currents have emerged, so that it is now possible to find exactly the one that fits one's own ideas. Meetings are easy due to the Internet and social media. And there are also numerous directions and movements among religions. Within Christianity alone, there are many diverse forms. The Protestant and Catholic denominations are accompanied by various other groups and sects.

The most diverse choices, philosophies of life and convictions meet. Although much of it has the same core, it is also so very different! And between all this, there you stand, and you have to make decisions. As you age, your options might reduce. Certain things are no longer accessible (e.g., study abroad programs for young people) or become unrealistic (e.g., education). But even for those over 40 with family as well as work responsibilities, a number of new opportunities have recently emerged that were unthinkable a few decades ago.

Example

Start trading stocks at the age of 60? Isn't that already too old? And as a woman too? "Pah, all prejudices!" thought Beate Sanders correctly when she started investing money in shares at the age of 60. She started with the equivalent of 30,000 euros and turned it into a fortune of around 2.5 million euros within 20 years. Her success gave her enormous status and made it clear that investing in stocks is realistic for anyone. She wrote books and participated in interviews, until in September 2020, she died of cancer at the age of 82.

So, perspectives are always there. Ordinary people write amazing stories. Sometimes they become famous. Sometimes it's enough for them to become happy. Most of all, people try new things to experience extraordinary things. Then they set their first goals. Once these are achieved, they move on step by step, raising the bar with each subsequent goal.

I hope I've managed to convince you that *you can really have everything you want*. The only thing is that you must plan your goals correctly and precisely, which brings us to the subject of this chapter. Planning your life and dividing it into stages will assure you reach your objectives as you move from one point to the next. But first we must determine how high your goals should even be. Everything that can't be planned, at least to some extent, is unattainable for the time being, but that will change as we go along. When updating your goals, you will notice when a previously unattainable goal comes closer to you. Then you will make changes. **At the beginning of your goal setting, it is important that you only set plannable and therefore achievable goals**. More about this in the following chapters. But everything that can be realistically planned, you can also implement. Let's say you realized this at the age of 16, then your path to becoming a millionaire would theoretically be a very simple one:

> ➢ Cram hard in school and get a 1.0 average.

> ➤ Graduate medicine with top grades and start working as a doctor.
> ➤ With average annual earnings of 60,000 euros per year, 1 million euros accumulates in less than 20 years.

That sounds too simple? But things *are* just as simple in theory! If there are no breakdowns and you consistently implement your goals, it is just as simple in practice. We will go in-depth in the rest of this book to help you set the goals that you really care about and no matter how high and how far away they are, you will be able to achieve them over time with as high a probability of success as possible. And one thing is sure: *You will find the answers within yourself.* No one can make the decision for you if you are wavering between multiple goals or options. Other people can advise you, but decisions about goals that concern only you, are only yours to make. With that comes the fact that you have to bear the responsibility for them too.

Hint!

Responsibility is a critical point. People who are not used to taking responsibility tend to lead an alienated life. The reason for this assertion is as follows: If you have to make a decision, but it is difficult for you, you ask others. If you are unsure or afraid of the matter in question, you can shift the responsibility to the person who advised you. Being able to shift responsibility may provide some peace of mind. But it does not help you to lead a self-determined life and to realize your dreams. Act and take responsibility! It is right now that your self-determined life begins.

Your environment exerts power on you

Your environment and you, you exert great power on each other. You can help or harm each other; whether consciously or unconsciously. Surely you have already had a conversation with a person who had a completely different character or interests to you. You didn't come to a common denominator and didn't feel entirely comfortable with each other. Over time, you would have found common ground and a pleasant relationship, but it didn't happen. Now imagine that there are people who are regularly confronted with such situations: Bullying victims are an extreme case. They find themselves in an environment that is not only antagonistic, but completely destructive. What are the possible effects of this on the person? She feels lonely, inferior, doubt and may even develop psychological problems.

Of course, there are also positive examples: People who can master so many topics of conversation and have such charisma that almost everyone is attracted to them. They are on top of their game, always have company, often have a strong sense of self-confidence and can hope for support in difficult times.

What if you find out that you can be the 2nd person described? It is up to you to build an environment that complements you perfectly. Even from the worst starting position you are able to build up a circle of family, friends and acquaintances in which you, and the people around you, feel good.

Your environment can be both a driver and an obstacle. This guidebook will show you the way to choose an environment that is as suitable as possible for your goals. You will be free to decide which people you allow into your environment. Advantageous are people you can trust and who support you in your plans. Mutual appreciation is of great importance, it should also be reflected in your choice of words, because emotional intelligence is very important.

Final task

The final task for the 1st chapter heralds your change; the change from a person with nothing but fascinating dreams that require a clear direction, to a person with absolutely precise goals and a pathway to their achievement. The first step is to take stock: write down in bullet points all the things that seemed particularly important to you in this chapter. Above all, you should write down things that you had not yet considered. Often the devil is in the details: Maybe the small lessons contain the answers to why you have not yet achieved your goals as you would have liked. Also, note the things that you obviously identify as deficits in yourself to achievement.

Step 1 | What must be?

As much as you may sometimes hate to hear it, *some things have to be done.* They cannot be prevented. Even if you would prefer to stay in bed in the morning, you still don't. Because work, lectures, the crying baby or other obligations make you act to the contrary. So, you do what you have to do. There are other **commitments** too, some of them are even necessary to exist. Others are more or less self-chosen, such as the job or the baby. The job, although self-chosen, is necessary to earn money. The baby needs an education to prepare for childhood and later adolescence and adulthood – this is also clearly a duty.

This chapter will help you identify your commitments and plan for them. Because before you can work on your wishes and dreams, you have to cover your mandatory program. Otherwise, it will be critical for your health, your ability to pay for things, or your family in the worst case. A very important lesson awaits you, one that is key to making your life more relaxed in the long run:

As much as it may seem today that you are trapped in your daily routine and that your obligations will never let you go, this impression is deceptive. Because in the long run, things about your obligations can be changed. This will give you the chance to live the life you dream of. A different job? Better salary? Passive income? A more relaxed family life? All within the realm of possibility, but only in the long term.

Exist

Since time immemorial in the history of living beings, the goal has been to keep one's own species alive. Survival and reproduction served to achieve this objective. Today, both are easier. Survival is no longer a bare struggle, as it may have been in the days of the Neanderthals. Reproduction is assured, even if not every person chooses to have children. Food is available in stores and in most countries the majority of the population can easily afford it. Medical care in Germany is good. Times of crisis, such as the Corona pandemic, have shown how well the German health care system is doing compared to other nations. The fact that it has **become easier to secure one's livelihood** provides **advantages** above all for people in the highly developed industrialized countries:

> ➤ More time! In the past, a lot of time was spent hunting and farming for people to be able to feed themselves. This time is now saved because food can be easily bought, and farming equipment is efficient. Fast food for fast daily routines also makes things easier for city dwellers.

> ➤ More safety! A few centuries ago, a simple flu could mean death. Today, diseases can be treated better, and the general life expectancy is increasing.

> ➤ More education! People are more informed about what happens in the body when a certain vitamin is deficient or what the effects of insufficient sleep are. This can prevent negative consequences for health and psyche.

Now, realize what tremendous advantages you were given when you saw the light of day in this age! Do this with a feeling of gratitude. Because gratitude is a basic building block for approaching life positively.

My experience

I once had a flu-like infection and no paracetamol or other antipyretic at home. On the 2nd day of my infection, my heart, beat over 200 beats a minute for several hours – you can't stand that for long! In fact, with this seemingly banal flu infection, the ambulance service had to come, and I stayed in the hospital for 2 days. In that situation, I at least came close to understanding what a privilege we enjoy by having medications today that completely cure previously fatal infections within a day or 2. In fact, people used to die at the youngest ages because of flu-like infections. Today, by comparison, we have it much better in most places.

Your existence and that of many other people in the German population has improved in the course of the last centuries and even the last decades. Many things have become easier, many things have become better. Of course, there are still inequalities in this country, crimes happen and there are huge income differences between rich and poor. But if you want to look at it optimistically and motivate yourself – and that's what I recommend you do, because it doesn't make sense to slow yourself down – then you come to the realization that things have improved for the low-income earners in society, too. After all, even low-income earners usually have a roof over their heads thanks to government support, their children can at least go to school and learn for a better life as well as work, and it's not uncommon for them to even own a plasma screen with a Netflix subscription to pass the time. It's not the rule, but it does happen. Low-income earners could only dream of this a century ago.

With the conditions of existence improved on the whole, scope opens up for people to ...

> Work on the quality fulfillment of their existential needs.
> Restructure here and there.
> Promote and support their goals.

Existential needs (food, drink, sleep, medical care, security etc.) are the basic building blocks on which all other goals are built. For example, you won't be able to work well if you don't sleep enough and rest doesn't make up the deficit. At worst, you'll make mistakes that cost you your job. Or you may follow through in the long run and keep your job, but eventually suffer mental illness because you overexert yourself. Unhealthy eating is a danger that can even lead to hospitalization or expensive dental surgery, for example.

I have had shocking experiences with the long-term negative effects on the psyche, which still shape my actions today: When I first started my own business, I put all my eggs in one basket. Old-age provision? I can take care of that when I'm older. At a young age, I first have to generate capital and grow my business. Public health insurance? Too expensive for young people, I prefer private health insurance instead. And plenty of sleep? You can catch up on sleep when you're dead I thought. What ultimately turned out to be precarious for me were the latter 2 points: Health insurance and sleep. I responsibly put a retirement plan into action 4 years later and did everything right. But with health insurance, I wasn't very forward-thinking. Although I had a history with my heart, I hid it and cheated my way into the cheaper insurance policy. I slept very little and often worked up to 60 hours at a stretch with the help of caffeine pills and energy drinks. Nothing happened to my heart, but instead to my psyche after about 2.5 years. I was exhausted, but I kept working anyway. At some point, various physical signals came to me, including headaches, digestive problems, and later even dental problems. The stress had caused several ulcers to develop in my mouth. Because I could barely eat, I was losing weight, suffering nutrient deficiencies and weakening my immune system. There I was, with super-cheap private health insurance, but a high annual deductible for medical treatments. I had to fork out large amounts of money for it. When I finally recovered after a year of doctor visits, treatments etc., I was as "wealthy" as when I started, and that's when I decided to become sensible. I focused on recovery and a healthy diet, upgraded my health insurance plan for reasonable benefits, and over the next 4 years got much further than before, because I was clear-headed, my body and psyche were recovered, and I could make the right decisions.

If I were to tell you that the quality of your steak or vegetable ratatouille determines how successful you will be, you would think I was crazy. Fortunately, I don't want to say that. Because lightheartedness and balance include buying the ready-to-eat pizza at the discount store and sitting down at home with your loved ones for a fatty and sinfully lazy evening watching Netflix. Instead, I advocate that it's important to maintain a healthy balance. At the end of the day, it's all the little things that add up and lead to results. If you are, for the most part, healthfully and sustainably meeting your existential needs, you are already doing a lot of things right towards furthering your goals.

Hint!

You picked up a book on setting and achieving goals. Now one of the first things you hear is that you should consider sleeping, eating, and other needs when setting goals. Isn't that missing the point a bit? You'll find that just the opposite is true. You should set aside a lot of time in your daily routine for these needs. If you don't take these needs into account and set yourself too many goals, you will either have to cut back on your sleep or relaxed eating, or you will have to cancel set goals again. So, take the existential needs and the following advice seriously. Your health and goal setting will thank you for it!

How important is the quality?

Quality in meeting existential needs plays a crucial role. Have you ever gotten out of a bed that was too small for you? Did you have muscle and joint pain afterwards? If so, please imagine that you also slept too little. The more often this scenario occurs, the less rested you will be. When it comes to sleep duration, scientists are largely in agreement: 6 to 8 hours of sleep is considered optimal. What's more, 6 to 8 hours even lets you live longer, as the *Ärztezeitung* reports with reference to a mammoth study with no less than 117,000 participants! Frequent sleepers who slept significantly longer than the prescribed amount had the following problems:

➢ physical inertia.
➢ Depression or frequent depressive states.
➢ Cigarette and alcohol consumption.
➢ Hypertension.

Extreme short sleepers, on the other hand, often suffered from diabetes and obesity. Otherwise, few illnesses were observed in short sleepers, except for the accidents. It is obvious that too little sleep weakens concentration.

Sleep duration is a crucial point for sleep quality. It should neither be too long nor too short, both are associated with disadvantages and dangers. For hormone levels, it is best to sleep in the dark, as it is in nature. In addition, the temperature of the room should be taken into account: Between 16 and 19 degrees is considered ideal, as this is the best way to activate the growth hormone somatropin after falling asleep. This hormone influences the repair processes of muscles, skin and hair. The question of a comfortable and ergonomic sleeping surface remains. Comfortable sleeping ensures faster falling asleep and more physical well-being during everyday life. The simplest solution is to buy a mattress and pillows that you find comfortable after a test lie. If you have the desire and the money for a professional solution, you can have the mattress and pillow individually adjusted to your body.

Other authors, such as Calvin Hollywood in his guidebook *Wer will, der kann!* (2018), emphasize the importance of getting enough sleep at the optimal time: *"It's really very, very rare that I ever go to bed after 10 p.m. Yes, there are certainly a few exceptions: when I have a long-haul flight and am traveling overnight, for example, or on New Year's Eve. But in general, my alarm clock rings at 9:30 p.m., telling me that I should now prepare for sleep. My goal is to always get between seven and eight hours of sleep so that I'm really in top shape the following day."*

Notice

Just so you really internalize what we're talking about here: You spend 6 to 8 hours a day sleeping in bed. As you get older, this duration decreases due to your basal metabolic rate decreasing. If you calculate with the 6 to 8 hours for the sake of simplicity, 25 to about 33% of your life takes place in bed! If this part of your life does not get the attention it deserves, the other parts will be negatively affected. Due to interactions (see Chapter 1: Humans and their environment are systems), poor sleep can even negatively affect half of your life. Therefore, take this section on sleep seriously and strive for optimal sleeping conditions.

When it comes to food and drink, with the right nutrition you will feel better, positively influence your health and increase the probability of physical as well as mental performance. The best way to demonstrate this is with the example of an athlete. Athletes need resources, the most important of which is energy. This is provided over a long period of time by carbohydrates. However, not all carbohydrates are the same. The sugar underneath only provides a short energy boost. Long-chain carbohydrates, such as those from whole grains and vegetables, are best for long-term performance. For the athlete, this recommendation may be especially true so that he can complete his marathon, but it also applies to employees in the office. If breakfast consists of only coffee in the morning and you have to polish off a pack of Haribo towards mid-morning to raise performance levels, something has been done fundamentally wrong. Because apart from a short performance boost due to the rapid rise in blood sugar levels, little comes of it later. The diet has no quality. Instead, the foundation for diabetes and obesity is laid.

To ensure quality in nutrition, the easiest way is to follow the 10 rules of the DGE:

1. Eat a variety of foods and, above all, integrate plant-based foods into a varied diet.
2. Eat at least 3 vegetables and 2 fruits daily.
3. Among the cereal products prefer the whole grain versions.
4. Eat milk and dairy products daily, fish up to twice a week and a maximum of 300 to 600 grams of meat a week.
5. Use predominantly vegetable oils to meet fat requirements.
6. Instead of sugar and salt prefer to season with herbs and spices.
7. Drink at least 1.5 liters of water per day. Otherwise, prefer calorie-free or low-calorie drinks, such as tea.
8. Prepare food gently to keep micronutrient content as high as possible.
9. Eat slowly and schedule breaks between meals.
10. Keep an eye on body weight and exercise regularly.

Feel free to read more about this. It is best to use the official websites of recognized institutes or professional literature as sources, because many Internet sources convey the information incompletely or incorrectly. Change your diet step by step. It is not necessary to do a 180° turn. In addition, here and there an exception and a sweet is allowed, because to mortify yourself by unnecessary abstinence does not make sense, as it lowers life enjoyment. A healthy diet optimizes your well-being. Therefore, do not hesitate to make modifications to your current diet slowly so that you feel good.

Well-being is also an existential need because living in pain and restrictions is difficult. You promote well-being through the aforementioned tips on sleep and nutrition. Hygiene and relaxation measures are also important.

Notice

If you've read my book on developing mental strength, you'll be familiar with physical well-being in a different context: Appreciation. Showing appreciation for yourself is a basic building block for becoming satisfied and developing the motivation and confidence needed for the tasks and goals ahead.

You have free choice in the methods you use to enhance your well-being. Relaxation methods such as meditation even have the potential to improve your quality of sleep. Here you can see the interactions that can occur in the human system from a positive point of view: By meditating, you are taking a measure that increases your physical well-being and at the same time boosts the quality of your sleep.

Other measures for increasing physical well-being include massages, stretching exercises, sports, walks, and yoga. In addition, hygiene increases your physical well-being. It is even a crucial part of health. Hygiene and health include, for example, having the recommended professional teeth cleaning twice a year at a dental office. It is the only hygiene measure for healthy people that really requires medical implementation. So, take it especially seriously, because operations on the teeth or even dentures can become necessary sooner than you imagine. This is unpleasant and expensive. It can even affect the achievement of goals immensely. As you can see, it's the little things that make the difference.

Restructuring methods and approaches

Here I have created a list of essential existential needs. Copy it on a sheet of paper and determine your priority commitments for a healthy life as well as estimate the time they would take up in your routine:

Must-Target	Notes	Time required
Sleep		
Nutrition		
Hygiene		
physical well-being		

The good news for you at this point is that you have leeway in scheduling these areas. When it comes to sleep, you can only choose between 6- and 8-hours duration, but at least you have 2 hours of leeway. In terms of food, there are the options to eat healthy convenience food or order in to save time, or to cook for yourself to save money. Now let's go over the methods and approaches to restructuring that help you gain time or quality in your existential needs.

Task 1

After you have transferred the table from above onto a sheet of paper, the work begins. Use the first list to document your behavior so far. Note how much time you have spent on each of the 4 areas each day. If you didn't do something every day, calculate from the week to the day by dividing the hours you devoted to one thing during the week by 7.

In my case, for example, the following picture used to come out:

Must-Target	Notes	Time required
Sleep		10 hours
Nutrition		2 hours
Hygiene		45 minutes
physical well-being		0,5 hours

I saw the biggest deficit in my sleep and physical well-being. I used to get only 0.5 hours of physical relaxation a day. My change was to sleep 2 hours less. This freed up 2 hours, one of which I invested in physical well-being. The other hour I saved to use elsewhere. This is how the following table was created:

Must-Target	Notes	Time required
Sleep		8 hours
Nutrition		2 hours
Hygiene		45 minutes
physical well-being		1,5 hours

Do the same task for yourself. While doing this, think about where you would like to make improvements, for example, to gain more time or invest more time in a better sense of well-being.

This task makes sense but is quite theoretical. In practice challenges arise: How do I implement my aspirations? One popular hurdle is getting up early: How do you manage to get up early? Most of the time, you've gotten into the habit of sleeping too long or sleeping too short. At this point, a challenging path of change awaits you. On the one hand, my book *Habits of Winners* will help you to successfully change habits. On the other hand, the following 3 tips should prove helpful:

1. Proceed step by step. For example, instead of waking up 2 hours earlier immediately, try waking up half an hour earlier for 2 weeks. Then increase to 1 hour, and so on.
2. Set hurdles for bad habits. By making it impossible to practice bad habits, it is much easier to change.
3. Reward yourself for successful small steps to increase your motivation.

As a supplement to this task, here is some information on how you can restructure individual areas: In the area of nutrition, for example, you can increase it if you find that you always have too little time to eat or cook. This will bring more quality and probably more freshness to your diet. If you find that you invest too much time in nutrition, you can think about reducing the quality minimally by buying ready-made food now and then or cooking less fussily. A good option to get food quickly is snacks on the go or deliveries.

Notice

These seemingly small things that you have planned and timed so far (sleep, diet, etc.) will determine whether you have 2 hours more or even 3 hours less each day to work on your dreams. Do not underestimate the importance these things. Because if you do, everything will go back to its usual course: You'll stay stuck in a hamster wheel and miss your goals partially or completely. Your success derives from the fact that you plan exactly and set goals. For this, you create a time frame by planning your existential needs. Especially for long sleepers, a time gain of 2 hours through shorter sleep can work wonders.

Standing firmly with both feet on the ground

Because life is not just about existing (that's the part of your commitments we just discussed), but also about having both feet firmly on the ground, the planning continues: What do you need to have both feet firmly on the ground? What goals do you need to set?

- ➤ Lifestyle financing.
- ➤ Protection into old age.
- ➤ Protection in emergencies.

If you don't have enough money on the side to finance your living without work, a job is necessary for regular income. The fact is: work costs time. Accordingly, work is an integral part of most people's agenda. Retirement and health care are also important, although these usually involve a financial cost instead of a time cost. The importance of retirement planning is especially evident in long-term goals: If you want to be agile and explore the world in your old age, you need a good pension. Protection for emergencies is provided by health insurance, liability insurance against damages and other necessary insurances.

If you are not yet satisfied with your main job, your future pension or other aspects of your life, you can make changes over time. Many individuals who neither achieve their dreams nor set them as a goal give into the misconception that their current job is for all eternity. They see themselves as trapped because they have had the training and have been in that particular job for a long time. But that's not right. As mentioned earlier, you can have anything you want! All you need to do is plan **the right long-term goals**.

A lot can be achieved in the long term

In most cases, it is not possible to change jobs from one day to the next. Let's say you're a painter or a nurse and you're unhappy with your job: today you're working your 8 hours and tomorrow you'll be working the same. You have no realistic chance of changing jobs from one day to the next, except in the unlikely event of winning the lottery. However, if you work towards a change on a part-time basis over the long term and plan it accurately, you are very likely to land your dream job in 5 to 8 years.

My experience

One experience I have already shared in another book in this series is my professional transformation. I must confess that I had it easier than other people. I worked as a lecturer only 3 days a week and still earned a full-time salary, so I couldn't complain. But the job was exhausting. I was constantly lecturing the same content. Opportunities for advancement were limited. So, I looked for change and found it: In addition to my job as a lecturer at the time, I built another self-employed business in online marketing, where I could expand my business any way I wanted. I had a positive vision and finally the courage to leave my previous job and try my luck in online marketing. Thus, over time, I obtained a job that I loved and still love today, as well as prospects that are unlimited.

Online marketing is not for everyone. You probably have a different dream or will find your own personal dream through the exercises in this book. It doesn't have to be your job that you change. You can also focus on other things. For example, you can resolve to no longer burden yourself with rent payments for a roof over your head. For this, you set yourself the goal of financing your own property. This way, your existential obligation of paying rent will eventually no longer be necessary. You eliminate a financial burden and lower your running costs by owning your own property.

So, it may be that today you still have to work 8 hours full time, pay the rent or fulfill other duties that don't suit you. But with a positive vision that is realistically achievable, you will have the chance to change your present situation in the long run. To this end, coming up is a passage that describes the classification of goals according to their time reference.

Time reference of goals

The classification of goals according to time is your key to fundamentally turning your life around. Many of the commitments that you can't change overnight and make you unhappy, don't have to be a long-term part of your life! You have the power to change your future and long-term planning is the key to this.

Companies divide their goals into short, medium, and long-term according to a time reference. The same makes sense with people. In the **short term, obligations** are pursued and as we have already mentioned they cannot be changed overnight. For a large part of the population this primarily includes their current full-time job and financing the roof over their heads. When there is too little money, too little time, or other resources in insufficient quantities, pursuing all of these activities is necessary in the short term. Nevertheless, even in the short term**,** you can **begin to move life in a different direction with long-term planning.** This means that while you are working your full-time job today, you can enroll in a degree program on the side, and thereby gain qualifications that will bring you closer to your dreams in 3 to 5 years from today.

To give you a better idea of the time horizons for short, medium, and long-term goals, here are a few specifications. There are no universal truths, but in business administration the following classification is generally used:

➢ Short-term goals are those that are to be completed within 1 year.
➢ Medium-term goals are designed to last up to 5 years.

➢ Long-term goals are all goals that involve time horizons of more than 5 years.

This time division can be applied to general life planning. Everything that you have to do now (short term) in order to exist, you do over the course of 1 year. That's why setting short-term goals is critical to long-term success.

In the medium term, on the other hand, up to 5 years is enough time to set the course for a new full-time job, a property or a general improvement in prospects. For example, a part-time degree program can be successfully completed within these 5 years. If it's a 3-year bachelor's degree, then within 5 years it's even possible to start the new job that matches your personal dreams, offers more opportunities for advancement and a better salary.

Lastly, the long-term goals: In 5 years, you can achieve anything that is realistic for your situation. If you are a well-earning employee with 3000 euros net per month, you can become a millionaire in over 5 years; here we are realistically talking about around 15 years. If you want to start a family, long-term planning gives you the chance to find a partner and work out a professional situation that will allow you to provide for your family. It is true that something like family planning can only be done for the long term to a limited extent if a partner has not yet been found. After all, falling in love is often accompanied by coincidences. Nevertheless, you can go out on a limb and set yourself such goals for the long term.

Notice

Even medium-term goals give you a lot of leeway. You would be surprised what people can accomplish within 5 years! Let alone in a period of more than 5 years, the long-term time frame opens up possibilities.

Now, these longer-term perspectives have the risk of unpredictability attached to them. Something can come up even with short-term goals, but these are often made up for within a few days or weeks. This is usually easy to do and plan for. The longer the time horizon, the more unforeseen things can happen, which makes medium and long-term goals difficult to plan for. You should therefore plan more generally for medium and long-term goals and have more time and financial cushion available so that you do not have to turn your entire goal planning upside down for unforeseen problems.

Practical use of the classification of goals according to their time reference

How does all this work in practice? How do you benefit from the classification of goals according to their time reference?

It's simple: First, write down all your commitments that we've talked about so far. You write down how many hours a day you have to spend on sleeping, eating, hygiene, full-time job, etc. and how much money you have to spend on food, rent, retirement plans and important insurances. This will show what you have to invest in your life in the short term and how much money and time is left over.

Next, you can take the medium, and long-term view: **How much of my time and money can I spare now to create my desired future in the medium and long term?** In line with this, you set your medium, and long-term goals: For example, you invest 3 hours a week in further training or start financing a property so that you no longer have to pay rent in the long term.

Your advantage compared to the people who have no idea about the time reference of goals: You have timed your desired future and are already carrying out activities today that you know will help you achieve your dream future in the long term! You plan all of this with concrete figures for the time required and the financial outlay, so that you don't overextend yourself with your goals and the probability of success increases. You will learn all this at the end of the chapter in the big final task. For now, you know what time is all-about and why it is important for you. People who don't have this knowledge – and unfortunately this is true of a significant percentage of people out there – plan without an overview of short, medium, and long-term goals. As a result, they only know subconsciously why they are doing something. As a result, they are less likely to be motivated. Another danger is that people set themselves too many goals because they don't have an overall view. They may set themselves so many goals that they cannot achieve them all under any circumstances.

Vision! See the positive in all the efforts

So far, so good: In the long term, an incredible amount can be changed in your life. If you set long-term goals that match your dreams, you'll be well on your way to living the life of your dreams. Most importantly, you'll be able to develop positive visions of your future. You no longer see yourself in the same place at the office every day until just before you retire. Instead, you see yourself traveling the world professionally or in a practice-oriented job – just as you wish. You can also develop positive visions for your family: Your long-term goals can be family-oriented, so that you and your loved ones manage to go on vacation more often because the financial situation has improved. It's also possible that your children will benefit from unique opportunities, such as studying abroad, because of the better living conditions that you provide.

Whatever long-term goal you set for yourself: Every long-term and concretely named goal that you tackle through your actions today helps you to develop positive visions. These positive visions provide you with tremendous motivation and follow-through. Your life gets a meaning!

Example

There is a speech by Arnold Schwarzenegger (successful bodybuilder, Hollywood actor, entrepreneur, politician) that garnered just over 10 million views. It was one of the speeches that went the most viral in the history of the Internet. He talks about success and about his early days in the US: 5 hours of training, work, university, 4 hours of acting school etc. Here is an interesting excerpt:

People used to ask me when they saw me training [...]: "Why do you train so hard –5 hours a day, 6 hours a day – and still have a smile on your face? The others are training just as hard as you, but they look unhappy. Why is there such a difference?" I used to tell people, "It's different for me: I'm reaching for a goal. Ahead of me is the title of Mr. Universe (biggest award in bodybuilding; note). Every repetition I do brings me closer to achieving that goal; closer to making that goal, that vision, a reality. [...] That's why I couldn't wait to do another 500-pound squat, another 500-pound bench press, another 2,000 sit-ups, another set. So let me tell you this: visualizing your goal and striving for it is fun and enjoyable. You need a goal in your life; no matter what you do in your life.

That's it: Visualize! Visualize your success and everything you do now, which may seem insignificant or puny in itself, will take on an incredibly positive meaning! As you do, you will be more likely to perform your duties consistently and quickly, in order to have more time for your goals and your dream future.

So, when you create a life plan, you make it up of small, short-term goals and larger medium, or long-term goals. The medium and long-term goals are always subject to change and adjustment. Just because you are currently doing a job that you may not like does not mean that this will be the case permanently. Therefore, in the medium and long term, every minute you can spare, you are working on your dream future!

The overall motivation is as follows: The 8 hours you spend at work today are the key to financing new prospects for yourself or to acquiring important skills for them. An example: A person uses a permanent position for 3 years after her education, although she hates the employer. However, she knows that she will learn a lot there and will then be able to start her own business with a high probability of success.

Internalize one thing: Even with a great dislike for your current commitments, you should be optimistic and focus on your mid, to long-term possibilities. Because these opportunities are your path to achieving your dreams.

Task 2

Long-term goals can be promoted through visualization exercises. You may have read about visualizations in my other books. They are a well-known method in mental and motivational trainings.

In visualizations, you put your goals down on paper in writing or in the form of a graphic. It's best to use intermediate steps: For example, write down the grade point average you are aiming for in your training on a sheet of paper and hang it on a wall at home. That way, you can always keep an eye on your success. This will unlock additional motivation in you. Alternatively, you can use your imagination by visualizing the state you want to achieve: If you close your eyes and imagine several times a day how you will reach the goal and feel the success at the end of a multi-year journey, you will create a positive vision that will make it easier for you to master the individual stages until you reach the goal. Think about and/or research on the Internet 3 visualization methods that appeal to you and support you in achieving your goals. You will work with these methods later.

Attention, the time is limited! Use it!

You probably know the many quotes about taking advantage of the little time you have. After all, at some point it would be too late for that. Some people think that these quotes are just truisms that will fizzles out. But there is a lot of truth behind them. Here are 10 sentences that can be very helpful:

The ten commandments of time

1. It is not too little time that we have, but it is too much time that we do not use. – Lucius Annaeus Seneca

2. When the time comes when one could, the time is over when one can. – Marie von Ebner-Eschenbach

3. Time that we take is time that gives us something. – Ernst Ferstl

4. Time does not pass more quickly than it used to, but we pass it more hurriedly. – George Orwell

5. There are thieves who are not punished and yet steal the most precious thing: time. – Napoleon

6. The people who never have time do the least. – George Christoph Lichtenberg

7. Time lingers long enough for the one who wants to use it. – Leonardo da Vinci

8. We live in a time of perfect means and confused ends. – Albert Einstein

9. Your time is limited, so don't waste it living someone else's life. Don't let dogma trap you. Don't let the opinions of others stifle your inner voice. Most importantly, have the courage to follow your heart and intuition. Everything else is beside the point. – Steve Jobs

10. Ordinary people only think about how they spend their
    time. An intelligent person tries to take advantage of it. –
    Arthur Schopenhauer

Each of these quotes expresses, in one way or another, that
the time we have is valuable. Orwell and Einstein emphasize typical problems of today's world, that we humans act too fast and
too confused, although the available means are actually perfect,
and enough time *is* present. Von Ebner-Eschenbach and Steve
Jobs ring the alarm bells and warn us to use the time while it is
still possible. Steve Jobs formulates in detail that it is necessary to
follow one's own goals for this. In doing so, one should not let
oneself be lured into a trap by dogmas. These dogmas are sometimes the thieves of time that Napoleon addresses in his quote:
dogmas and people are thieves who rob people of their precious
time and go unpunished. Seneca and da Vinci give consideration
to the idea that enough time is always present, as long as one really
wants to use it. Schopenhauer notes differences among people.
Thereby it is a sign of intelligence to use the time and not "only"
to spend it – to act meaningfully, purposefully and for a concrete
purpose to a concrete benefit.

Some of these quotes are so simplistic that they ignore numerous factors. But that's what can help you think outside the box:
For example, I dislike quote VI, which says that people who never
have time do the least. It's pretty simplistic in that form, general-
izing, and unfair to the many exceptions. But when I think about
it a little longer, I develop a particular interpretation of the quote
that I can do something with: The quote criticizes the fact that
one talks one's way out of certain things; under the pretext of not
having time. In reality, however, one does have time. In fact, even

today I find situations in which I show this behavior, although it would be better for me not to talk my way out of it and to spend an hour working, reading, doing sports or something similar.

Task 3

You have 10 quotes. Sure, you don't agree with all of them, or you find some unfair. But there is at least a little bit of truth in each one. Write the quotes on the left side of a piece of paper and leave space on the right for comments about them. Afterwards, think about each one. The question you will have to answer for each is: "How can this quote help me improve the way I manage my time so far and thereby further my goals?" The goal here is that you openly consider how you can improve. These quotes will help you to look at things from different angles.

The purpose of this assignment and the explanations given so far is to show you how limited time is in a person's life. Why does this topic belong in this chapter? It's simple: In your life, an incredible amount of time is spent on your obligations! Working, preparing and consuming food, health, keeping your household in order... In fact, these things are a must. I was downright shocked when I observed and recorded over the course of a week how much time even the most ordinary chores take up: Cooking, vacuuming, laundry, ironing, etc. Leaving these things out, however, is not an option. After all, living in disorder, with poor health and eating a lot of convenience food reduces your prospects for the future.

My experience

What should appeal to you at this point is the fact that by consistently working towards your goals, you can buy yourself time. That's what I did when I was drawing a higher income and no longer wanted to completely take care of the household. I still did the ironing, laundry, office stuff and cooking myself. For vacuuming and mopping, on the other hand, I hired help. In the garden, I had a neighbor's boy do the most tedious work for me. He earned 10 euros pocket money every hour and I no longer had to weed or mow the lawn but could finally work on the terrace. By delegating this work, I bought myself about 5 additional hours of time each week. Since my income had increased significantly, I could easily afford it.

You will be able to delegate certain work and gain time. However, this requires accurate planning which starts with your commitments. Everything that has to be done, is done – that's it! The time required should be calculated as accurately as possible.

After that, you have time left over to work towards what you really want. We will deal with planning this time in the next chapter by defining your desired goals. It becomes clear that the time most people have to work on their dreams and desires is actually rather limited – at least in the beginning.

An extreme example: Person A sleeps 10 hours and works 8 hours. Including 1 hour to and from work, there are only 5 hours left to organize the day according to his own will. Over the course of the day, 1 hour is spent on eating and half an hour on household chores. That leaves only 3.5 hours.

➢ *Do you really want to be person A?*

A positive counterexample: Person B sleeps 6 hours. But she otherwise has the same daily routine. The fact is that by sleeping 4 hours less, she has 4 hours more time to work on her dreams and desires. She works on improving her professional situation, which will allow her to earn more and work less in 2 years. She shortens her daily work hours to 6 and allows herself an extra hour of daily sleep as a reward for the intense period. In total, she now has 6.5 hours more of life than person A.

➢ *If you want to be Person B, then you've gotten the gist of this book so far, and you'll be fighting for every spare hour in your daily life or goal planning.*

Final task

Start planning your own goals! Based on what you've learned in this chapter, start by making a list of your commitments. Take stock of how you would prefer to manage your commitments in order to use the time and financial resources given to you as efficiently as possible. In the following steps and chapters, this goal planning will of course be supplemented by your desired goals. As you can see in the instructions for the task, you can already start thinking about long-term goals. For now, however, the focus is on planning your commitments. First and foremost, define the following things precisely in terms of time and financial expenditure:

➢ Work
➢ Household duties

- ➢ Possibly family duties
- ➢ Cooking or eating
- ➢ Hygiene
- ➢ Sleep
- ➢ Relaxation and deceleration (e.g., lazing around, reading, massages, hobbies)
- ➢ (other) living expenses; separated by individual items such as rent, insurance, etc.

Which of these things do you need to include in your planning, and how much time and money do they cost? What do you plan to change based on the advice in this guide? (e.g., cutting back on sleep time, cooking more fresh food). Determining and planning these commitments in your daily life creates the framework for you to work on your desired goals in the next chapter and, for example, initiate long-term-changes.

Instructions for performing the task

Hanna works 8 hours a day, 6 days a week. Apart from that, she sleeps an average of 9 hours a day. She needs about 10 hours a week for the household. Cooking for herself and her family takes 2 hours a day. On the side, Hanna takes the children to school before work, which takes half an hour daily (from Monday to Friday). The weekly hygiene takes about 6 hours of her time. She earns 1,700 euros net per month. After expenses for rent including utilities, groceries and a few things for the kids, that leaves 300 euros a month to save. The spouse Jonas can contribute 200 euros per month, the rest of the money he spends on his hobbies and his share of food and rent. Most of the time Hanna and Jonas spend the rest of the money on vacations, trips or clothes because there are no other plans for it. Sometimes Hanna is dissatisfied in her life because she has no hobby to pursue. Until now, there was a lack of time – at least that was the thought. Now she wants to reschedule so that she no longer spends everything on consumption, but perhaps finances a property. She would like to involve Jonas more in the household and thus gain time. In addition, a somewhat shorter sleep duration is the goal. And maybe there is still a retirement plan in it. After all, the finances don't look that bad.

*The **new planning** in terms of the task proceeds as follows:*

Activity	Time spent per week (in hours)	Financial return per month	Financial expenditure per month
Work	48	1.700 euros net	–
Child benefit (2 children)		400 euros net	
contributed by spouse	–	200 euros	–
Household duties	7		
Cooking	14		
Take children to school	2,5		
Hygiene	6		

Sleep	49		
Real estate financing (incl. ancillary costs) instead of renting	-	-	1.000 euros
Food and other private expenses	-	-	900 euros
Retirement provision	-	-	100 euros
Total	126,5	2.300 euros net	2.000 euros

From the current planning it follows that from 168 hours in the week, 41.5 hours are still free after deducting the scheduled 126.5 hours. This corresponds to almost 6 hours per day! Based on her financial and time possibilities, Hanna sets herself the goal of saving her remaining 300 euros per month in order to be able to finance her own property soon. She discusses the matter with Jonas, who agrees to contribute his 200 euros as well, and is enthusiastic about the idea of financing a property. Since, with real estate financing, the rent payments would be void, despite the investment of the saved 500 euros, money would still remain, so that it would be economically intelligent planning. In 2 to 3 decades – so the long-term realistic plan – the real estate would be paid off and there would be no more financial burdens in rent or credit rates. In parallel, a supplementary private pension plan is to be taken out for around 100 euros a month. Hanna also plans to involve her spouse more in the household than before. The spouse agrees to the plan. This will give Hanna time for a hobby or certain relaxation practices. The next chapter continues with more detailed planning of hobbies and wishes.

Step 2 | What do you want?

Once your commitments are recorded, the program is complete for now. But keep the list from the final task anyway because you will still be working on it as we go along. This is your 1ˢᵗ list of commitments from which we determine the subsequent steps. Starting in this chapter, with step 2 – establishing your wishes and dreams.

If life were only about what has to be done and didn't correspond with your dreams at all, it would likely be quite unbearable for many people. Successful people emphasize time and again how important it is to be enthusiastic about your path. Sleeping, working and eating, are activities that serve to solve problems. People sleep so they can relax and recharge their batteries, otherwise they'd be tired and incapable of functioning properly. Work serves to solve the problem of financing your life while giving you a role in society. And eating and drinking serve to solve the problem of energy needs and sustenance in order to perform and survive.

Out of problems, and forwards to your dream world – that is the motto of this second step! Get inspired, try things out and find your passions. Make real what you have been dreaming about for a long time. And here comes the juicy bit: the easiest way to make your dreams come true is to apply the consistent planning that you have already begun to learn about. It isn't for nothing that there are training plans in the gym, dances with simple steps for the beginner in dancing, ranking with belts in martial arts, a clear sequence of teaching contents in language learning, a certain sequence of skills that are learned one after the other in pottery.

Start planning your desired goals as accurately as you learn to do certain activities in textbooks or courses. This will help you implement your desired program more consistently and acquire skills more quickly. Every now and then, people quickly lose interest when they try new things. Possible reasons are that things don't suit them or that there are obstacles that crop up. You can counteract this by planning thoroughly. This chapter tells you how to do this. In this way, you will have a high probability that your attempts at new hobbies and interests will be successful first time around.

Let yourself be inspired!

What needs the goals should satisfy

There are certain completely natural needs that humans being have. Consequently, it is appropriate to integrate them into your planning process. Please do not misunderstand this chapter, while it introduces you to those needs in detail, the goal is not to prescribe them to you. Of course, you alone decide what to put on your wish list. The following serves solely to open your eyes, so as to prevent you from disregarding these needs, that could result in you becoming dissatisfied and ultimately failing to achieve your goals, despite having done some excellent planning.

There was a phase in my life when I was on a good path, and I was experiencing professional success. I had given up my teaching job and was working in online marketing. While at the same time I started a degree program, which I successfully completed.

I had regained my old discipline and increased it. Consistent goal setting was a matter of course, and achieving my goals worked like clockwork. But I overlooked one important component in all of this: my fellow human beings. With increasing success, I became so ambitious that I planned every aspect of my life in minute detail, depriving myself of any spontaneity. Social contacts didn't even happen by chance anymore. I had no fixed time scheduled for socializing, nor did I have any spontaneous time available for it. Eventually I became tired of realizing of my goals, and dissatisfaction arose in me. It was no wonder, because I had been distancing myself socially for over half a year ... until I was almost living for myself, alone in my own hyper-disciplined world. I allowed myself a few hours of free time every day, but the problem did not solve itself, as I slowly despaired. What could it be that made me feel so demotivated and powerless? I learned the reason when I received a surprise visit from 2 old friends. During their regular visits over the course of 2 weeks (they were on vacation in my area and often imposed themselves on me, which is why we met frequently), I regained more zest for life and motivation. All this time I had overlooked a central need in my planning: Man is a social being.

Because we are social creatures, the recommendation at this point is that you give enough space to social needs in your list of desired goals. How much you plan for this in your everyday life should depend on how much contact with other people you already have through your commitments (e.g., work and family). If you interact with people frequently at work and your colleagues appeal to you, you can take more space for your free time. Family and friends still have a high value and should not be neglected.

Social goals and their importance

If it's up to needs researchers, then social goals must play a central role. Companies know the same thing, which brings us back to the entrepreneurial aspect of goal planning. Companies set their goals not only in terms of orders, production, sales figures and expansion. In recent decades, corporate social responsibility (CSR) has increasingly come to the fore. This expresses a company's responsibility in the social sphere: companies are obligated to create a pleasant working environment for their employees, taking their needs into account. And indeed – even in the supposedly capitalistic and profit-oriented companies – there are abundant traits of humanity nowadays. Based on models, man is seen as a pool of skills and abilities. Accordingly, he should be enabled to develop further and realize himself.

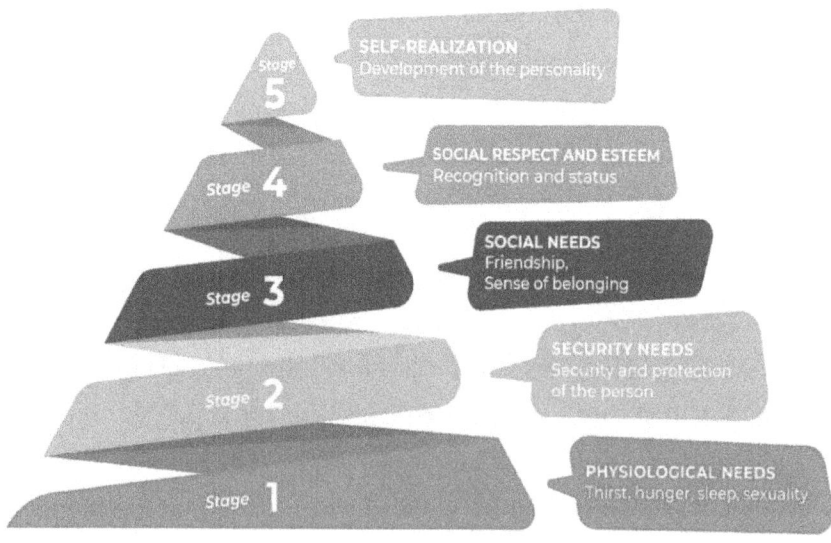

Figure 5: Maslow's pyramid of needs

Maslow's pyramid of needs is a prime example of the position of social needs in a person's life. It is used in business administration but is equally important for every private person when setting goals and planning their own life. The pyramid has 5 levels. On the 3rd level from the bottom comes social needs. This means having certain contacts and being able to talk to them. One level above, on level 4, is the need for social respect and esteem. In other words, a distinction can be made between the need to talk to people and the need to be respected and valued by them.

In fact, the second is especially important: Who, if not the people around you, could effectively convey a feeling of respect and appreciation to you? You yourself, of course. But if you consider that doubts arise in everyone from time to time, it is good to be able to rely on people in your environment to talk you out of them. In this way, you gain confidence in difficult phases and are stronger than if you were on your own. Wolfgang Schmidbauer (2012) finely formulates this important aspect:

"Man is indeed a vertebrate in his physique, to which bones and ligaments give a firm structure. But psychologically he resembles insects, whose bodies are soft on the inside and at the same time supported and protected against the environment by an outer shell. We are psychologically dependent on being strengthened from the outside. Without symbolic confirmation or confirmation rooted in interpersonal contact, we lose our inner support."

This explanation gives you an indication as to which direction social goals should take: Ideally, you build an environment in which you make each other strong. This mutual strengthening does not have to be based exclusively on praising each other. In addition to words of praise, the focus could be on raising proportionate justified criticism and presenting it constructively.

Make new contacts and deal with people properly

You may be shy and have a small circle of friends. Or you may be so outwardly focused that you have created a large circle of friends. The important thing is not the size, but the quality of it. Meaning the feeling you have when meeting the people around you: Do you feel good around these people or not? If yes, then you have a good environment. If not, there is room for improvement. So, you could set yourself a goal to work on improving your circle of friends. Giving you the opportunity to deepen existing relationships and to look for new friends too.

Try to create a sense of reciprocity in everything positive you receive: if a person compliments you frequently, look for the person's qualities and give him or her legitimate compliments as well. If a family member always stands by you, you stand by that person too with everything you can muster. In a healthy environment, it is important not only to take, but also to give. That way, your positive relationships are likely to last longer.

What is wholly undesirable is frequent grumbling, comparison with others, competitiveness among friends or family members, frequent lying, and so on. Of course, there are exceptions. Every once in a while, competition among friends is beneficial, such as when it pushes both people towards improvement and is done fairly. Great rivals have turned into great friends in this world. It can also be normal to have no time for friends when you are busy improving other aspects of life. But apart from those few exceptions, the thoughts and actions listed at the beginning of this paragraph are generally not helpful.

I once moved in a circle of friends that was counterproductive to my happiness. If I am not to point the finger, I'd say simply that that group of people did not fit my character. One of my best friends always steered the conversation towards his professional field. And if you took the bait, he used it as an opportunity to belittle you. Another friend came from a different culture. This is an interesting thing in itself but can be a problem if he puts his culture above everything. Accordingly, he presented himself as limited and maladjusted in his views on various topics, which was a problem in that he spoke disparagingly about the female gender and belittled my views. In the family, on the other hand, I had a radical pessimist with whom I had a lot of contact: my father. As long as I did not change anything in this circle of family and friends, I always had problems: I didn't feel valued. I didn't experience support in my goals. When I addressed these issues and wanted to find solutions, none of the people concerned showed any insight. I became more and more dissatisfied as a result. Ultimately, reducing my contact with these people and even cutting it off completely in some cases helped me. I took more time making new contacts and made sure that there were similarities in character or at least openness to talk about differing points of view.

Task 1

It is normal not to get along with certain people for various reasons. Write down all the people in your circle of acquaintances, friends and family, one below the other, on a sheet of paper in the left column. For each person, think for 5 minutes about how you feel after having contact with them. In the right column, on the line corresponding to each name from the left column, record on a scale of 1 to 10 how you felt after meeting that person. With "10" meaning you feel absolutely great. Any person who receives less than a "5" leaves you feeling uncomfortable for some reason. Think about what this might be and how it threatens your goals and psychological well-being. Based on this assessment, determine the right actions to take:

> With which people do you engage in an open conversation that reduces problems in your interpersonal interaction?

> What can you do to help create a better feeling with that person in your conversations and meetings with them?

> With which people should you possibly break off contact? Is it worthwhile making new contacts?

> What social goals do you have and what people contribute to you achieving them?

Can social needs be unimportant?

I have already given an example of my own personal experiences highlighting the difficulties I had with social contacts. While I find it hard to imagine that it is different for other people, my own ideas naturally do not lend sufficient foundation to the argumentation in this book. Therefore, based on further experience and scientific research, we explore the question: *Can social needs really be unimportant?*

For you, clarification of this question is especially important if you doubt the previous explanations about the importance of social goals. Accordingly, you might also ask yourself: *"Why should I set myself any social goals with the help of this guidebook, when I don't care about my environment? I'm just going to do my thing, aren't I?"*

Some people have this way of thinking. I also had it. It led me into misfortune, as I already explained. If we go by the findings of psychologists, sociologists and other scientists, a similar verdict emerges – social needs are important for human beings. Or going further – they increase the prospects of a healthy life. Too much loneliness makes people ill, according to an article in *TAGESS-PIEGEL.* A distinction can be made between emotional and social loneliness. The former occurs when one does not have a steady partner and thus no close reference person. Social loneliness, on the other hand, affects those who are completely alone and have no contacts at all. Both forms of loneliness cannot be generalized because of people's individual reactions. But the fact of the matter is that whether it is emotional or social loneliness, it can lead to psychological problems, and even physical ailments. For example, the article in *TAGESSPIEGEL* goes on to report, citing research results from the University of Chicago, that when a person is rejected by others, the same regions in the brain react as they do to physical pain.

But what does loneliness mean? At what level of rejection, and other forms of lack of contact with people really constitutes loneliness?

Kim Bartholomew's attachment theory offers an answer. According to this theory, there are 4 different types of attachment:

1. Secure type: develops fulfilling relationships quickly and does not worry about being alone.

2. Anxious type: afraid of the possible negative consequences of social contact and risks little, although this usually leaves him lonely and feeling exactly what he fears.

3. Possessive type: close connections to fellow human beings are his goal, which is why he already reacts very sensitively to minor rejections.

4. Rejecting type: does not want to be dependent on others, nor does he want others to be dependent on him, which is why he enters into few relationships.

Admittedly, this classification into types is very simplistic. However, you can get some helpful information from it. On the one hand, the types reveal some advantages and disadvantages of loneliness; for example, the lack of dependence can be seen as an advantage. For another, the types impressively show that there is no one form of loneliness. Considering the fact that many more attachment types could be found, loneliness has to be considered in a differentiated way.

Task 2

This task serves to clarify a question: Do you feel lonely? When you set your social goals, you should clarify this question. What counts in the assessment is purely your emotional state. Because what you feel, reflects your social satisfaction, or shows a present dissatisfaction. Therefore, keep a diary for 2 weeks starting today and question various situations in your everyday life with each entry (at least 2 entries a day). Did you feel lonely? If so, when was it and why did you feel lonely? Even with small signs of loneliness, you should make an effort to look for solutions following this task. Set a goal that fits your problem. Examples: Go out more often with existing friends, join a club, or find new friends.

A small hint with reference to the first task: Loneliness can also stem from the fact that you do not have people in your environment who can understand certain emotional states and give you the wrong support. Therefore, when setting your social goals, try to analyze your needs carefully.

Example

A fitting example of this is therapy groups: Even the best circle of friends cannot always give the right advice to a person addicted to cocaine, a dry alcoholic, or a rape victim. After all, you have to have experienced some problems yourself in order to be able to empathize with an affected person and give good advice. Therefore, look for special interlocutors for special concerns. This radical example can also be applied to smaller issues. For example, there may be circles of friends who do not share your enthusiasm for a small hobby. So, try to find social contacts unique to your hobby. There is certainly a suitable Facebook group for every hobby, no matter how small, where you can find like-minded people and exchange ideas about your passion.

At the end of the day, this is exactly what it means to consider one's social needs in goal setting and to build a good environment for oneself: **Matching your own interests, goals, and activities – no matter how small they may be – to an appropriate set of understanding interlocutors!** In this way you learn as much as possible and can reach your goals better. After all, people should be there to help you. Finally, it should be mentioned that you can of course do certain activities all by yourself and keep the enthusiasm anyway. Time for yourself should be available on any given day anyway. A good balance between contact and alone time is optimal. You find this balance for yourself by trying things out. Just remember that being completely alone is never good in the long run, according to scientific findings.

Find desire goals

Now let's move on to defining your desired goals. First of all, it is important to distinguish between the terms: For this guide, desired goals are defined as everything that you do because you want to do it. These can be individual activities (e.g., hobbies, meeting friends) or long-term professional and private goals (e.g., new job, owning a home instead of renting). It is anything you do outside of your commitments. Commitments were the main topic in the last chapter. The main topic of this chapter is *desire goals*. These goals are closely related to your social goals because in your personal life, unlike at work, you have the freedom to create your social environment. So, try to set your desire goals based on the first 2 tasks in this chapter and matching the findings from them. In this way, you will balance 2 important components of your personal life – social and activities. You'll be able to balance any social deficits from your must-do goals (e.g., if you're rarely around people at work) with your desire goals.

There are a number of desired destinations open to you, from a wide variety of fields:

> ➤ Sports (including team sports, martial arts, athletics, gymnastics, fitness, jogging).

- ➢ Art (including pottery, sculpting, painting).
- ➢ Dance (including hip-hop, couple dance, group perfor- mances, ballet).
- ➢ Nature (including gardening, involvement in a nature con- servation club, hiking, biking).

These areas, which are still quite hobby-oriented, are supple- mented by others that can serve specific purposes. Should you have the desire to practice a different job in the long term, then there are still desire goals in the field of education: courses, areas of study, training etc. Sometimes just learning a new language is enough to get better prospects and a better salary in your current job.

Example

The mother of a good friend has been an outpatient caregiver for over 30 years. She goes from house to house caring for pa- tients who need it. She is an employee for the German Red Cross. Advancement prospects are definitely there, they always have been. The catch: the friend's mother is an immigrant and although she learned the German language relatively quickly, she makes mistakes now and then in minor grammar. Additionally, because she speaks with a slight accent, she feels ashamed. The fact is that this would not stand in her way one bit and promotions have been suggested to her several times. But she refused, because it would be embarrassing for her to make mistakes when writing texts in a higher position. Now she is about to retire. She loved her job be- cause she could help people. But she regrets not having taken ad- vantage of the opportunities offered to incorporate her own ideas and visions into the company, and not having been able to finance a better way of life.

In this case, it would have helped to attend a German course. Maybe it wouldn't even have had to be a course, but even just a simple app on her smartphone to improve her language skills. Come to think of it, even that might not have been necessary. She had the promotions assured anyway because offers were forthcoming. Shame and fear stood in her way, in this case, irrational shame and fear.

If you are unsure what your desired goals are, then the best thing to do is to start informing yourself. The more trade magazines you read, documentaries you watch, hobbies or further education you test (there are always free test phases), and the more you are always on the lookout for something new, the sooner and faster you will find something suitable for you.

What could be the reason why you can't think of any desired goals? One possible scenario is that you are already satisfied with your life. Another possible scenario is the lack of a concrete idea: Maybe you lack a positive vision of your future life because you have been trapped in your personal hamster wheel for too long. You may be afraid to take responsibility for yourself and to set your sights on your goals. Another conceivable cause is the classic problem of the digital age: You have too many ideas and set yourself too many goals at the same time.

If you are currently satisfied with your life, look for small areas of improvement. If you don't find any, then you probably already have the right "must" and "want" goals. This means that you can use the advice in the other chapters of this book to optimize your planning, but otherwise leave everything as it is.

The situation is different if you are dissatisfied with your life:

➤ Do you regularly miss your goals?

➤ Your everyday life is too much of a burden for you?

➤ Your job, your free time, and the people around you leave you with too many negative emotions?

➤ You lack ideas for creative pass-times, and it seems like you are wasting your life?

Exactly for these problems the following contents have been designed to inspire you, to point out your talents, and to provide you with concrete instructions on how to choose suitable desired goals.

Example

U.S. actor Denzel Washington, known as a unique character actor, and for his involvements outside of acting, spoke several times to college graduates. His motivational speeches are listed on several YouTube channels in a row with those of the greatest entrepreneurs and politicians out there. In one of his speeches, he made a very important point: He said that *what matters to* us as human beings is *not* always how *much* we have, but *what* we have. However, it is more important to do what you love in life and what is right for you. By following your passions and building on what you already have – whether it's character traits like patience or resources like money – you increase your chance of success.

Be inspired and courageously try new things

Often people do not follow their desired goals because there is some uncertainty or improbability associated with it. From this we can infer the central advantage that commitments have: Living the life one has to live – working, sleeping, feeding oneself, taking care of the household, taking care of one's health – is associated with security and normality. One does not step out of line. Accordingly, you rarely have to explain yourself to people. If you are puzzled at this point, the following example will explain what is meant: Imagine you are observing 2 people. One person works 8 hours a day, then goes home and makes his dinner. The rest of the time is spent watching series on the couch. The other person works 8 hours, also has a mini-job and is doing distance learning in parallel. She is often exhausted because she manages a heavy workload. That's why she uses Sundays for extensive relaxation. With which of these people would you be more likely to object to the daily routine? Usually, it's the second person who has 2 jobs and is studying at the same time. Because having such a workload, seems abnormal.

But since when is not normal automatically bad? As long as you feel that your regeneration is sufficient and you make good use of the small time-outs during the day, you can have a busy schedule and still be satisfied and recovered. If you want to find your true desired goals and make maximum efficient use of your lifetime, please get inspired! Dare to go unfamiliar ways. Possibly this entails that you try out new things. Do not be afraid of it.

Example

On goal setting, Denzel Washington recited an anecdote in one of his speeches. He was talking about a task on an IQ test: In this test, there are 9 dots in 3 rows inside a box. The task is to draw 5 lines with a pencil without lifting the pencil. The crux: the 5 lines are supposed to connect all the 9 dots. This task can only be completed successfully if the lines are drawn to the outside of the box. With this example, Washington appeals to students to think outside the box; that is, to pursue even unusual lines of thought and act accordingly.

The desire goals are what make you leave your comfort zone. For these goals, you go the extra mile in your life. You no longer just do what you have to do, but what is close to your heart. If you want to succeed in this desire program and achieve the goals, your goals should come from your heart. Afterwards, think of these wish goals as exactly what they are: a wish planning exercise in which you are purposeful but feel no pressure. Who cares if you miss a free throw at the next handball game in one of Germany's lowest leagues? Who cares if your correspondence course goes to waste? Maybe it just wasn't the right thing for you. You still have a full-time job and all the security you need in life.

The desire goals are waiting for you. They are waiting for all your creativity, your courage, your enthusiasm, your passion, your vision, and your dreams. Do not be afraid to make mistakes! Don't think about having to justify to others why you do or don't do a certain hobby! Be open to even the most outlandish hobbies and ideas, because maybe there is just the right thing for you, hidden in one of the insane ideas!

Task 3

Start working on a preliminary list of desired goals. For this purpose, take a blank sheet of paper and write down all the goals that you would like to achieve. The exact time planning up to realization as well as the weighing up process, comes later. For now, just collect goals. When making your preliminary list, try to incorporate your findings from the social-needs tasks. Which desired goals are appropriate for meeting your social needs? Also, if you are unhappy with your full-time job, rent payments, or other obligations in your life, consider what opportunities there are to make long-term changes based on desire goals. Goals like financing a home, traveling more often, studying while working, continuing your education, and similar goals are absolutely right on the money here. More advice awaits you in the coming subchapters. Your list of desired goals may be extensive.

Personal hobbies and talents – great opportunities lie dormant here

Ever thought that hobbies and talents can become a profession? It's not the rule, but it is possible. Especially in today's times, it's easier to monetize hobbies and talents. Let's say you have handyman skills and put it on your wish list to refinish an old piece of furniture every day. You sand down an old cabinet, prime it and repaint it. You cover the inside of the cabinet with fabric. The result is a French Provence style masterpiece. As a joke, you get the idea to put the cabinet up for sale on *eBay Classifieds*. You end up making a huge profit on the sale, because people are willing to pay for unique products that exude personality. Over time, you get the idea to share your artwork on social media, create an online store with a simple modular system, and build a small business. As a sideline, you earn a high 4-digit amount per year. What's more, you're doing something that's close to your heart and that you enjoy. You receive recognition via social media. This also satisfies your social needs.

Hobby and talent = profession

This simple formula can work if you want it to. If you find it too stressful and would rather let your hobby, be a hobby, you are of course equally free to do so. Whether as a profession or for fun, promote hobbies and talents anyway! Do more of what you enjoy. Develop your talents. Work to perhaps turn your hobby into a profession. Not only hobbies and talents are important: expanding your knowledge and interests also make excellent additions to your list. These tips will help you find and set appropriate desired goals.

Notice

Practicing hobbies should never become stressful. Otherwise, they end up not serving as relaxation and filling you less and less with joy. Ideally, objectives concerning your hobbies should be formulated as loosely as possible. Leave room for spontaneity. As soon as you notice that the hobby is stressing you out in some way, or that it is taking up too much of your time so that you can hardly relax during the day, you should tone down your goals.

"One day your time will come. At your deathbed will be not only friends and family, but also the other companions of your life: your talents and abilities. They will tell you that it is a pity that you left them unused. It was clear from the beginning that you would eventually pass away. The talents, however,

could have outlived you. Now, unfortunately, they will be buried along with you." – Denzel Washington (U.S. actor)

With this quote we conclude the statements of Denzel Washington. With this sentence, the actor encouraged students to use their talents and abilities as well as possible. Mistakes are all too normal in the process. Even big mistakes can happen. But what matters in life is to have the courage to make mistakes. And when you fall, always fall forward, and keep going. Just don't fall back ...

Turning old into new – skills over time

In your search for desired goals for comprehensive goal planning, one last piece of advice awaits you: never get into the habit of definitively writing off a goal based on past experiences. If you couldn't do something in the past or were talked out of it, it doesn't necessarily have to be wrong for you today. Over the years, many things may have changed in the way you think and act. It may be that activities that were unsuitable for you 5 to 10 years ago suit you today.

Author Bernhard Moestl also addresses this issue in his best-seller *Der Weg des Tigers* (2013). He cites an experience from his own life: He was repeatedly told in his environment that he had no manual skills. What's more, he didn't enjoy doing manual work. He therefore often let other people go ahead with the work in question. He was convinced of his own inability. One day he found himself in a situation where he was forced to renovate a photo studio. Helpers were not available. The hardship of the situation led him to try himself. He took it upon himself to forget his perceived years of incompetence and take on the task with an open mind. The result: all the renovations looked perfectly satisfactory. Apparently, he didn't have 2 left hands after all.

What Moestl wants to say with this example, and what he comes directly to later, is the fact that in the course of time every human being undergoes further development. Why should the human being not learn new abilities in the context of further development? Quote from Moestl: *"But it is a fact that we learn and develop further. And that today we might be able to do things with ease that would have been impossible for us 10 years ago."*

This state of affairs can be explained transparently in 2 words: **Transfer benefits**. If you learn certain things or activities in the course of your life, you also benefit from them in relation to other activities. For example, a person who can already play 10 instruments can learn each additional instrument with less effort than a person who does not yet play any instruments. In addition, there is another phenomenon that is unfortunately little researched scientifically: if you have tried an activity for a while and then take a longer break (whether years, months, weeks), you can learn the activity more easily after the break. Some learning concepts make use of this, pointing to long-term memory: if you cram through an activity at all costs, you will only retain the sequences in short-term memory and have a harder time recalling them. In contrast, people who deal with the content regularly are able to store it in long-term memory, from where it is easier to recall once it sits.

Task 4

Transfer these insights to your desired goals by thinking about whether there are things you would like to do but are doubting your abilities. Think back to your childhood: was there anything there, in your youth, or in your young adult life that you very much wanted to do, but for a variety of reasons it didn't work out? If so, write it down on a blank piece of paper. Then, for each of these things, think about why you didn't master it or couldn't make it work. Then answer the question of whether it could be different today. It is best to try out the activities without obligation. This is the best way to find out whether an activity that didn't suit you in the past suits you better today. If so, add it to your preliminary list of desired goals.

From mere goal to action

How many desired goals do you have now? What comes into question for you? In what do you want to rediscover yourself? If you have formulated some wish goals with the help of the previous tasks and contents in this chapter, the question now arises as to how to operationalize them:

How do you translate your wishes and dreams into actions? How many wish-goals can, or should you set at the same time in order not to overwhelm yourself in view of the parallel existing obligations?

It's a little easier with your day-to-day responsibilities. For example, a certain amount of time is usually set aside for your work. Your superiors or the boss take over the task allocation directly. Household chores, on the other hand, can be planned flexibly and are usually done when there is time – or they are not done at all ... Nevertheless, chores usually require a little less planning than voluntary goals.

When it comes to your desired goals, you are the boss: you determine which goal you choose, how you divide it into intermediate steps, and finally, how you achieve it. You also determine the quantity of goals. You are responsible for your goals. Of course, as many people do, you can prefer to listen to other people's advice and follow their wishes in your life. Or you can do nothing at all. Then you have no responsibility and don't have to plan anything. But then this advice has done nothing. It's time to act and tackle your dreams. For this, it is essential that you take responsibility for your goal setting and actions.

It's time to take responsibility

If you've been reluctant to take responsibility for your actions, now is the time to rethink. You are faced with several options for dealing with the effect your environment has on you. In all the options for goal setting that you have gathered from the first 2 steps of this guide, the environment will play a role. The reason for this is that pretty much every goal involves other people. Even if you keep something like a diet to yourself, sooner or later friends, family or co-workers will notice that something has changed in your eating habits. For some it will be a reason for praise, but for others it will be a reason for blame.

Example

You shouldn't always take praise and criticism seriously these days. An amazing example is the reactions to an Instagram post by plus-size model Ashley Graham. The woman has her curves and medically she is overweight, but she accepts it. She is happy with it and works successfully as a model. An extensive fan base admires her. So far, everything is fine. Now Ashley Graham has apparently nevertheless sporty hobbies. Practicing sports, but still staying true to her overweight figure and being happy with it, do not contradict each other. Nevertheless, when she posted a photo of herself at the gym, she gathered plenty of criticism from her followers. She no longer remains true to herself and does not stand by her body it was said sporadically. This form of criticism is inappropriate.

This example is not intended to start a debate about the justification of sports, obesity, or physical ideals. It is only meant to illustrate that nowadays people are sometimes so strongly focused on one point of view that they can no longer differentiate. So, it can happen that even with – from your point of view – highly praiseworthy goals you get to hear a lot of criticism. Be prepared to hear perhaps the strangest and most absurd criticism of your decisions. After all, the philosophy of the critics in the example would mean that no overweight person can be proud of his figure if he practices sports. But doesn't every person have the right to practice sports hobbies in public?

There will always be criticism. It helps to listen to this criticism. The more meaningful the criticism seems from your point of view, the more it may be included in the decision about setting and pursuing goals. But the decision is always yours or yours and the other people involved. Negative circumstances in the environment may arise sooner or later. You decide whether you want to complain and pass on the responsibility for the decision or whether you want to live your dream life on your own initiative despite the unavoidable resistance. As soon as you realize your personal responsibility and act accordingly, you will realize that you have the ability to influence and control your environment and decide how far you will let *it* influence *you*.

Refine your list of desired goals

When making your list of desired goals, it is first and foremost important that you write down what is realistic and plannable from your current point of view. It doesn't matter whether the goal is short, medium or long-term. After all, you divide the goals into intermediate steps for better operationalization anyway. More about this awaits you in the 4 steps of this book, when you precisely formulate your long-term planning.

Estimate time required

After formulating realistic goals, you need to find out how much time is behind your desired goals. This is the only way to choose the right amount of goals to pursue at the same time, so as not to overburden yourself. If you choose too many desired goals in addition to your commitments, you run risks. On the one hand, it is possible that due to the large number of goals, none of them will be implemented properly and the commitments will suffer. On the other hand, it can happen that you pursue all goals well for a while, but then you are too busy and mental and physical fatigue sets in, which completely slows you down.

Therefore, the next step after writing down your desired goals is to estimate the time required for each of them. It can be the daily time spent, but it can also be the time spent over a longer time horizon. For example, when traveling, it's hard to measure daily time because you don't travel every day. Here, it makes more sense to report the monthly time spent.

Important: Estimate the time required realistically and generously. This also includes preparatory measures, such as packing the sports bag or shopping in advance for an excursion with the family (e.g., provisions and tent for a camping weekend). If you want more general knowledge and use your smartphone as a knowledge library for that, there's no need for preparatory measures. Regular trips to the library, on the other hand, require preparatory measures. Nevertheless, there are also goals that do not require additional time, such as quitting smoking. If anything, they give you more time because you no longer have to buy cigarettes. In your list next to each goal, note how much extra time it will cost you.

Final task

Revise the list you have worked with so far in the 4 tasks of the chapter. You have written down desired goals. Now cross off the desired goals from the list that do not fully convince you. Also, cross off the goals that don't seem realistic at all from today's point of view. It doesn't have to be a "goodbye", because maybe the goals will become realistic in a few years or months. For now, however, they are not and do not belong on the list. Next to each remaining desired goal, enter numbers that describe its priority. The number "1" represents the highest priority, "5" represents the lowest priority. Also, write down the amount of time you expect to spend on each goal. The quantity of your goals does not matter at first.

Instructions for performing the task

Let's take Ingo as an example, who, while reading this chapter, identified the following desired goals for himself in the individual tasks:

➢ In tasks 1 and 2, he has none because he is very satisfied with his social environment.

➢ In Task 3, he has entered as goals a better salary at his full-time job, which he intends to achieve through further training and the associated acquisition of new qualifications. In addition, in Task 3 he has formulated the goal of resuming playing table tennis in the club. In fact, he quite misses this passion from his youth.

➢ Task 4 brought Ingo to the realization that he had always been told that he couldn't cook. The origin of this claim is quite ridiculous because he has only once failed to cook a dish; stupidly when he cooked for his entire circle of acquaintances. Accordingly, the mishap had great repercussions. Because Ingo has a lot of time, especially on weekends and sometimes in the evenings, he takes it upon himself to try cooking every now and then. This way he can possibly give his wife a nice surprise.

Ingo sets the priority numbers for his desired goals as follows:

➢ Advanced training: 1
➢ Table tennis: 2
➢ Cooking: 4

Obviously, improving his professional situation is most important to him, but taking up his old hobby is almost as important.

Lastly, in Ingo's eyes, cooking is more of a nice add-on that he passes the time with when everything else is going well and he has a lot of available free time for it. Therefore, cooking has a lower priority. Based on the priority numbers, he determines the amount of time that is highest in training. He sticks to the curriculum: His advanced training should take a year and a half in total, with a recommended learning time of 20 hours a week. To be on the safe side, he adds 5 hours, most of which he spends on weekends off. Table tennis is scheduled twice a week, for a total of 1.5 hours per training session, so that 3 hours a week are spent on it. But wait: You surely remember that preparatory measures should also be included in a time planning. For Ingo, this means that for 3 hours of table tennis per week, one and 1.5 hours of preparatory measures (packing a bag, traveling there and back) have to be added. So, it costs him 4.5 hours of time per week. Cooking is less important. For Ingo, it would already be enough if he could find 3 hours on each of 2 weekends a month to cook 1 or 2 dishes; so, we are at an estimated monthly time expenditure of 6 hours.

This information is not yet binding. But they already give a direction as to what is important to Ingo and how much time is required. This will enable him to refine his objectives in the following steps or chapters of the guidebook and ultimately draw up a precise overall plan for his goals.

Step 3 | Filter and decide – what will you do?

Filtering is the step that helps you figure out which of your many goals to tackle first. You have already applied 1 filter in the 1st step of goal setting: The "must" filter. These are the goals or duties you will be forced to pursue because you need them for your life. They are relevant in planning because they limit the time and energy available for your other goals.

We leave out the "must", i.e., the obligations, for the time being. We will start at the end of the 2nd step, namely with your desired goals – **List 1**. Ideally, after the last exercises, you will have a list of several goals. Great enthusiasts and visionaries may have 20 goals, modest people may have 2 or 3. The amount doesn't matter as long as everything you care about is written down.

The more goals you have, or the more time individual goals take, the sooner you will notice the dilemma that often arises for unsuccessful people without clear goal planning: The goals may collide with each other, and if you want to pursue all your desires, an enormous amount of time is required. You may not even have that much time available. Do you experience the same problem?

Whatever is on your wish list, it must not overwhelm you. Therefore, filtering becomes necessary. For this, take your list 2 with desire goals and your list 1, with obligations. Write down how much time your commitments take up each day. Normally, with a

40-to-48-hour job, you won't have more than 3 to 5 hours during the week to work on your desired goals. You realize what's coming up: filtering. How do the goals interact with each other? This is one of the questions that will be clarified in order to optimize the goal selection process.

There are several methods to help you with filtering. I have 4 methods ready for you. You don't have to use them in this order. Accordingly, you don't have to do the individual tasks in this chapter in order. It's a good idea to read through the entire chapter first and then decide which methods you want to try. This is the best way to find the right filter method for you.

Filtering method 1: Search complementary targets

From my studies I have taken the brilliant approach of subdivision and filtering according to goal relationships: Goals are in different relationships to each other; for it to help you in the implementation, already a subdivision into complementary, conflicting, and indifferent goals is sufficient. Does it all sound too scientific? No problem, let's make it easier ...

Complementary goals are compatible with each other. They support each other. By pursuing 2 goals that support each other, the achievement of 1 goal simultaneously promotes the achievement of the other goal. This is beneficial to you when it comes to pursuing more than 1 of your goals. This is because when you have 2 complementary goals, it is easier to implement. For example, for the list above, it would look like this:

> ➤ The goals of "dieting" and "exercising more" are 2 different goals but support each other.

> ➢ Quitting smoking and sport can also be seen as complementary, because sport distracts from the difficult smoking cessation (keyword: addiction shift), so that ideally it is carried through more consistently and successfully.

> ➢ Not complementary, on the other hand, would be for working people to do distance learning and weekend trips at the same time. After all, distance learning requires a large investment of time. If you don't invest part of your weekends, you'll have a hard time successfully completing your studies while working a 48-hour job at the same time.

When you set complementary goals, you have the chance to accomplish more goals from your wish list in the time you have left each day. Always make sure that you don't choose complementary goals just because they complement each other, and you can do as much as possible. They have to be really close-to your heart. So: Don't just add new goals to your list at the drop of a hat that complement the other goals! Instead, strictly follow your list of commitments and desired goals.

It is also helpful to identify **conflicting goals**, i.e., those that interfere with each other. This will give you information about which goals you should possibly not pursue at the same time. An example I just mentioned: 48-hour job as a commitment and distance learning and weekend getaways as a desired goal. In rare cases, this approach can work, but in a full-time job with working hours on Saturdays, weekend trips and distance learning are conflicting, because both eat up a lot of the remaining time.

The **indifferent goals** are those that do not influence each other. After knowing about complementary, conflicting, and indifferent goals, it suggests itself that you prefer the complementary goals in your plans, because this way you can work off your desire goals best. If you are particularly concerned about a goal that is difficult to reconcile with the other goals, then you should think carefully about whether this goal is really worth giving up all the other desired goals for, or vice versa and then think about which ones could be better out off for a later point in time.

Task 1

Look at your lists of commitments and desired goals. Consider what relationships emerge among the goals. On a separate sheet of paper, write down which goals are complementary, conflicting, and indifferent to each other. Since you have to meet your commitments anyway, ideally you will start from this and determine which desire goals are most compatible with your commitments: Which desire goals are complementary to your commitments? Which desired goals are more likely to conflict and should be avoided for the time being?

Filtering method 2: Match targets to character

Every person is unique. Individual characters entail individual goals. That's why you're reading this book – your individual and external advice hasn't satisfied you yet. Now you are looking for answers within yourself. In view of this, there is hardly anything better than to think a few basic thoughts about who you really are in the first place ...

Sometimes the answer to this question is easier than the answer to the question of what you want to do. Do you perhaps manage to categorize yourself right off the bat, for example, as a family person, a career person, a sports fanatic, a social person? Of course, in a way, that's pigeonholing, which is simplistic, and maybe you don't want to categorize yourself that way. However, sometimes simple pigeonholing gets you further than complicated thinking.

Example

If you enjoy being around people frequently and can think of few things better than spending your time with friends and family, then it suggests that you have a strong social streak that you could further promote with your goals. Or maybe you are the complete opposite of a social person? Do you have a specific passion (e.g., music, art, sports, IT, gaming, technical literature) and set a career path in mind where relationships play little role for you? In this case, it would be a good idea to take a path in which you promote your skills straight away. You are a career person with high ambitions.

A character cannot always be classified as simplistically as in these 2 examples. And yet, pigeonholing is useful now and then. Because if you have no ideas at all about which goals from the list best suit you, and balance is already assured, you simply choose the simple way of pigeonholing: characterize yourself with one word, choose the most appropriate goal, and try it out to see if it suits you.

However, there are characters who are particularly complicated and for whom pigeonholing cannot be applied. Perhaps you know it yourself from your own life: You are torn between 2 things. On the one hand, you want nothing more than to work in your dream career, but on the other hand, you care a lot about your family. What now? Which goals should you choose? If you can't decide clearly, then set the goals in a balanced way. For example, your work already covers a large part of the "career" area. It would be a good idea to choose less career-oriented goals among the desire goals, but to improve your social situation instead. Adapt your goals to your current character and check regularly every few months to see if your goals still suit you. There are plenty of impressive stories of career people who thought to themselves after a few years or decades: No, this is not what I want. Their character changed or they realized that there was another side to them from the beginning. They quit their jobs and traveled the world or devoted more time to their families.

My experience

I always face enormous challenges when selecting new targets because my character is so multi-layered. No doubt this trait has various merits, but sometimes it makes things more difficult. So, it is with me for goal setting. I almost never avoid trying activities for several weeks or even months before setting goals. Adapting goals to character can be highly complex and require permanent mindfulness to make the necessary changes. What helped me were regular self-tests. There are many of these available on the internet. You can take self-tests for your job, personality, suitable hobby, family and for numerous other fields. Feel free to try out a few of them. They are especially advantageous for people who find it difficult to assess their character. They give advice on even the most contradictory character traits and the most ambivalent answers, which may be perfectly applicable.

Method 3 to filter: Favor the influenceable goals

You know when you've got it all figured out and planned great, but success also depends on other people who are just unreliable? Most of the time in studies, school, work, and team sports – everywhere there are dependencies – there is this one group partner who ruins all the work. It can be the same with goals. Because some goals can't be influenced just by you.

The model *Three Circles of Influence* according to Stephen R. Covey provides a better understanding. It divides the goals into 3 spheres of influence:

> ➢ controllable by me alone
> ➢ Influenceable by me
> ➢ concerns me

If a goal is **controllable by you alone,** then you can work on it and don't have to consult with anyone in your approach. According to Covey, these are the goals you should prefer. The central advantage is absolute sovereignty, the central disadvantage is absolute responsibility. Regarding responsibility, this guidebook has already given 1 or 2 important pieces of advice: Even though it is cited by Covey as a disadvantage, it still comes with many advantages. Because if you take responsibility, you are also in control. That's exactly why you are absolutely independent with a goal that is controllable by you alone. A perfect example can be found in Calvin Hollywood's guidebook *Who Will, Who Can!* (2018).

Example

Hollywood talks about how his son came back home after school and reported that he had detention. The reason, he said, was a fight with another boy. Hollywood's son managed to get the other boy blamed. Nevertheless, both boys got detention, which Hollywood's son thought was unfair. The father explained the problem to his son: the moment he shifted the blame to the other boy, he relinquished control of the situation and became dependent on him. If he had accepted at least part of the blame, he would have been able to argue better in front of the teachers.

Admittedly, for many individuals, responsibility is something that comes with a queasy feeling. Many individuals resist having control and responsibility over a situation. After all, this results in obligations and full liability for mistakes. The good thing is that with desire goals that are controllable by you alone, you are accountable only to yourself.

Next, there are the **goals that you can influence**: These are goals whose success you influence, but which you don't completely control. Be attentive at this point because these goals make up a large part of your life:

➢ Family decisions are goals that can be influenced by you, but not controlled by you alone.
➢ Finding a spouse is a goal that is highly dependent on another person.
➢ Goals for team sports or hobbies with others are ideally made with the agreement of all concerned.

> ➤ When starting a business with another person and running the business, there are all kinds of goals ahead that are not determined by you alone.

Family goals and the search for a permanent partner in particular require a great deal of consideration for others in the formulation and implementation of goals. For example, even the most charismatic and eloquent people do not necessarily find a partner for life in a hurry or within the targeted time frame. Such goals, which can be influenced by you but cannot be completely decided, should only be on your goals agenda if they are a) particularly important to you and at the same time b) complementary with other goals.

Example

Your goals are "travel" and "find friends". The former can be controlled by you alone, the latter can only be "influenced" by you. Therefore, it is best if you do not plan the second goal in a binding way but integrate it into your everyday life. Fortunately, "traveling" and "making friends" are possible complementary goals: For example, while traveling, you can try to meet people along the way. This would be a way to pursue a goal that can only be influenced without much effort.

Lastly, the **concern-me goals**: These types of goals are irrelevant because they are outside of your decision-making power. They cannot be influenced by you, or only to a limited extent. Working on these goals would be like an enormous effort that does not pay off.

Conclusion: It's all about your life and how you shape it. Get the most control over your life by choosing goals that are fully within your control. For the rare goals that require you to coordinate with other people (e.g., family, friends), make sure that you all communicate clearly and in detail with each other about how the goal is to be approached. That way, you're sure that people will go along with it. Here, once again, the system characteristics become apparent. Especially with goals that are not fully controllable by you, many unforeseen interactions can occur when pursuing goals.

Task 2

Look at your list of desired goals. Review and write down on a piece of paper which of the desired goals are controllable by you alone. Mark these goals clearly because they are to be preferred. Then write down the goals that can only be influenced by you. Ask yourself whether it is really worthwhile to plan these goals, where your success depends on other people. If they are important family goals, then write down some of these goals, of course. After all, a happy family life requires compromise in living together. Nevertheless, try to plan and choose the majority of your desired goals so that they are controllable by you alone – full responsibility, but full independence and control!

Method 4 to filter: Focus on your strengths

Focusing on your strengths will not only help you filter but may also add a few new goals to your list. You may even change your previous basic attitude with this filtering method. Because many people who don't succeed or are longing for success are characterized by the problem of focusing on their weaknesses or being blinded by their weaknesses. If you change your mindset and focus on your strengths from an optimistic point of view, you may make better progress. Various sayings from successful people go argumentatively in this direction:

> *"Those who work with their strengths become stronger."* – Ingo Krawiec
> *"Success consists in having the very skills that are in demand at the moment."* – Henry Ford
> *"One should not consider the worth of a man according to the great qualities he has, but according to the use he makes of you."* – La Rochefoucuald
> *"Think rather of what you have than of what you lack."* – Marcus Aurelius

So, what counts in life is to focus on your strengths. Why should you let your weaknesses stop you from doing something you're not good at? Maybe because others instigate you to do it. But no, that's enough! You finally take responsibility for your actions. You decide what you want to do. Your strengths should come to the fore. Promote them and – you remember the last chapter – regularly try things that you couldn't do before. Because you may have gained new skills in the meantime without knowing it.

Of course, if there's something you particularly like but haven't mastered, you may develop and learn new skills. Ideally, however, the majority of your goals should be those that are compatible with your strengths. That's the best way to move forward.

Task 3

What was your previous mindset? Have you undervalued yourself and stood in your own way because you thought too much about your weaknesses? If so, then turn the tables now: Think about what your strengths are **and** what you'd like to do. Mark each goal that meets these 2 criteria in your wish list of goals.

Final task

You now know various different methods of filtering. Finally, apply all of them, whether you have already done the 3 tasks in this chapter or not. Once you have done all 4 methods, you can do an overall evaluation, and decide on the desired goals that seem best to you at the moment, and that fit your time frame. Make sure you don't calculate too tightly and don't forget to take into account your commitments. Speaking of commitments: Now is the time when you can better make modifications in scheduling your commitments to give yourself more space. Cutting your sleep by an hour or 2 to make more time for your desired goals is worth doing now. Because now you have an overview of your desired goals and commitments – that is, your complete goal program – with the associated time commitment. Through this overview you can bring the commitments and desired goals even better and more precisely in line with each other. All desired goals that do not fit into your schedule because of the commitments, you put aside for the time being. You can schedule them for later as part of the long-term planning in the next step.

Instructions for performing the task

Theo currently has the following commitments:

➢ Sleep: around 8 hours a day so far (a bit more on weekends).

➢ Hygiene: about half an hour a day.

➢ Full-time job: 5 x 9 hours a day during the week (including 1 hour a day to and from work).

➢ take care of his children: just under 2 hours a day to take the children to school and pick them up again, as well as playing and reading to them in the evening.

➢ Preparing and eating food: sometimes the wife does it, sometimes Theo; all in all, it takes about 1.5 hours a day.

During the week, 3 hours per day remain for the pursuit of desired goals, because 21 hours already have to be factored in for obligations. On weekend days – minus the 9 hours of work and plus just under 2 additional hours of sleep – there are about 10 hours each day. So, Theo has 3 hours a day from Monday to Friday and 10 hours on Saturday and Sunday.

Additionally, as a person with an affinity for music, he has the following desired goals with an estimated time commitment:

➢ learning to dance with the wife; every Tuesday and Thursday 2 hours each (+ 0,5 hours in total for going and coming back).

➢ Learn to play the piano; 1 hour each Monday and Friday (+ 1 hour total to and from).

➢ Spend more time with friends because most of the time is spent with family; do something with friends for 5 hours on each of 2 Sunday evenings a month.

➢ Find more time for relaxation and promote well-being (e.g., through massages, wellness); book a wellness program every weekend for 3 hours and once during the week for 1 hour (+ 1 hour total to get there and back).

➢ travel around the world (only possible during vacation).

You can already tell from the goals that Theo and his family are not short of money. After all, anyone who books wellness programs twice a week, travels the world and wants to learn to dance and play the piano professionally must have quite a bit of money at their disposal. In fact, Theo and his wife are top earners.

Nevertheless, goal planning is not advantageous because, especially during the week, there is hardly any time left for anything other than the scheduled activities. Although the desired goals do not go beyond the scope of time availability, Theo knows that a tightly scheduled plan is associated with disadvantages. Even if schedules include partial hobbies, there should be plenty of free, unscheduled time in a sustainable plan. After consulting with his wife, Theo determines that learning to dance is out of the question. After all, someone has to take care of the kids, so they both can't be away at the same time. So, Theo and his wife decide to attend intensive dance classes on the 4 vacations they have together each year.

➢ Thus, "dancing" and "traveling" become complementary goals.

➢ On the condition that Theo gets up an hour earlier every day and looks after the children more intensively in the mornings, his wife agrees to him learning to play the piano 2 evenings a week.

➢ Spending more time with his friends on the weekend *and* booking wellness programs is not okay for Theo's family. Much of their time together would be lost and the wife would have to take care of the children for almost the entire weekend. That's why everyone decides by consensus that Theo will do one thing. He commits to meeting up with his friends more often. From time to time, he goes to wellness with the friends, which makes the goals "more meetings with friends" and "more wellness" complementary.

➢ Even doing an hour of wellness during the week is out of the question after consulting with the wife. Instead, they both decide to give each other a massage or a soothing bath every now and then in the evening. This brings them closer together physically, something that was often lacking in their marriage.

We realize that because of his family, Theo has a lot of goals that he can't control on his own. Instead, he has to discuss almost everything with his family. Nevertheless, compromises can be made in which Theo's wife has plenty of freedom and can sometimes do what she likes. The bottom line is that Theo has made some goals complementary or incorporated them into his other day-to-day obligations. It seems like little has changed in the daily routine because a lot of the desired goals have been shifted to vacation time. But meeting his friends more often and living out his musical vein – these goals, which are important to him, have been achieved. Within families, you just have to bake smaller rolls now and then.

Step 4 | Carry out long-term planning

If you set your goals for the short, medium, and long term and follow them consistently, your whole life will follow a plan. Through filtering, from the last chapter, you have decided which goals you want to tackle first. By doing this, you have chosen an order in which to address each goal. Long-term planning gives you the opportunity to also take into account the desire goals in the plans for which you currently do not have time. Because the planning is long-term and knows no restricting time horizons.

For example, you've realized that the fastest way to make changes to your full-time job is to start setting the course now. Because your full-time job is a significant part of your life, it makes sense to start planning here: What goals will help me improve my full-time job (e.g., continuing my education to increase my salary and prospects) or get a new and, in my eyes, better full-time job? (e.g., going to college, getting a different education, starting my own business).

In addition to a full-time job, long-term planning also helps you in your private life. You can plan together with your spouse when and under what conditions you would like to have a child. Example: First increase savings, create better living conditions and then plan the offspring.

Although this 4th step is mentioned in reference to "long-term planning", it also includes short-term planning. Because long-term planning definitely includes short-term plans anyway – at least if you want to be really precise and thus more likely to succeed. Long-term goals require a division into intermediate stages. These intermediate stages are again divided into smaller stages and then further subdivisions take place. Without intermediate stages, the danger that you will stray is great.

If you want to put it piquantly, but also consistently and correctly, then you come to the realization that there is basically no separate short-term planning. It does exist, but it is part of a higher-level long-term plan. Accordingly, the people most likely to achieve their goals are those who consider how to do short-term planning in conjunction with long-term goals. This gives even the smallest short-term goals an overarching larger meaning. Consequently, motivation is highest to achieve the goals.

With all that you have gathered in the previous chapters of this book – all your commitments and desired goals, your duties and dreams – you should now create a long-term plan in which one cog meshes with another and the smallest goals become long-term puzzle pieces. They become puzzle pieces of a fascinating and impressive project that every human being has to master – life.

Ranking of goals

The foundation that helps you to bring order and clarity into your planning is the division of the goals according to their ranking. This is where what, many authors in books and on websites, and numerous coaches and psychologists, suggest comes into play: the division of goals into stages. In business studies, at least 4 stages are regularly used for larger goals:

- ➤ The **overall goal** is what you want to achieve in the end.
- ➤ The **intermediate goal** is subordinate to the overall goal.
- ➤ The **subgoal** is subordinate to the intermediate goal.
- ➤ At the bottom of the chain is the **stage goal**, which is immediately tackled as a short-term goal.

Goals divided into stages keep your stamina and motivation higher. Imagine you want to lose 20 kilograms. Such a diet takes time, especially if it is to be safe from a health point of view.

Let's start from something conceivably impractical: You don't have a scale at home, and you don't weigh yourself all the time. As a result, you are in the dark and don't know what your goal is. As a result, you can't see any intermediate successes in front of you. Your stamina and motivation decrease in the face of the stresses and strains of dieting, with no certainty of whether they will pay off. Because you do not weigh yourself.

In contrast, you can now imagine a person who weighs himself every week on his diet and sees the kilos fall. He has the certainty that the diet works and can be happy about getting closer and closer to his goal.

Stages and precise summaries of intermediate steps on the way to your goal bring it to the point: your success so far, your progress, your stamina. You'll be more motivated to fight internal and external resistance and still pursue your goal. Doesn't that sound appealing?

Therefore, a ranking is established for each major goal. This ranking tells you which individual steps you need to take to achieve the goal. Here is an example of a ranking for the goal of quitting smoking. It is assumed to be a medium-term or even short-term goal (see: "Time Reference of Goals" from Step 1 of this book), because consistent smoking cessation is possible within less than 5 years.

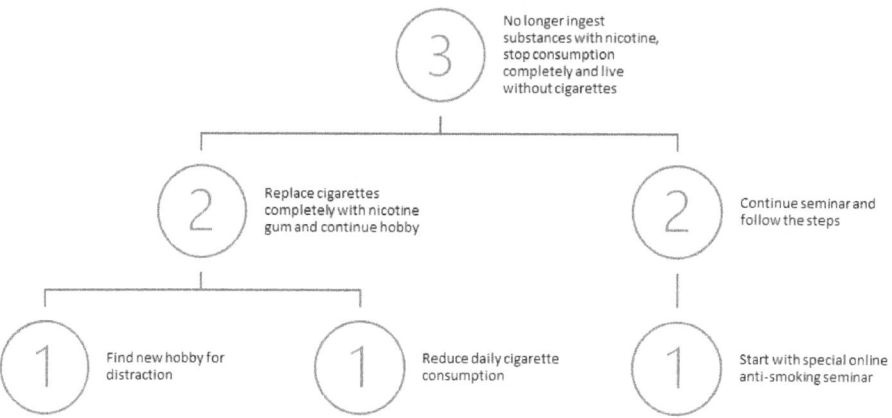

The numbers 1 represent the first short-term goals that are formulated: You start smoking cessation by consuming fewer cigarettes and taking up a hobby to shift addiction or distraction. For 2, there is the professional online seminar that gives you further advice on how to carry out the smoking cessation. After that – it can be for example after 2 months – the seminar is continued according to the instructions of the seminar leader. Meanwhile, the cigarettes are completely replaced by nicotine gum to improve the cessation process. After, for example, 8 months, the cigarettes can be completely discontinued. For the time being, weaning is then successful.

This is how a ranking works: What has to be done first and for how long? What comes next and how long does this step take in turn? This step-by-step approach to the goal is essential in order to carry out all the necessary steps, not to disregard anything important and to stand there successfully at the end.

Example: Nina establishes a hierarchy

Let's now relate the ranking of goals to an example. The example will be used throughout much of this chapter to adequately demonstrate how to bring your list of goals to completion in long-term planning. Nina has set 10 goals for herself. She has not necessarily formulated the goals precisely, but she has a sufficiently concrete idea of them:

- Lose 20 kilogram
- Stop smoking
- Earn more money
- Take more time for the family (parents and her 2 brothers)
- Gain more general knowledge
- Travel more often
- Try something new more often
- Create order at home
- Find steady friend
- Do more sports

Nina has noticed so far that quitting smoking and dieting are not compatible. In a way, they are conflicting goals. Because imagine how difficult it is to quit 2 vices at the same time: Giving up both smoking and snacking immediately and simultaneously is a strong imposition on one's will. For the time being, Nina has therefore decided on the diet that is more important to her.

Continue with the other goals: Nina can pursue the desires for more general knowledge and more money simultaneously through distance learning, which is why she makes them complementary goals.

Nina also promotes her diet through sports.

Who knows – maybe she'll find the steady boyfriend she longs for while playing sports? So, Nina decides not to prioritize the goal of finding a boyfriend.

She makes more time for her family by taking smaller day trips with her parents and brothers. For this purpose, she uses 2 weekend days per month and the holidays during the year. On these few days, she takes a break from distance learning to allow herself enough rest.

Thus, she has set the goals and defined which goals she will tackle first and which she will put off for now. She also considers the following ranking of goals:

Overall objective	Interim target	Subgoal	Stage destination
Lose 20 kg and do more sports	Have lost 10 kg by the end of the sixth month	From the tenth week enroll in the gym and lose half a kilogram per week	Lose half a kilogram every week; initially through a change in diet

Higher earnings and more general knowledge	Complete distance learning and apply for new job	Complete first semester on schedule within six months	Start with distance learning to gain qualifications for a better paying job, and set aside 2 hours each evening to study
Take more time for family, travel more often, and try new things	After 6 months, take a multi-day trip or vacation with the family for the first time and make the vacation rich in experiences and activities	Make concrete plans for 2 weekend days -> The motto is to spend time together outside of the usual environment and with new activities if possible.	Discuss 2 weekend days off with family members each month
Create order at home	After 6 months, if necessary, muck out on 1 or 2 days off.	Do household chores for half an hour every day –1 hour after returning from work; 1 hour each on weekend days.	Getting into the habit of always hanging up clothes after returning home, doing the dishes immediately after a meal, and otherwise cleaning up any messes that

			have been made right away
Find steady friend	If there is no success for 2 years, reconsider planning and seek advice.	If the stage goal didn't work, try classic places for singles to go (e.g., speed dating, special events, bars)	First do all the other things; because already through gym, distance learning and traveling you can meet people
Stop smoking	After the 3 months, use lower-dose nicotine products and wean off slowly	Use nicotine gum, patches, or other special products and reduce amount of cigarettes smoked during first 3 months of cessation	If health permits, then do not start smoking cessation until 2 years after the successful diet, so that no "addiction shift" occurs

What is Nina doing with her ranking?

On the one hand, she sets complementary goals (lose 20 kg and exercise). On the other hand, she makes goals complementary by making her planning specific: For example, higher earnings and more general knowledge are not necessarily complementary goals. However, by doing distance learning, she makes the goals complementary. This is because the study program provides her with the desired general knowledge through the large number of inter-disciplinary modules and insights into other subject areas, while the bachelor's degree enables her to pursue a profession with higher earnings.

In addition to skillfully choosing complementary goals (she combines a total of 7 goals into 3 goals), she postpones other goals. This is evident in finding a steady boyfriend and quitting smoking. In the case of quitting smoking, she notes a conflicting nature with losing weight. In themselves, the 2 need not be mutu-ally exclusive, but if Nina were to do both at the same time, she would have to cope with various cuts from one day to the next – at least that's how she lays it out for herself argumentatively. The advantage of this plan is that she can "enjoy" smoking for 2 more years and put less pressure on herself in setting her goal. With the goal of finding a boyfriend, she initially refrains from clear plan-ning. This is because she recognizes the spontaneity behind this goal: *when* you meet a man can be difficult or impossible to con-trol. True love, which is what Nina is looking for, cannot be forced. So, she realizes that she may already meet her future steady boyfriend while doing new sports activities, meeting her family, or traveling. In case this is not the case, she has formulated a few "contingency plans" in the intermediate goal and sub-goal.

Nina trades off the goal of creating order in the household and keeping it tidy with small windows of time. If you look at it soberly, this is exactly the right choice. Because if you constantly keep things tidy and immediately put them in the right place, wash the dishes or start the vacuum cleaner, you won't usually have to spend much more than 30 minutes a day tidying up.

Overall, by combining several complementary or potentially complementary goals and deferring 2 of them, Nina is only working on 8 desired goals at a time. Since she combines almost all of the goals in some way with at least 1 other goal, it feels like Nina is only working on 4 goals at a time. At the same time, she is pursuing commitments such as her job. In parallel, she integrates social contacts into her life through family and sports. By being mostly free on weekends, she creates plenty of relaxation and space for spontaneity. The time windows that remain for certain obligations (sleeping, eating, hygiene) fit well into the schedule and do not allow stress to arise at all.

What you learn from the example for your planning ...

First and foremost, you learn from Nina's example that pursuing complementary goals offers enormous advantages. You can pursue several goals at once and use your time more efficiently. Goals don't always have to be complementary by themselves. You can make them complementary by choosing actions to achieve them that benefit both goals. This is what Nina did with the goal combination "higher earnings & more general knowledge".

Furthermore, you should not strive to complete all goals as quickly as possible. If you feel no time pressure and have some freedom in prioritizing and completing your goals, then take plenty of time! Nina, for example, has retained the option to readjust in her interim and sub-goals: If she hasn't lost the 10 kilograms after 6 months, she makes a few changes in her planning. You can see this in the table above.

Last tip: Don't assume that everything will run optimally. Those obstacles and problems will occur is absolutely normal and very likely. Nina has understood this. If you do the math, you'll find that with half a kilogram of weight loss per week on her diet, it would by no means take her half a year to lose 10 kilograms. She has left herself almost a whole month as a time buffer, so that if there are problems – especially at the beginning some can occur – she won't jeopardize reaching the intermediate goal. This buffer also has the advantage that if it goes according to plan, she will lose more weight than formulated in the interim goal. This can lead to a positive surprise effect and Nina is most likely more motivated on the way to her goal to also take the 2nd half of the path and lose the additional 10 kilograms.

Task 1

Take your lists of commitments and desired goals from the previous chapters. Rank each goal: How finely do you divide each goal so that you can easily work through its stages and stay motivated? Also create a ranking for the desired goals that you have postponed and do not write on your agenda for the time being. Because later you will come back to your desired goals. Then it is practical to have the appropriate ranking directly.

Time reference of goals

You are already familiar with the classification of goals according to their time reference from the 1st step of the book. It was relevant to introduce this aspect earlier. Feel free to reread the section because the contents are very important for long-term planning. Then continue at this point with your lists and the following example.

Example: Nina sets a time reference

A classification of the goals by time reference, as in the following example, can of course make sense *before* the ranking is determined. However, the approach chosen in this guidebook is that the ranking is formed first. The reason for this is that the ranking leads to a meticulous and quite meticulously executed subdivision of the overall objectives. In this way, the duration until the goals are achieved can be better estimated.

Let us now look at the example of Nina, how she divides her goals according to time reference and how the previous formation of a ranking helped her in this. She still has her 10 overall goals, from which she summarizes the complementary goals and for which she calculates the following time horizons:

Overall objective	Planned duration	Further notes	Time reference
Lose 20 kilograms and do more sports	1 year and 2 months	Plus, another 4 months to prevent the yoyo effect	medium-term
Higher earnings and more general knowledge	3 years (duration of studies)	After 3 years, likely up to 2 more years to get a better paying job	medium to long term
Take more time for family, travel more often, and try something new more often	1 month for organization	Organize in the first month and maintain regular activities month after month thereafter	short term

Stop smoking	1 year to stop smoking cigarettes; then prevent relapse through new positive habits	Do not start until 2 years after weight reduction	medium to long term
Create order at home	At the latest after 8 months (to have completely cleaned out)	Start immediately and create a little more order every day	short term
Find steady friend	With a natural approach, something should come up within 2 years	Cannot be planned precisely; intensify efforts only after deadline of 2 years	medium-term

What does Nina do when time-referencing her goals?

After ranking them, she writes down how much time her goals take. If she reads "short-term" in the right column, she knows that she has to check the respective task more closely on a daily or monthly basis. Strictly speaking, this example is incomplete: A good classification by time reference would be for Nina to list all short-term, medium-term, and long-term goals in 3 separate tables. With these 3 tables, it would be possible for her to check the intermediate status in different time windows:

➢ For example, Nina would look at the table with the short-term goals every day or every week.

➢ For example, she could look at the table with the medium-term goals every month.

> ➤ Last, Nina would look at the long-term goals chart once a year.

With the 3 tables divided by time reference, Nina would have a strict separation of the different time references. She would not be driven crazy by medium-term goals but would regularly enjoy the progress on her short-term goals. In turn, she would look at the medium, and long-term goals at regular, but more widely spaced, intervals in order to monitor the intermediate statuses and to tighten up the short-term goals in good time if there was a threat that the goals would be missed.

When Nina combines all this with visualization, she has the ultimate motivation booster. If you imagine that she checks off the short-term goals, day by day or week by week, draws them in a diagram and thus sees how she has come a few percent closer to the long-term goal again through a few small measures, then you understand that the subdivision of the goals according to time reference in combination with a clear ranking is optimal for staying motivated and consistently getting closer to the big goals with small steps.

What you learn from the example for your plans

Dividing your goals by time helps you to move forward in small steps. If you list all short, medium, and long-term goals in 3 different catalogs (books or notebooks), you have a clear separation. You then look at the list of short-term goals every day or week. As you achieve them on schedule, you can check them off one by one and see how fast you're progressing. This is a psychological trick: Why keep looking at the long road to the big goals? Why get discouraged by the many tasks that lie ahead? By working through the short-term and easier goals, you'll move forward much more easily and lightheartedly.

Task 2

You, too, plan according to the time reference of goals. It is best to set up 3 catalogs as described. The 1ˢᵗ catalog concerns short-term goals, the 2ⁿᵈ medium-term goals and the 3ʳᵈ long-term goals. Create the catalogs and determine for yourself how regularly you want to look into a catalog. It is obvious to look into the catalog with short-term goals in short intervals (e.g., every week). And then? Well, then you'd better start directly with the pursuit of your goals according to your planning! Why wait when your dreams are within reach?

Subdivision according to target importance

The target meanings have some parallels to the time reference. Here, there is a division into strategic, tactical, and operational goals. **Strategic goals** are the long-term goals that are **formulated rather generally**: Improving your income situation, getting your first property, etc. They are fundamental to your overall life. Depending on what your strategy is – making a career, being a family man, helping other people, etc. – you set the strategic goals and formulate them based on the tactical goals.

Tactical goals usually concern the medium-term time horizon. They **summarize which activities are necessary to achieve the strategic goals**. You can get a good impression of this from the examples mentioned above. If your strategic goal is to get a better job with a higher salary, your tactical goal with a medium-term time horizon is to study or train to achieve that goal.

Last but not least, there are the **operational goals**, which are both short, and long-term in nature. On the one hand, they are there to carry out your current mandatory program of work and other commitments. In addition, the **operational goals detail the medium-term goals, which will help you achieve the medium-term goals and thus get closer to the long-term goals**. To follow up on the previous example, in order to complete your studies and find a better job later on, it is necessary to enroll in a university and start studying in a timely manner.

Hint!

What is the actual connection between all the presented subdivisions of goals according to time horizon, goal significance and ranking? The connection between all these things is that they make adequate goal planning possible in the first place. You have strategic goals in life to bring you closer to your dreams? These goals are long-term. It is necessary to divide them into tactical goals and to operationalize them. In other words, you set operational short, and medium-term goals in order to act in a goal-oriented way. Ranking the goals helps you check off one task at a time, motivate yourself, and keep at it. If you follow through with the steps and stay on schedule, your tactics will work so that you achieve the medium-term goals and consistently move toward the long-term goals. Also, if you go through all of these things in your long-term planning and break down all of the goals by time horizon, goal importance, and ranking, you'll notice any inconsistencies. In this way, you realize that you may have missed some important aspects. Consequently, you correct your objectives.

Monitor regularly, evaluate, and change if necessary

Of course, you need an overview of your goals. Because let's be frank and honest: Even with the greatest motivation, you may overlook individual goals. To prevent this from happening and to ensure that you proceed according to plan, there are 3 main methods for monitoring:

- ➢ Handwritten on a piece of paper or in a book
- ➢ Use of specialized apps
- ➢ Use of comprehensive programs (e.g., project management)

We have handwritten your goals and monitored them in almost every task in the book up to this point. The reason you use pen and paper is scientifically based: It causes people to think more carefully about what they write. They select better and accordingly think more carefully about the content. This helps you to think more intensively each time about whether you really want the respective goals.

In addition to handwritten recording, you are free to use digital helpers to record and monitor your goals. Because people tend to use a lot of digital applications every day, I recommend the handwritten version. One thing is clear about this: if you write out all the goals and write complete sentences, it's going to take a lot of effort on your part. That's why a trend has emerged in recent years around the so-called *bullet journal*. You can find all imaginable and important information about this way of keeping a diary and recording your daily tasks at the URL "https://bulletjournal.com/". The author Ryder Carroll has even written a compre-hensive book on this topic. The trick to his way of recording tasks and goals in writing is to work with different types of **bullet points,** which make everything clearer and easier and saves time.

Task 3

The choice is yours: either find out how the *bullet journal* works and try it out on your goals. Or come up with your own way to make it easy to handwrite and monitor your goals. After all, writ-ing out your goals in complete sentences and keeping up with them on a daily or weekly basis is exhausting in the long run. Also, when documenting your goals, use your energies sparingly and make it easy rather than difficult.

As a contrast to the handwritten approach, there are the digital helpers. Apps for the smartphone and desktop applications for stationary PCs are plentiful. Because there is an oversupply, it is difficult to find good programs. I myself have only worked with one application, but on a daily basis, as a supplement to handwrit-ing my goals: Asana. It is a program that can be used on the PC and laptop as well as on smaller devices. I always used it on the laptop and the smartphone. This way I always had an overview of all my tasks and goals at home and on the road. The handy thing is that you can create multiple projects. For example, one project can be named "Personal Life" and the other can be named "Ca-reer". This is a rough subdivision under which you can list your more detailed goals. It's best to look at the program yourself and find your own way to use it. Because there are various ways to create projects and thus subdivide the goals. The program itself lists in table form, and on a project-to-project basis, indicates which tasks are still to be carried out and which goals they are subordinate to.

Another list of useful apps can be found in the book *Richtig priorisieren* (2014). If necessary, you can also try them out. Some of them specialize in individual functions. Here are 5 promising apps:

> - *Things* for iPhone and iPad users to manage themselves
> - *aTimeLogger* a time tracking app for the iPhone
> - *AWD Time Logger* a time tracking app for devices with the Android system
> - *Eisenhower* as an app for the iPhone to set priorities
> - *Tenplustwo* as a stopwatch app with great utility for unloved tasks (after 10 minutes of work time always comes 2 minutes of break)

Apart from handwritten journals and apps, there is another method of monitoring, which at the same time is highly valued in personal development. This is the visualization method: You already learned about it in *Task 2* from the *Step 1* chapter in this book. Use this method especially for the goals you don't like. The visualizations will keep you better motivated and in a better mood. One possible visualization would be the *progress pie*. It is best to hang visualizations clearly visible on a wall in your home.

Finally, one important question remains: how and when do you change something about your goals?

This is exactly what monitoring is for: to change the objectives if necessary. The central problem with changing goals is that one is not always quite sure whether the goals are being changed rightly or whether it is the wrong decision. It often happens that people pursue their goals well and consistently, but still abandon them. Then it is said that it was too difficult. But was it really?

There is no general formula for when goals should be abandoned. Obviously, you should not pursue goals that you don't care about or that don't do us a reasonable favor that would justify the effort. Pursuing such false goals should not happen anyway if you follow the advice and guidance in this guide. Now, it is possible that even if you follow the right goals and the instructions in this guidebook, at some point you may feel the urge to change individual goals ...

It's permissible and important to make changes when you realize you have too hard a workload. Especially in the 1st few weeks of new goal setting, it is not uncommon to realize that you've taken on a bit too much. Slowing down the pace now is helpful. Either you eliminate less important goals, or you reduce the pace.

Another situation in which objectives change is changes in one's own character, certain ways of thinking, and life circumstances. A prime example of this is provided by author Eric Adler in his work *More of Life* (2014): A person sets himself the goal of being the most successful representative of his company. On the way to this goal, he meets a woman with whom he begins a relationship. With this acquaintance, the focus in his life shifts abruptly. In such situations, it is also not wrong to change one's own goals or, under certain circumstances, to cancel them completely.

This is not the end of the situations that justify changing or canceling goals: there are goals that you take up even though you are not sure that they really fit you and the situation in your life. Even reading this guide and following all the helpful advice, you may find yourself uncertain about your future. In that case, the tip is: try everything that appeals to you in the slightest. Try new things. Sometimes it is only possible by trying and observing. Find out by doing which goals suit you and which do not. Have the courage to break off goals and set new ones if something doesn't appeal to you on the 1st attempt. Important: Don't break off at the 1st hurdle, but patiently give it a chance.

I hope these few hints can help you figure out when you should and shouldn't break goals. Basically, though, there is no general formula. You'll have to intuitively decide for yourself when it's appropriate to change goals. However, keep in mind that if you are more than 50% of the way there, or if your goals are costing you a lot (e.g., distance learning), you should only abandon them in the most extreme cases.

Final task

If you have completed the tasks in this chapter, the long-term planning is already done, and your goals are set. Ideally, you have already started tracking your goals. What could the final task be about? Now it gets interesting with regard to your environment: Given that all your goals are in place, you can talk to those around you about your objectives, get opinions and, if necessary, redesign the environment. Ask what people think of your goals. You can accept constructive criticism and make changes. If you have completely new goals in life, try to make new inspiring acquaintances related to your respective goals.

Closing words

Each reader writes their own story. You have the piece of paper, the pencil, and a set of ideas. Now you decide which story you want to write. Your goals will be based on that. Do you want to write the story of a career person who has extensive know-how and is self-actualized in his work? Do you want to reach people and spread your views? Does your heart, beat for your family and do you define your life by their happiness?

Whatever path you choose: You can walk it and achieve all your goals, as long as you set them realistically and ensure a certain balance. Every person needs this balance in his life. Not everything can revolve around one goal if you don't want to miss out on too much in your life. This is how scientists, psychologists, needs researchers and many other groups of people who have something to say in the field of personal development and goal setting see it. Therefore, the biggest takeaway from this guidebook is that, as different as we may be, at our core we all have the same needs and require the same components in life. These include existential needs, physical and mental well-being, a social environment, and the opportunity for self-actualization. How much of these things we need, however, is an individual matter.

Think about what you consider important in your life. Create a careful plan with goals according to the instructions in this book. Because setting and pursuing goals without a plan is almost impossible. Unfortunately, a surprising number of people take such a path. Consequently, they stray in some areas of life or even in their entire life. They do not get the most out of their lives. Sometimes talents remain unused, sometimes people even go astray out of desperation. Some might have had the chance to make a positive mark on entire nations or even the world, but let their lives pass aimlessly.

In our childhood, there is usually no need for a plan, because a large part of life is determined by others. The school, with its curriculum and teachers as the enforcers, provides us with one framework, while parents, with their upbringing, provide the other. Already here we can see that when parents let the leash loose, it is not uncommon for children to neglect their school duties and fail to achieve the goals there. When one part in a person's system is not functioning, interactions occur that can also negatively affect other parts. So already in childhood it becomes clear how finely and closely the system "human & environment" works. In adulthood it is then exactly the same issue, only that you have to take more responsibility yourself.

Have the courage to take responsibility by setting your own goals. This is probably the greatest challenge: leaving your comfort zone and making your own decisions. It is all too likely that mistakes will be made in the process. After all, a lifetime is long, and especially in anyone's early 20s, experience is limited. But at least they will be your mistakes – they will be your hallmark, and you will be able to tell about them later to help or warn other people. Besides, each mistake lowers the probability that you will make more mistakes. Finally, you learn.

Think about what adjustments you would like to make in your life. Who knows – maybe thanks to this guide you'll realize that you already have everything you want? In the pursuit of more, many an ambitious person has noticed that it doesn't really have to be more. So don't let yourself be blinded by certain ambitions within yourself but take into account the big picture in everything – within yourself and in what affects you from the outside. I wish you so much luck with this!

References and further reading

Literature Sources:

Adler, E.: *Mehr vom Leben – Die 12 Naturgesetze zum Erfolg©*. München: Südwest Verlag, 2014.

Hollywood, C.: *Wer will, der kann! Wie du deine Ziele schneller und einfacher erreichst.* Heidelberg: dpunkt.verlag GmbH, 2018.

Moestl, B.: *Der Weg des Tigers.* München: Knaur Verlag, 2013.

Proske, H.; Reichert, J. F.; Reiff, E.: Richtig priorisieren. Freiburg: Haufe-Lexware GmbH & Co. KG, 2014.

Schmidbauer, W.: *Die gelassene Art, Ziele zu erreichen! Abschied vom Erfolgszwang.* Freiburg im Breisgau: KREUZ VERLAG, 2012.

Online sources:

Asendorpf, J. B.; Banse, R.; Wilpers, S.; Neyer, F. J.: Diagnostica 1997,43, Heft 4, 289:313, *Beziehungsspezifische Bindungsskalen für Erwachsene und ihre Validierung durch Netzwerk- und Tagebuchverfahren.* Göttingen: Hogrefe-Verlag, 1997, von https://www.psychologie.hu-berlin.de/de/prof/per/downloads/Bindungsskalen.pdf

Carroll, R.: The Bullet Journal Merthod, von https://bulletjournal.com/.

Clauß, M.; Kern, C.: Südwest Presse, *Multi-Millionärin durch Ak-tien: „Börsen-Oma" aus Ulm ist tot.* (29. September 2020). https://www.swp.de/suedwesten/staedte/ulm/beate-sander-ulm-tod-burch-krebs-vermoegen-boerse-boersen-oma-aktien-millionen-51893466.html

Deutsche Gesellschaft für Ernährung e. V., *Vollwertig essen und trinken nach den 10 Regeln der DGE.* (Download vom 25.02.2021, 19:44 Uhr). https://www.dge.de/ernaeh-rungspraxis/vollwertige-ernaehrung/10-regeln-der-dge/.

Müller, T.: ÄrzteZeitung, *Wer sechs bis acht Stunden pro Nacht schläft, lebt am längsten.* (28. Dezember 2018). https://www.aerztezeitung.de/Medizin/Wer-sechs-bis-acht-Stunden-pro-Nacht-schlaeft-lebt-am-laengsten-232317.html

Ries, F.: https://www.fabianries.de/. *Das Lebensrestaurant.* (1. November 2015). https://lebensrestaurant.de/lebensres-taurant-geschichte/

Schmermund, K.: Forschung & Lehre, *Warum wir wieder mehr mit der Hand schreiben sollten.* (04.02.2020). https://www.for-schung-und-lehre.de/forschung/warum-wir-wieder-mehr-mit-der-hand-schreiben-sollten-2504/

Stanzl, E.: Wiener Zeitung .at, *Was die Handschrift im Gehirn be-wirkt.* (10.02.2015). https://www.wienerzeitung.at/nach-richten/wissen/mensch/734175-Was-die-Handschrift-im-Gehirn-bewirkt.html

Washington, D.: YouTube-Channel von AlexKaltsMotivation, *WATCH THIS EVERYDAY AND CHANGE YOUR*

LIFE - Denzel Washington Motivational Speech 2020. (Download vom 25.02.2021, 19:50 Uhr). https://www.y-outube.com/watch?v=tbnzAVRZ9Xc&t=260s.

Weiss, B.: Der Tagesspiegel, Einsamkeit macht Menschen krank. (01.09.2012). https://www.tagesspiegel.de/wissen/psy-chologie-einsamkeit-macht-menschen-krank/7080868.html

ZSH GmbH, *Effizient lernen: die vier besten Lerntechniken für Zahnme-dizin-Studenten.* (23. Juni 2020). https://www.zsh.de/blog/lerntechniken-zahnmedizin-studenten#_Toc42861265

THE MIND POWER SYSTEM

Success Through Mental Strength and Positive Thinking

How to Build an Unshakable Winning Mindset in 6 Steps

by

Patrick Drechsler

Table of Contents

Introduction

Your supervisor at work criticizes you. He doesn't like the draft you submitted. What's more, you handed it in not a day before the due date. "Timed pretty tight, huh?" he provokes with a mischievous grin on his face. You know he has something against you. *It doesn't matter when you turn in the draft, as long as it's on time!* But he just has to say something anyway. Or maybe he's right? After all, you never managed to take criticism well, always letting it affect you personally. By the end of this harsh workday, through your entire evening off, and into the next few days, you are seething inside; you feel insecure, and you don't feel like working – all because of some criticism from a superior who doesn't like you.

Exhausting superiors and a lack of critical faculties are only a couple of the many difficulties that people tend to suffer from. Have you ever experienced wanting something badly enough, but you just lacked the discipline to achieve it? You kept putting off that thing that was so close to your heart until eventually, your dream fizzled out? Instead, you stayed on your hamster wheel and there you remain, hoping that this book will give you the consistency to realize your dreams in the future. I'm here to tell you that *it will*.

This book will show you the right way to deal with those superiors who have it in for you, through the cultivation of *mental strength*. Being mentally strong means being resilient. Resilient to deal with losses such as financial hardships or the death of a loved one. That doesn't mean that you can't cry and grieve. But it *does mean* that you won't lose your motivation, zest for life and confidence because of it.

In all of our lives, we face challenges that require us to embody mental strength in many different ways – challenges are unavoidable. But what we can change, is our ability to deal with them effectively.

This book will show you how to deal with all of the challenges that life can throw at you. It will show you how to develop mental strength and how to focus that strength effectively. It will present you with numerous, real life examples to learn from, as well as giving you a holistic guide to developing mental strength generally. The first chapter gives you valuable knowledge about the different elements that go together to form a strong mind. And this is followed up in the subsequent chapters by a complete **Mind Power System (MPS)**; a 6-step guide that equips you with the mental strength to deal with a large variety of situations. If you follow the steps laid out in this book, you *will* become happier, more successful, more crisis-proof and much more optimistic.

Mentally strong: what it brings you, what it means and how you get there

The benefits of mental strength mentioned in the introduction are only a small part of what you can accomplish as a mentally strong person.

Let's look at some cases of famously successful people. Public figures such as Sylvester Stallone, who was broke and facing homelessness, Thomas Hitzlsperger, who was one of the first footballers to come out as homosexual, or Coco Chanel, who worked her way from a convent to become a world-famous fashion designer, are prime examples of the power of mental strength. There are mentally resilient people all around you too. People in tough jobs that pay poorly. Who, despite the meager salary, are able to provide for their families and even live an enjoyable life outside of work – isn't that admirable? Or, if we take teenagers who are going through puberty while being worried about a seriously ill parent, somehow they still manage to pass their school exams with flying colors, doesn't that deserve the highest praise? What about single parents who have been widowed after the death of a spouse, who do twice or even 3 times as much work as other parents, and still have to explain to their child why the other parent is missing – isn't this also the epitome of mental strength?

Mental strength brings you progress and resilience!

Maslow, in his pyramid of needs, clarified that personal development and self-realization are the only real growth needs that people have.

Each person has their own view of what personal development is but every person will encounter challenges along the way in whatever they do. Whether one starts a family, devotes oneself fully to sports, business or any other pursuit, sooner or later problems will arise. But as you develop mental strength you will make progress through negatively and positively perceived times. Resilience will increase, and you will not break down in the face of challenges, instead continuing on to achieve your life objectives.

In the beginning is the challenge

Challenges, obstacles, and strokes of fate in life are actually defined by your positive or negative reaction to them. *Positive emotions with bad strokes of fate? That's easy to say on paper, but hardly true in real life!* You may be thinking to yourself. For now, you're right. Anyone who learns of a serious illness or loses a family member will definitely not feel positive about it. But while negative emotions are there and have to be accepted, strength can still be gained from these situations.

There are individuals who let life pass them by without savoring it and taking advantage of the many opportunities they have. Then, when they are diagnosed as having only a few months to live, after the initial shock, they finally decide to take advantage of life – in the face of death came the realization that they wanted to live. Furthermore, there are cases in which loss releases unimagined forces in grieving individuals and they suddenly turn their whole lives upside down. For example, a single father and widower who gives his child all the love that the mother had wished for her child on her deathbed; bad fathers transform into model fathers overnight. Bad students who became model students for the sake of their deceased fathers and made a successful career for themselves. Brain researcher Gerhard Roth calls these *teachable moments*: moments that touch a person so deeply on an emotional level, that they are animated to change their previous behavior from one moment to the next.

Example

Christiano Ronaldo is a world renowned football player. He has won numerous national and international titles with clubs he played for. At the beginning of his career, he was a great talent, and his father was proud of him. However, his father died early and did not witness his son's rise to fame. In recent years, Ronaldo repeatedly stated on social media and in interviews that he dedicates all his success to his father. He has even burst into tears on television several times. Even now, at the age of 34 (as of November 2020), which is high for footballers, he is still one of the best in his profession, scoring goal after goal and remaining an absolute leader. How such ambition, discipline and physical prowess have been maintained late into his career can only be fully explained by considering the importance of his father's death. This is a great example of a *teachable moment*.

People who go through these moments are not necessarily always mentally strong. Sometimes they suppress their grief through discipline, which is not healthy for the psyche; but that's another topic. For now, it should be noted that a stroke of fate can strengthen a person's mind and spur amazing and uncanny achievement.

Other challenges that people face in life fit into the description of *self-imposed challenges*. Examples of this are moving home and the resulting new lifestyle, new projects at work or diets for weight loss: In contrast to externally generated, uncontrollable strokes of fate, professional and private challenges are partly self-inflicted. One sees something positive in the challenge in this case, which is why the decision is made to face it. These types of challenges look more harmless compared to the previously mentioned strokes of fate, but they should not be underestimated. For example, the impact of a move on the psyche of children can be significant.

Example

In a study, researchers led by Roger Webb of the University of Manchester analyzed data from children in Denmark born between 1971 and 1997. The focus was on the effects of moving on the children once they reached adulthood. The more frequently moves occurred during childhood, the higher the chances of suicide attempts, mental illness, drug addiction and violence when they became adults. Surprisingly, the parents' financial and social circumstances did not seem to play a role in it, with all of the children being equally affected. Similar findings were made by psychologist Shigehiro Oishi, whose comments were published in the *Journal of Personality and Social Psychology* (2010, Vol. 98). Children who were moved around tend to replicate the same radical changes to the course of their lives when they become adults, especially in the case of children who were moved at the age of puberty.

The conclusion to this is that moving can be a major challenge for people to deal with, and can have potentially strong effects on their future lives. It can be noted that some children also have a different experience and emerge from the move stronger. They learn to adapt quickly to new environments. These and other lessons from the move carry over to later life.

Challenges, obstacles, strokes of fate and other events in life thus put us humans to the test in a variety of ways. Our task is to face up to the challenge as quickly as possible and to find a way of dealing with it. If we succeed in this, we have the chance to grow. By not breaking down and giving up, we demonstrate mental strength. The more often this happens in different life situations, the more we strengthen ourselves in general, so that we can defy an increasing amount of challenges more quickly.

What would life be without these challenges? Such a life would be impossible on the one hand, and on the other hand it would lack a certain charm. Every person on this planet loses loved ones at some point. And if one doesn't lose them because he doesn't have loved ones, there is no social environment surrounding him that makes life worth living. A life without friends and family? Desolate, without support, without succor, lonely…

Even the smaller challenges in life are unavoidable: Sooner or later, every person has to take care of themselves, which is already a challenge with work, cooking, keeping things in order, and all the trimmings. Those who cannot take care of themselves because of an illness have the illness as a challenge.

Despite all this, let's assume that there is a life without challenges and unforeseeable strokes of fate: How could we then still prove our mental strength? Would life still be worth living? This is simply food for thought for you ... left unanswered. Feel free to make your own ideas about it.

The fact is that there are always challenges and strokes of fate that act as a gauge of our mental strength. Those who demonstrate mental strength continue to develop and harden themselves for the further stages of life. The experience gained can be shared with other people, which increases the beneficial aspects to be found in our challenges.

When we talk about strength of mind, we can distinguish it into 2 categories: offensive and defensive. Offensive is when we set goals and move to achieve them. They are challenges that we accept voluntarily. Defensive mental strength is resilience: the ability to catch ourselves after losses and defeats and to respond to unexpected challenges.

Resilience: You feel security in difficult phases

Resilience is the psychological ability to withstand critical situations and crises. Resilient people deal with challenges better than non-resilient people. If they resolve the crisis or continue life in a new way as a result of the crisis, people are considered resilient. The prerequisite here is that they do not let themselves get down and they tackle the crisis comparatively quickly, without letting negative emotions hold them back for too long.

The foundations for resilience are laid in childhood. In his work *Training Resilience* (2020), Max Janson points to the following factors in childhood that would promote pronounced resilience in adulthood:

- ➢ Children have the courage and openness to talk about their emotions.
- ➢ School performance is better than expected.
- ➢ Intact family life.
- ➢ Parents of the children are working.

According to Janson, poverty or wealth would play a subordinate role. If anything, children from wealthy households are expected to have lower resilience in adulthood because they may be "overprotected" by their parents; a factor that stands in the way of resilience. Fittingly, there is a study by U.S. developmental psychologist Emmy Werner that sparked the beginning of resilience research. As part of her study, she observed the development of 700 children in Hawaii who were growing up in poor conditions. What was striking was that despite the conditions (violence, substance abuse, and low levels of parental education), 1/3 of the children grew up to become socially integrated and employed adults. What almost all of these children had in common was the presence of at least one familiar caregiver in their environment who was responsive to their needs.

Whether in childhood or in adulthood, resilience can be trained. The environment plays an important role here because it can teach, strengthen and support. On the other hand, it can of course have a negative influence. In this guide, you will learn how to build a resilient environment. The fact is that resilience is important in difficult phases of life: become resilient and you will find the motivation to live in difficult times!

Example

U.S. President Joe Biden (as of November 2020) has an impressive resume. Despite his political success, he has always remained down-to-earth. Reportedly, since he was a teenager, he still frequents the same diner in his hometown, where he talks to and shakes hands with "normal" people – that is, people who are not prominent or famous in politics. He has served as a senator for about 50 years. He has made a name for himself as a backdoor deal man. He has been able to obtain quite a few betterments for low-income earners and minorities this way. What puts his down-to-earth, successful and people-oriented resume in an even more impressive light is the fact that he has already had to cope with several strokes of fate in his life. His first wife and his daughter died in a traffic accident. He himself was left alone. He started a new family with his second wife. One of his 2 sons from his 2nd marriage died in the war. How was this man able to stand up again and again and deal so exemplarily with Trump's attack in their TV duel when he called Biden's son, who died in the war, a "failure"? He responded matter-of-factly, without bursting into tears or lashing out. The man is resilient! That's why he always found meaning in life and became increasingly successful even in old age.

You grow; maybe even beyond yourself

Resilience is a defensive form of mental strength because it responds to life crises that are not self-made but come about via external factors. In addition to resilience, there is an offensive form of mental strength that is multi-faceted: ambition, discipline, consistency, determination and other factors that spur us to setting goals and challenges for ourselves. Those who set themselves a goal and want to achieve it against all odds, prepare their own challenges. The person in question does this because he or she hopes to gain more advantages than disadvantages.

An example of this would be signing up for a club, taking piano lessons, or going on a diet – a person does not experience a stroke of fate, but makes a conscious decision to take on a challenge. A motive for this could be to learn new things and to expand one's abilities. In the case of dieting, the person might have realized that he has a problem with his body weight, which considerably reduces his well-being and can be dangerous for his health, and thus makes the decision to go on a diet.

These offensive forms of mental strength testify to a love of life. The more pronounced the mental strength, the longer the person sticks to the self-imposed challenge. He or she draws lessons from the mishaps or defeats, improves and starts again. People who have this kind of mental strength are open to new developments in life and have adaptable ambitions. They often outgrow themselves through self-drive because the will is stronger than the potential hurdles.

Mental strength in interpersonal interaction

Mental strength is evident in how one responds to attacks or stands by others in their challenges. Just like in the example of Joe Biden, strong people do not let their emotions control them and attach little or no importance to verbal attacks.

When in the position of helper, mental strength gives you the opportunity to assist others by putting yourself in their shoes. Either you have already been in the same challenging situation as the person you intend to help, or you can draw conclusions about the person's state of mind based on your own similar experiences. In the latter case, there is a so-called transfer performance: You transfer your experiences to other areas of application. Because you are mentally strong, you are able to give people authentic advice and have high credibility. A person who has mastered crises tends to be believed more than people without this experience. By helping others, you are likely to secure help for yourself in the future.

Let's start with interpersonal interactions where you are verbally attacked by other people. They may insult you, put obstacles in your way, or harbor other bad intentions. Either because they are specifically angry with you, or they are angry with people in general. With mental strength, you are 1st and foremost able to not let yourself be swayed from your convictions. Do you remember the introduction that talked about your supervisor criticizing you unfairly? There are cases like that. Mentally strong people deal with it, recognizing that there is a lack of objective opinion behind the criticism. They stick to their convictions and do not attach any importance to the criticism as long as it is not objective: the joy of work remains, and the evening is never clouded by the irrational supervisor. Mental strength in defense against verbal attacks is therefore a question of faith in oneself: Do I believe in my abilities? Am I convinced that I can do the job? Do I believe so much in the path I have chosen that I will "do my thing" with maximum determination? With mental strength, this belief returns.

What does it mean to be mentally strong? What do you need for that?

Mental strength is a kind of cocktail of character traits and situational capacities. There isn't one specific form of mental strength, but different types in relation to the different challenges in life. For example, there are people who are mentally strong only in relation to certain activities. A person who goes to the gym regularly, always puts away the weight plates and leaves everything clean, can have the biggest mess at home.

The subtle differences and many details related to mental strength already give you an initial insight into how to train and develop it. If, for example, you succeed in keeping order at work or in sports, but not at home, then you have a situation-related mental strength. One approach to training or improving is to apply your mental strength to other situations in your life. Step by step you adapt your strengths from work or sports to your home. How this can be achieved will be the subject of this guidebook.

If you want to be mentally strong in as many situations as possible, it is a good idea to reflect on your behavior in the relevant situations and identify personal deficits. Then you work on solutions. The 1st step in the next chapter helps you to take stock of this. It pays to work on individual character traits, because there are specific types of character traits that favor mental strength. To train this "cocktail of character traits", you will...

1. ...select character traits specific to your own life.
2. ...train specific important universal character traits.

A few examples of point 1: A person who gives speeches in front of an audience or plays in professional sports will depend on having "nerves of steel". There is no place for nervousness and stage fright in this situation. Therefore, nerves of steel need to be acquired. People in creative fields require mental strength to deal with customers wishes, even if they do not correspond to their own creative ideas. Teachers depend on having good resistance to student bullying and require a great deal of patience.

Notes on the 2nd point: Universal character traits are motivation, discipline, self-confidence, solution orientation and network orientation.

Motivation

"Motivation refers to processes in which certain motives are activated and translated into actions. This gives behavior a direction toward a goal, a level of intensity, and a sequence of events." — (Stangl, 2020)

Intensity is an important keyword: the more intense the behavior, the greater the motivation. The greater the motivation, the more likely you are to realize your goals. When you want something, you perform more convincingly. The more you want it, the stronger the motivation. A distinction is made between extrinsic and intrinsic motivation: Extrinsic motivation is when you are motivated by another person, or the motivation depends on some other external factor. Since the motivation does not come from you, dropping out is more likely and mental strength against resistance is lower. Intrinsic motivation is when you motivate yourself because *you yourself* want something.

To keep motivation high, you should...

➢ ...know what you really want.

➢ ...derive personal benefit from it.

➢ ...prioritize, so that you offer the greatest focus to what is important to you personally.

Steps 1 and 3 in this book provide guidance in this regard.

Discipline

"Discipline comes from Latin and stands for instruction, discipline and order. Discipline is the act of following rules or regulations. Self-control is called self-discipline." (cf. Brockhaus 1988, p. 553)   — (Stangl, 2020)

If discipline means following rules and regulations, then who sets the rules and regulations? Ideally you yourself, which establishes the link to the previous section: self-imposed goals and desires have the greatest motivation, which in turn has a positive effect on discipline. Motivation influences discipline and vice versa, although they are 2 different things. One is motives that justify (motivation). The other is rules that must be followed even without a reason, for example because they are based on social norms or are a basic requirement for one's own life (discipline).

Since discipline does not have to have anything to do with motives, it is often associated with activities that do not suit you. Discipline, then, is the ability to do anyway, something you don't like doing. This ability, in my experience, is often overestimated, but is helpful in the 1st steps and every now and then in between goals. Let's take a thing that is really close to your heart: You like to pursue it, but at some point, there comes an intermediate stage that you are not good at and don't feel like doing. A suitable example would be a psychology course: You love the theory and dealing with people, but the module "statistics" with the mathematical part doesn't appeal to you at all. Now your motivation, which is great in relation to the course of study, but low in relation to the module, is sinking. The catch: You have to complete the module successfully if you want to continue your studies. Motivation is more important than discipline in the whole study program, but in this one module your discipline matters. Are you doing something you don't feel comfortable doing to achieve your big goal? If yes, you've demonstrated mental toughness. If no, you're failing and, despite being highly motivated overall, you've blown the course because of that one module. Too bad.

Discipline is important so that whenever obstacles arise, you keep your motivation high and resist the obstacles. For high discipline, it is beneficial if you...

> ➤ ...keep reminding yourself of your motives.
> ➤ ...find relaxation in difficult times and reduce your worries.
> ➤ ...control your impulses to be less deterred by challenges.

Especially steps 1, 4 and 5 in this book will help you.

Self-confidence/self-awareness

"In psychology, the term self-awareness is understood primarily as self-esteem, i.e., awareness of the importance and value of one's own personality, primarily implying an emotional assessment of one's own worth." — (Stangl, 2020)

Self-esteem equals self-confidence – that's the equation, if Stangl's specialist lexicon, has its way. This equation is plausible in that people who assign themselves a higher value are more stable. Take a person who has already received several employee of the month awards: The awards were given by the entire team and reflect the opinion of all employees as well as supervisors. The person is of high value to the company. With the awards, it is even proven in writing. In addition, the person enjoys his job and even works on optimizing his skills in his free time. Due to the permanent increase in the quality of their work, the person's self-confidence rises. The regularly repeated awards are proof of this. Friends and acquaintances praise the person for what he or she does. Suddenly a critical voice arises, which is not even sufficiently supported by factual criticism. Does it shake the person's self-confidence? Not even remotely. It's different with a person who is criticized around the clock, feels uncomfortable at work and regularly makes mistakes: Here, even the smallest hint of criticism – no matter how implausible – can cause the already battered self-confidence to hit a new low.

Self-awareness means ascribing a high value to oneself. What "high" means at this point is something each person must decide for themselves. In general, it is about feeling important and capable in who you are and what you do. Self-confidence makes you believe in your own abilities or in yourself in general. The stronger one's self-confidence is, the less one's beliefs can be shaken. It can be learned because it grows with the challenges mastered.

For a strong self-confidence and self-esteem, it is significant that you...

> ...surround yourself with people who will encourage you in your goals and desires.

> ...gradually and consistently work on and improve your skills.

> ...with increasing success nevertheless remain grounded, because otherwise self-confidence can degenerate into arrogance.

In particular, steps 2, 5, and 6 in this book will help you with these aspects.

Solution orientation

"Solution orientation is an attitude that helps us in every situation in our lives. Instead of circling around a problem again and again with our feelings and thoughts and researching its causes, we can also simply examine what works well." — (Heller, 2013)

Do not despair of problems but focus on solutions – this is the motto of solution orientation. It thus stands for optimism. Where solution orientation has an advantage over optimism: it is well thought out. While optimism also has the negative blind optimism, a solution orientation is linked to thinking about solutions. The thought process counteracts naiveté. For example, a typical statement with optimism would be, "It'll work out *somehow.*" Solution orientation, on the other hand, would ask one of the following questions, in the words of Steve de Shazer's solution-focused brief therapy: "Suppose overnight, while you were sleeping, a miracle happened, and your problem was solved. How would you know? What would be different? How will others know this without you saying a word about it to them?" The answers would be concrete and would help solve the problem.

For a solution-oriented approach, it will help you if you...

➤ ...live in the present and, starting from your present point of view, determine your possibilities for action.

➤ ...hold on to your determination and overcome obstacles with thoughtful methods.

➤ ...accept the current situation and do not act hastily.

Steps 1, 3, 4, and 5, among others, will help you achieve these behaviors and mindsets.

Network orientation

"Good social relationships are vital for people and are one of the most valuable resources for inner resilience. Having a stable social environment, maintaining contacts, and seeking support when challenges arise are healthy behaviors to draw on in critical situations." — (Heller, 2013)

The social environment can motivate and demotivate. It can help or hinder the acquisition of new skills or the improvement of these skills. Furthermore, it has the potential to relieve you of difficult tasks completely in some cases or to assign you additional tasks. Your environment is an exciting thing because it is a factor that you can only partially work on. To a considerable extent, you have to work with what is given; after all, you can't change people at the drop of a hat, and can, only to a limited extent.

Optimization in the social environment comes through your openness and your willingness to make contact. Openness means that you talk about your feelings and don't hide anything. This is because people can behave best towards you if they know your circumstances and your current condition. Suppose you are imitating a strong person: even though you feel weak, people will treat you like a strong person because you give them the impression of strength – more criticism and less praise is usually the result. This is likely to further weaken your actually sensitive attitude. Honesty is an essential input that optimizes the output from others to you. Being sociable as a 2nd factor helps you to regularly expand your environment and make new contacts. This is your key to dynamically adapting your environment to the changes in your life.

Honesty and openness lead you to succeed in your network: Pointless pride should give way to an admission of one's own excessive demands. Help should be accepted and offered in return in order to establish a mutual culture of helpfulness between oneself and other people. With increasing interaction, people become accustomed to each other and learn how best to approach each other in conversations in order to criticize and support constructively, so that motivation and self-confidence are strengthened.

For a successful network orientation, it is beneficial for you to...

- ➢ ...value other people and stick to the people who show you appreciation.
- ➢ ...openly share your emotions and needs with others.
- ➢ ...as your success grows, never forget who helped you achieve it and always remain grateful to those people.

First and foremost, steps 2, 3, 4 and 6 in this book will help you maintain such a network.

Groups of people who can be taken as an example

My experience

For me, it was mainly learning from a model that brought me success. I was able to gain insights into the vitae of numerous people who had been in a similar situation to mine. I learned from their experiences, which saved me from making certain mistakes myself. Certain groups of people excel in mental strength. Due to profession, life circumstances, their own decisions or other factors, these groups of people depend on mental strength for a successful interpretation of their role. They are trained or train themselves to meet daily demands.

As a little inspiration for you, before getting started, I've compiled 5 groups of people that I've taken as examples and highlighted what I found motivating and inspiring about them. The step-by-step instructions in this guidebook have been laid out in the same way in which I achieved mental toughness and would recommend to anyone. Combining that with the 5 groups of people and their regular characteristics contributes to a balanced, holistic approach.

Single parent

Mothers or fathers who are single parents have to perform an overwhelming balancing act. The less independent the child is due to age, illness or developmental stage, the more difficult this balancing act is to accomplish. Either work is done alongside parenting, which presents a time problem. Or the parent does not work and receives financial support from the state, which in turn reduces the financial possibilities.

According to findings from interviews, those who are successful single parents often have the following mental strengths: They talk openly about their feelings and are more willing to seek support. The reason for this is that friends and family more often have to take care of the child because there is no (spouse) partner to support them. Accordingly, the inhibition threshold to interact with other people about various concerns is lowered. Furthermore, as a mental strength, there is a considerable amount of self-responsibility: all decisions regarding the child are made by the single parent. In addition, decisions concerning one's own life and that of the child are made by one's own responsibility. This increases determination and sense of responsibility. Single parents who develop these qualities exhibit strong self-confidence and a network orientation.

Sportsman

Professional and extreme athletes have to withstand psychological pressure. Professional athletes perform in front of tens of thousands of spectators. If you add television, their performances are often in front of millions of people. Extreme athletes usually have nowhere near that many live spectators, but often go to the extent of fighting for survival in their sport. Over time, they harden to such an extent that fear fades out or doesn't even appear anymore. They live fully in the moment and deliver their top performance.

The tragic suicide of former national soccer goalkeeper Robert Enke should prove just how much pressure celebrity athletes are under: He threw himself in front of a train, leaving behind a wife and child. The strain was so great that not even his family could be a support to him. Despite these obstacles, suicides in professional sports remain a marginal phenomenon. The reason for this is that mental training and discussions with psychologists are an integral part of the sport. Fear is overcome. Doubt and pain are transformed into positive feelings. Successes serve as a booster for self-confidence. One's own abilities are consistently worked on in order to improve. Discipline is a matter of course through professional training. Those who are not disciplined will be fined or suspended.

Leaders

Leaders – whether in business, politics, or any other segment – must demonstrate mental toughness when it comes to making decisions with far-reaching implications. Dozens, hundreds, thousands and even more people can be affected by decisions made by one person. It must be admitted at this point that decisions are never made completely alone, because in larger companies and in politics, teams always consult and co-decide. But the final signature and the final decision usually fall on one person. Managers have different levels of scruples. Some don't care a bit about their workers or the population and do what is good for themselves. The others attach importance to the workers and the population and want to improve their working and living conditions. Especially the latter type of leaders, who care about others, can be plagued by pressures, worries, fears and doubts. Mistakes can cause remorse. But everyone makes mistakes. Over time, top leaders tend to realize this, which is why they develop a high level of acceptance toward the current situation – acceptance is a particular mental strength. A solution orientation to improve the mistakes or to further develop the company or the state is fundamental, the network orientation ensures successful cooperation with the consultants and employees.

Warriors / Soldiers

Imagine saying goodbye to your family (parents, children, wife or husband, brothers and sisters, grandparents, etc.) before going to work and not knowing if you will come home alive the next time. Developing the mental strength to cope with this tremendous uncertainty and fear is probably unimaginable for a large percentage of people. The fact that it is unimaginable is not only due to the nature of the circumstances, but also due to the current living situation here in Central Europe. The overwhelming majority of the population was born after the Second World War and has witnessed wars only from a distance. The situation is different in the USA, for example, which has participated in more wars with a larger contingent since the Second World War than Germany, for example. This is not a discussion about whether the military involvement of states or individuals is justified or not. Instead, it should be noted that due to decades of peace in Central Europe, it is often not considered that in other parts of the world it is an everyday scenario that people have to say goodbye to their families and face one of the most feared challenges in living memory: the fight for life and death. Mental training is nowadays a logical part of the education and training of soldiers. In most cases, soldiers are highly motivated because they identify with their home country and want to serve it and the people in it. The motivation and loyalty is so great that they are willing to sacrifice their lives for it – at least that is the ideal scenario. This mental strength, as well as the art of living in the present and maximizing life with family before deployment, are common strengths found in soldiers.

Teen

Teenagers are not to be envied. Although they have far more prospects than adults in terms of age and life expectancy – assuming they are in full health – they find themselves in a complicated in-between world: child or adult – who are they? One relaxing evening, as I was roaming through the offerings on Amazon Prime, I discovered a film (*Chemical Hearts*, 2020) that is, at its core, about a love affair between 2 teenagers that is ill-fated to begin with. In one scene, the problem behind being a teenager is put into fascinating and apt words:

"Think about what it means to be a teenager. [...] Both parents push you to succeed. Your friends push you to do shit you don't want to do. Social media is pushing you to hate your body. It's hard; even if you're a well-adjusted kid from a good family. [...] As a teenager, you're kind of wandering through a no man's land. You're caught somewhere between childhood and adulthood, and the whole world is telling you to be as mature as possible and to please develop yourself. But as soon as you do that, it's, 'Shut up!'"

When the wild dance of hormones is included from a medical perspective, the simple words take on a scientific foundation. Adults can learn a lot from teenagers. Above all, this includes the ability to withstand a storm of emotions and roller coasters of feelings.

The most important things in a nutshell

➤ Through mental strength, one attains better prospects for progress because challenges are accepted and overcome.

➤ When difficult phases of life or crises occur, mental strength helps to find your way back into life.

➤ Mental toughness is also the key to creating a positive environment in which you feel good and make others feel good as well.

➤ Universal character traits that promote mental strength are motivation, discipline, self-confidence/self-awareness, solution orientation, network orientation.

➤ There are groups of people who naturally display mental strength. Some examples of inspirational and usually mentally strong people are leaders, single parents, athletes, soldiers and teenagers.

➔ Observe these groups of people in your personal environment well in order to learn from them and visualize the universal character traits as well as their expression in you! This is how you initiate your transformation into a mentally strong person.

MPS Step 1: Live, Respect and Enjoy the Present

The present is decisive. With dissolute thoughts of the past, you let yourself be distracted by things that you can no longer change anyway. Certainly, it is important to reflect on what has happened and learn from it. This will be a part of this chapter. But it should happen exclusively in designated windows of time so that it doesn't dominate every moment of your life. Instead, you should spend the majority of your moments in the present. Because within the present you work on the future at the same time: Your actions in this moment change the following moment. So, you could say that the present is your chance to create a better past and to shape the future according to your wishes. Thereby, the unconditional focus on the present is purposeful. This is not so easy, because often people get distracted by thoughts. How is the focus concentrated on a certain moment? You will learn this in this chapter by means of exercises and explanations. First, let's take a more detailed look at the benefits of living in the present:

1) Best performance and greatest mindfulness through high concentration

If you let the past distract you, you'll have a harder time delivering a top performance. While you're worrying about outstanding bills, yesterday's disputes, and embarrassing moments, your head will be somewhere else. If you focus on the here and now, you'll perform at your best in the current situation.

That's mental strength: Don't get distracted but clear your head and deliver convincing performances!

2) Capture the beauty of the moment

There is always something going on around you that is worth paying attention to. The couple kissing shows that despite the many conflicts in this world, love still has a place. The girl playing with her dog shows that fun can be achieved by the simplest of means. The well-trained man jogging testifies to the fact that performance is rewarded, and hard work can pay off.

This is mental strength: To renounce the negative influences of everyday life and to discover for yourself the many beautiful and positive things in order to maintain a pleasant view of the world!

3) Gain insights for and about yourself

Only when you live in the present and think about yourself and the things around you can you gain insights that will move you forward. It is very important to think about the past. But what is going on in your mind right now, at this moment in time, in the context of the environment and the current circumstances, gives you the most current insight into your inner self. In retrospect, you never feel as intensely as you do at the moment.

This is mental toughness: to listen inside yourself and recognize what is really important to you in order to use all your resources to achieve realistic dreams!

Living in the present also helps to escape stress. Because stress is the harbinger of the future. The more you think about things you have to do, the more likely you are to put yourself under pressure and be in a hurry. But it should be different... Because while you're sitting on the park bench, for example, and taking time out for 10 minutes, you've decided for yourself that you're going to relax in those 10 minutes. Relaxation can only happen in the moment. Get rid of all the ballast from your head!

With thoughts of the future comes not only stress. Dreams relate to the future. They are an important motivation and incentive to put your plans into action. However, it becomes problematic when dreams degenerate into fairy tale castles. Mastering the balancing act between realistic dreams and concrete goals in life is not easy. Some people don't manage it at all. They build fairy-tale castles while life passes them by – day after day, month after month, year after year. To live in the present means to live one's dreams. An important tool for this is having realistic dreams, which are transformed into stage goals and pursued with the actions of the present.

Expectations, like stress, are the harbingers of the future. They are linked to the condition that you reach a certain goal in a certain time. On the one hand, the problem with expectations is that they can be disappointed. On the other hand, expectations are an important orientation and a benchmark about whether you are on the right track to achieve your dreams. So, what should you do – expect or not expect?

All the topics mentioned and expected results are waiting for you in this chapter. It is the 1ˢᵗ step because the present is your starting point. Become the master of your present situation!

From today the present counts for you

The introduction to this chapter is practical. Exercises are the best way to get a feeling for what living in the present means. By learning step by step to focus on the present moment, you will be better able to understand the rest of this chapter on your path to mental strength. Exercises, aside from helping you focus on the present moment, have several other benefits on the path to mental toughness.

Sport is an element of the following exercises. It helps you develop mental strength in different ways, depending on the sport. If you perform in front of spectators, at best you'll develop nerves of steel, which can also help alleviate or eliminate your stage fright at work. In team sports, you may gain friends who are sympathetic to you. They motivate you and make you believe more strongly in your abilities, which increases your resilience in difficult phases of life.

In addition to sports, special relaxation exercises are useful. One example is Progressive Muscle Relaxation. PME was developed by the American doctor Edmund Jacobson (1885–1976), who was looking for solutions to help nervous people relax. Lowering nervousness is a good sign of developing mental strength. But can PME confirm the hopes? Today the method is well researched. As early as 1994, 66 controlled studies by Grawe et al. showed that PME is helpful as a component of therapies. The greatest effect was found in the therapy of anxiety disorders and psychosomatic diseases (such as hypertension and chronic pain).

The recommendation to you now is to make use of relaxation exercises on the one hand and sports on the other, in order to better switch off and find your way into the present. Below you will find a selection of 3 exercises, from which you should choose only 1 and practice it regularly for a week. In addition to these exercises, it is optimal to try to exercise for 30 minutes every 2 or 3 days. You are welcome to do the exercise in your own home. You have plenty of sports to choose from, just adjust the intensity and technical requirements to your performance level. Try to do this activity every 2 to 3 days for 30 minutes over the course of a month. If you like it, you will increase the frequency and duration of the activity by yourself.

The following 3 exercises are special and serve specifically to focus on the present. Most of the time, the goal is to create relaxation. For you, relaxation is an important element to let the worries and thoughts of the day slip away and to find yourself more easily in the present.

Exercise 1

PME, according to Jacobson, runs alternatively in short or long forms. The short form has the following sequence:

1. Take 30 minutes in a quiet and undisturbed room. Assume a comfortable reclining position. Wear loose clothing. It is best to set an alarm clock so as not to be distracted by looking at the clock.

2. Close your eyes at the beginning of the exercise. Begin to inhale and exhale evenly and at a steady pace.

3. Firmly tense the muscles of the body for 5 to 10 seconds. Then relax for about 30 seconds. Repeat this sequence several times.

In the long form, the procedure is different for the 3rd step. You don't tense the entire musculature of the body, but individual muscles. For example, you start with the hands and slowly work your way to the forearms, then tense the arms completely. After the arms, tense the arms and chest muscles. Continue like this, adding another muscle group to the previous ones, step by step, and in the end the whole body is tensed. There are breaks in between. Feel free to guide yourself through in your mind during the exercise. Tell yourself which muscles to tense and count the seconds. During the contraction you can repeat "hold" several times. Finally, say "release" and relax before starting the sequence again.

Exercise 2

Meditation is a Far Eastern method of sitting in a comfortable posture. The focus is solely on the moment. Any distraction is to be avoided. Beginners are advised to concentrate fully on breathing during the first few meditations. This is to help distract oneself from the thoughts of everyday life.

1. Sit comfortably in a seated position on the floor. Make sure that you are not sitting on your lower legs and that all vessels are well supplied with blood. Otherwise, you risk your legs falling asleep.

2. Sit upright to open your chest and breathe better. Keep your head straight ahead and close your eyes. Let your arms rest loosely in your lap.
3. It is advisable to set the alarm clock here as well. Because meditation is rather monotonous, beginners should practice with a shorter duration, twice a day, in contrast to PME. 10 minutes is appropriate.
4. Inhale deeply at the beginning and hold the air for 1 to 2 seconds. Then exhale again. With each breath, try to imagine yourself going deep into your inner mind. With each exhalation, imagine yourself getting rid of the worries of everyday life.

Exercise 3

The ESA technique is used for emotional stress relief. It is specifically designed for difficult phases of life or stressful moments of everyday life to clear the mind of negative thoughts.

1. Lie down or sit down comfortably.
2. Let one hand touch your forehead very lightly and keep the other hand lightly on your belly button.
3. Close your eyes, breathe in and out calmly and evenly for a while.
4. Now imagine unpleasant thoughts and images roaming through your mind. Hold each thought and image briefly, taking this moment seriously, but after a few seconds of holding, imagine sending the thoughts and images away to distance yourself from them.

If the question remains with you, what influence all these exercises have on the present, it is understandable. To clarify the question, let's first list a common feature of the exercises: They all help you distance yourself from the hustle and bustle of everyday life and the challenges that lie ahead. These influences are replaced by the activity at hand, which usually puts you fully in the moment. In the beginning it will take practice for the meditation, PME or other method to work as they should. With time you will become more and more aware of the present. And now it gets really interesting: Because immediately after the exercise you are usually clearer and more focused in your thoughts. You see the world with different eyes, so to speak.

My experience

I used to try to increase my focus at work by consuming energy drinks. After a few months, I started having problems with my blood pressure. Consequently, I decided to get back to the roots! I renounced substances containing caffeine and taurine. Instead, I meditated, as recommended by millennia-old traditions. At first, I found it difficult to concentrate. However, by focusing on breathing, I had an anchor that helped me shut off all other thoughts. After 15 minutes of meditation, my concentration was better than after several energy drinks. I was setting an insane pace. To this day, meditation is my preferred way to fully focus on the moment.

The focus you take away from these exercises carries over to other activities: At work, you're more focused. In conversations, you pick up on the important little details. You're more efficient when you're studying. When you have to carry out procedures smoothly, you succeed more cleanly. The more often you do the exercises, the more you train yourself to be attentive in general.

Start today and you will succeed in living more and more in the present with each passing day.

Interim summary

Special exercises are the best 1ˢᵗ step you can take to focus your awareness on the present. Through regular practice, you learn to be in the present even beyond the exercises. You'll be less likely to be distracted in your activities.

How you gain insights through mindfulness

Presence requires mindfulness. The exercises mentioned above will help you to achieve it. Continue them regularly to experience lasting change. The more attentive you are in the individual moments of your life, the more insights you will gain about yourself.

Example

You are sitting near the center of a big city park. The weather is sunny and draws lots of people to spend time in the park too. Imagine that your personal mental strength coach comes and sits down next to you on the bench, and asks you the following question, "What's happening here right now? What's going on in the park?" Your answer is, "Nothing." Your coach just shakes his head and says, "That's wrong. In fact, there's a lot going on."

First, it is interesting to determine how a person arrives at the answer "Nothing is going on." The reason is simple: there is nothing "special" going on. Children are playing, couples are kissing, pensioners are feeding the pigeons – all ordinary things for now, things that have been seen many times over already. This is how the answer "nothing" comes about. There are many people who would answer in the same way. But this has nothing to do with mindfulness. Mindfulness would mean observing every detail around you, revealing situations that hold surprising details:

➢ The children are playing, but they do it in a completely different way than usual for their age. A child falls and immediately everyone rushes selflessly to help him get up. They put the fun of playing on the back seat.

➢ A couple is kissing. But both are easily over 80 years old. Since when has the intimacy shown by this kiss been natural at this age? *Maybe they've even been together since their youth...* You think and begin to develop an interest in the couple's life story.

➢ The pensioners are feeding the pigeons, but the horde of youngsters that is approaching is preparing to chase the pigeons away. They run towards the pigeons and drive the pensioners into a rage. What a spectacle!

There is always something going on that is worth watching. And sometimes simple descriptions, like in the 3 bullet points above, hold fascinating details or surprising twists: In the course of your observations, you can, on the one hand, gather insights about yourself, and on the other hand, gain relaxation and improve your mood. You gain relaxation, for example, if you are able to apply this precise power of observation to the shortest of breaks: You don't think about the fact that the break in the office only lasts 5 minutes and that you don't feel like working afterwards. Instead, you're fully in the moment, relieving stress and being soothed while you sit. By being less stressed, you gain more patience, balance, and mental strength.

How can you gain insights about yourself from observation? By mindfully observing the moment with all its trimmings, you begin to think about various things and your attitude towards them. It becomes an automatism. You also get ideas to try new hobbies or transfer observations to the professional context. Being mindful of the moment promotes insights about yourself and what's happening around you. Observations give you plenty of material to question yourself and your current situation. "Questioning" at this point does not mean that your current plans and actions are bad. Rather, "questioning" should be understood as a generally useful action. Because if you don't question whether everything is still going according to your innermost wishes, it can happen that you ignore the dynamic developments of life and maintain your present course, even though a few changes would do you good.

With all that you have now learned about mindfulness, you can already do exercises:

➤ Use the short breaks in everyday life to observe and think about the things around you. This is an excellent alternative to pulling out your smartphone and stumbling across negative news or other bad influences on it.

➤ When you are bored in the near future, think about whether there is something to observe. Because as you now know: There's always something going on. This promotes your creativity in many ways.

➤ Be attentive to people: If you are mindful, you will recognize that your colleague has changed something about his or her appearance. Praise the person to start a conversation with your fellow human beings.

So, mindfulness has multiple benefits. There is one exercise that has the most important function for you personally, the epitome of mindfulness towards yourself in fact. It takes you into the deepest reaches of your consciousness. It brings out thoughts that you unintentionally withhold from yourself. It shows you the path that you really want to take in life. The exercise is: the Inner Dialogue.

In a world full of distractions and permanent accessibility, listening to yourself is worth its weight in gold. The Inner Dialogue helps you to do this. It works wonders and can bring you from the wrong path to the right one or – if you already have the right path in mind – make you stick to it. Inner Dialogue may strengthen your resolve to go through with certain undertakings because it shows that you really want what you are doing and are grateful for it.

Hint!

Gratitude is an essential point in your life anyway. The more grateful you are, the more you remind yourself that you are happy or at least satisfied with what you have. This attitude is balm for the soul. It can alleviate depression and offer support in difficult phases. Also, gratitude suggests to you a certain kind of wealth. It doesn't have to be wealth in the form of money. How about wealth in health, great family, or other benefits you get to enjoy in your life? You will appreciate yourself and your life more with a grateful attitude and be more confident too.

To practice Inner Dialogue, sit down in a comfortable chair, sofa or armchair, making sure that it is quiet around you for the entire duration. Switch off devices that may cause distraction and choose a time frame for your practice. Think about your daily life and about certain aspects of it that are currently affecting you, especially on your thoughts and feelings towards them. Have the courage to question whether what is currently happening is in your best interest. Can you perhaps change something in your favor? Ideally, at the end of the Inner Dialogue, you will realize that you are happy with everything you are doing. The purpose of the Inner Dialogue is to intensively deal with yourself. When you are done, recall 5 facts for which you are grateful and repeat them several times.

Exercise

Conduct the Inner Dialogue as a ritual regularly at fixed times. Keep a diary of your thoughts as it allows you to trace your emotions back several days, weeks, months, or even years, giving you a solid overview of your development.

Interim summary

Live in the present to be mindful of the many stimuli and wonders around you. They inspire you and change your present for the better if you let them. Through Inner Dialogue, also be mindful of yourself to find out if you like the present in its current state.

Realism and fairy tale are clearly separated

The principle of the Inner Dialogue helps you to distinguish between realism and fairy tales. Based on your insights, it will be easier for you to set realistic goals and have realistic dreams. It becomes clearer to you where you stand and what you can expect.

Consequently, you don't build fairy-tale castles that make you live in a dream world somewhere other than in the present moment.

Example

You are currently in debt but you dream of being a millionaire. The fairy tale dream in front of your eyes, makes it difficult for you to see the small, realistic steps necessary to reduce your debts first. Because as long as you have debts, you have to pay the high overdraft interest or reminder fees, and you cannot find your way out of your precarious situation. Your dream castle is also your prison at the same time. Through the Inner Dialogue, you remind yourself that you want too much and you realize that it's better to think in small steps. In this way, you will eventually work your way to being debt-free, whereupon you will have more opportunities to invest your money profitably. This is the way you are most likely to become a millionaire. But dreaming of being a millionaire at this point would be counterproductive. You have to get out of debt first.

Inner Dialogue promotes insights, but on its own does not guarantee that you will quickly escape from the fairy-tale castle. For this, you need other methods too. And here's just the thing:

Exercise

1. Write down everything you dream of – even the most absurd things. Take your time, using the Inner Dialogue in a quiet environment.
2. Now write down how much time you have available every day and how much of it is lost for duties that you *have to*

perform. How much time is left for the realization of your dreams?

3. Check whether it is realistic to realize your dreams in a timely manner with the time available to you and your other resources (e.g., money, your own abilities, health condition). Stay away from dreams that are far beyond your time and other capacities. Cross them off the list. In the Inner Dialogue you will probably discover several little things that are attractive substitutes for unrealistic dreams that have been crossed off.

4. The list should contain dreams or rather smaller goals that you can realize in a relatively short time with your actual resources. These smaller goals may be related to a big dream and bring you closer to it. Just make sure that they can be achieved in a timely manner and that they are not so far away that the journey seems long and arduous. Make it easy for yourself!

5. Create a step-by-step sequence with your stage goals to tackle the realistic dreams. The more you achieve, the closer you will get to your bigger dreams. Update your goals regularly; especially when you reach them and new goals are needed.

What is useful in this context is to take a cue from people who already achieved their dreams. Which person is suitable as a role model? What can you learn from other people in relation to your individual stage goals? Celebrities, people from world history, people from your circle of acquaintances and others you can think of can be included. The advantage of people who are in your immediate vicinity is their availability: unlike celebrities, they are available for conversation, so that an individual approach to your needs is possible. This process of seeking out and orienting your-self to role models is known as "learning from the model". It is a psychologically recognized method in which it is only important that you choose models who are in a similar situation to you. For example, a person who has not had to struggle through life as you have, but has had everything laid at their feet, is not a suitable model for you.

Gretchen question: What does all this have to do with life in the present?

For one thing, setting realistic goals and moving away from unrealistic dreams promotes a connection to your current situa-tion. If you orient yourself to your current situation and create concrete plans for your future actions, you are most likely to be successful. Setting good plans already means, to a certain extent, living in the present.

Second, scrapping unrealistic dreams helps you live in the mo-ment. After all, you don't have the distraction of dreams that are unlikely to come true at this point in time. Instead, you devote yourself to realistic goals that you actually approach – precisely because they are realistic and appropriate to your current situation.

Take a book or a hard drive as an example: you need to leave as much info as possible for a person to master the challenges ahead. The hurdle is that both book and hard drive have limited space for information. Do you choose to leave info about work steps that are 8 years in the distance and don't currently matter? Or do you leave the person with information material that starts with his current situation and shows him step by step the way from here to his better future? Rather the latter, isn't it? So, think of your mind as the hard disk. The fewer dreams or things that lie in the distant future are stored in it, the faster and smoother the hard drive runs.

Interim summary

Your life today will be positively influenced by banishing from your mind everything that currently has no relevance. Dreams are not forbidden, but they should be realistic. Then you will be more motivated, focused and most likely to deliver a good performance in the present.

Expectations are important, but only belong in the present to a limited extent

Expectations play a basic role in the present because they concern the future. You don't expect anything from an event that has already happened. You may have an expectation of the outcome of the event that is taking place, but that is still in the future and could distract you from the present moment.

Example

You have an important performance in front of an audience. But while you are delivering it, you are actually thinking all the time about how it's going to turn out and expecting it to be a good outcome for you. The problem here is that you distract yourself with your expectations, resulting in confusion or mental lapses.

This being said, you may have noticed that at the beginning of this subchapter that I said expectations play a *basic role* in the present, because they concern the future. So, what is the appropriate way to deal with them?

Expectations as a guide

With all the focus on the moment, it must not be disregarded that expectations can serve as orientation. They are identical to goals or smaller milestones you set for yourself. For example, if you have a milestone goal to be more disciplined in completing your work or study assignments by the end of this month in order to have more free time, your expectation is that you will achieve that goal. So, expectations have the role of giving you a direction.

If you had no expectations, you would have no goals.

If you didn't have goals, you would have a harder time motivating yourself.

If your motivation were low, the likelihood of success would decrease.

You realize at this point that expectations used appropriately, serve as a benchmark for determining your success as you set milestones to achieve a larger goal. These milestones are associated with the expectation of mastering them.

What if this expectation is not fulfilled? Then you haven't reached your milestone either. As a consequence, you might make course corrections in order to avoid further failure. So, expectations in this sense help you to monitor your successful progress.

Expectations should not be completely discarded. Because expecting something from the next 3 months in order to assess your own performance is beneficial. Accordingly, the crux of the matter is not whether you have expectations, but *when you have expectations.*

Have expectations – this is the right way to do it!

Imagine you are sitting with your best friend in your favorite café. You haven't seen each other for several months and you are having a chat. One topic that arises is your plans for the future. You talk about your upcoming bachelor thesis. Your goal is at least an A average, because you believe you have the necessary qualities, you are normally pretty good in your studies, having an A average in previous subjects. Now think for a while and decide whether it is an appropriate expectation.

The answer is that it's absolutely an appropriate expectation – it is a goal that you set for yourself. It only becomes problematic when you allow yourself to be distracted by your expectations in the present while you are actually performing a task because you should be free to focus on the moment. Applied to the example of the bachelor thesis, it means that while you are working on it, at best you don't waste a thought on your expectation. Otherwise, you will distract yourself, make careless mistakes or even bigger errors, be unable to think clearly and risk your A-grade.

My experience

I used to be a talented soccer player. If I had understood back then how mental strength is developed, I might have had a great career. But that's a thing of the past. What matters to me is that my expectations on the pitch got in the way. In training sessions and several hours before the game, I formulated expectations and set goals. That was good. But the problem was that on the field, I kept thinking about the expectations and let them take me out of the moment. I worried about not meeting the expectations every time I received the ball.

Situation	Orientation guide	Distraction
Sports: You have a game.	If you set training goals and expect to achieve them, it's productive.	When you're playing, you're thinking all the time about whether people are rating you the way you expect them to. You're distracted by that.
Social / Love: You are dating a person for the first time.	You formulate a plan for the interview before the meeting to make it interesting and be prepared for questions.	You're sitting across from the person, thinking all the time about whether you're coming across as charming as you planned. Because of these thoughts, you are not in the moment and unable to listen to the person.
Job / School / Study: You carry out a project.	You set a plan for the stages of the project and work through them according to your expectations.	During the project, your thoughts revolving around the outcome will get you off track.

Expectations are orientation and distraction at the same time. They are an important orientation if they show you the way in the present and a distraction if they distract you from your task. Therefore, formulate expectations, but do not let them dominate your mind.

Interim summary

If you have expectations and they are disappointed halfway through, you are condemning the moment. This takes you away from taking the minimum chance of success. Therefore, when performing a task, always stay in the moment without expectations. Deal with expectations and their evaluation when you have the time and peace of mind to do so.

MPS Step 1 in brief

> ➤ Great attention should be paid to the present. Because the past is over, and you should leave it behind. The future, on the other hand, cannot be influenced and should be approached without fears or queasy feelings.

> ➤ By focusing on the present, the past is let go of and the future is shaped. Because the best way to live the life you dream of in the future is to act purposefully in the present.

> ➤ Useful exercises to develop sensitivity to the present and greater focus on the moment at every stage of daily life are PME, meditation and ESA techniques. Sports, gymnastics and breathing exercises of any form are also helpful.

> ➤ Whoever lives in the moment and pays all attention to the present, gains many insights about himself and his surroundings, making it clearer what his wishes are and how he would like to live.

> ➤ By focusing unconditionally on the present, distractions are reduced: Expectations, worries, fears and other hindering thoughts occur less or not at all. Therefore, the present principle helps you to perform at your best.

➢ Concentration on the moment, reduces stress levels. Resulting in better mental balance and relaxation, which can also improve health conditions.

→ Living in the moment leads to concentration. Concentration makes you forget your own weaknesses. So ultimately the present principle provides mental strength!

MPS Step 2: Know your value

Not badmouthing yourself or one another is an artform in life. Badmouthing is an easy trap to fall into, when any person can research information online and be a know-it-all. It is admirable and commands the greatest respect when you can discover a person's value despite their flaws. Or even better is discovering the value of a person in their flaws!

➢ Overweight: Ever heard of the artist Peter Paul Rubens, who artfully staged female curves and made them fashionable? In the past, for example during the Renaissance in Central Europe, a plump body was considered a symbol of prosperity and performance.

➢ Knowledge gaps: Every gap is an opportunity to gain new knowledge and enrich oneself. Many smart people have fewer such opportunities because they think they already know everything or feel less incentive to learn.

➢ No money in the account: It doesn't matter. Because you certainly have other strengths. Maybe you're eloquent. Maybe you have an incredible amount of knowledge. Maybe your wealth of experience can't be topped. And by the way, if you don't have any money in your account, you can't lose any...

Everything that is negative also has a positive side. Everything that is positive also has a negative side. You decide which side you want to see. Of course, it should not be ignored that some situations are an exception to this rule. If you always look only at the positive side, you run the risk of hiding from things you need to improve in your life. This chapter, therefore, does not teach you to always look through rose-colored glasses. It teaches you the ability to exercise a healthy measure of appreciation and criticism towards yourself as well as towards other people.

Developing appreciation requires clear reference points

Appreciation doesn't come from anywhere: it must be based on the recognition that a person has value. The more convinced you are of a person's value, the more appreciation you will have for him or her. To put it simply, you need reasons to value a person:

➤ Does the person have certain physical or mental abilities that demand recognition and respect?

➤ Does the person have character traits that speak for him or her?

➤ Has the person succeeded in achieving certain goals on his or her resume?

These points are easy to understand up to this point. Should a person have trained his memory to be photographic, then he deserves appreciation. If the person has succeeded in completing training, he also deserves appreciation for it, regardless of what kind of training it is. Here is the crux of the matter: an academic who has completed a course of study and may even have a doctorate is held in higher esteem in the eyes of many people than a person who does track construction work on railroad tracks. The academic is considered to have a higher value. A reference point is taken on the basis of which the person is judged.

Do you know which people will most likely make the most intriguing acquaintances and make others feel better about themselves?

Individuals who see the specialties in what appears to be the least prestigious profession and recognize that this profession must also be learned.

People who are willing to go beyond initial uninteresting aspects to further explore the interlocutor and discover impressive details in the course of conversation.

People who are capable of being enthusiastic about any kind of special circumstances that distinguish another person.

These insights apply when thinking about yourself, and to conversations with other people. If you try to open yourself to the details of every single clue, you will recognize even in the simplest professions, the simplest activities and the finest character traits why every person is special – and should have their strengths valued!

My experience

In a phase of life when I was not succeeding at anything, I denied my mistakes and criticized other people. I was so meticulous in my criticism that it was unbearable. So, it was no wonder that almost my entire environment turned away from me and showed me little appreciation. A vicious circle of lack of appreciation developed, with which I and my entourage beat each other up. My dissatisfaction almost degenerated into depression. When

I took distance and practiced writing down positive things about myself and others and repeating it several times, there was a change in my mindset. People were surprised at how respectful and benevolent I became toward them. As a result, they almost automatically showed me more appreciation as well.

Connection between optimism and appreciation

Appreciation is best developed when you approach things with optimism. Optimism means positive thinking. If you believe that something will turn out well, you are in an optimistic mood. If you think optimistically, it will be easier to see the value of a person or thing even where it is hard to see. The reason for this is that the optimistic person views the world through a filter of confidence, enthusiasm, and love of life. This filter leads to a more willing engagement with other people and their finest qualities. An optimistic person will be able to see something good even in the weaknesses of the interlocutor or in his own flaws.

Example

You're having a hard time with math class. Luckily, you have a teacher who cares about his students. He gets on the level with his students by trying to understand what life is like for a teenage person these days. The confusion of hormones during puberty, the expectations of home and teachers to be an adult and face challenges – these things and more make it difficult to always deliver a top performance. Then, when one subject doesn't suit you – in this case math – the barriers to good performance are all the greater. But the teacher is an optimist. He believes that he can get a few percent more out of you. He comes to this conclusion because of your good performance in physics, which is partly similar to math. He devotes himself to you more intensively and tries to create parallels between mathematics and physics. In the process, he gives you a smile or 2 in appreciation and deliberately makes a mistake himself to take the pressure off you.

What principles about appreciation do you learn from this example?

1. Optimism is what drives you and makes it easier for you to develop appreciation.
2. Getting on the same level as people and not appearing aloof is elementary to getting through to the person. To do this, it is often necessary to try to put yourself in their shoes.
3. A smile helps because it gives familiarity and warmth. It is a positive way to express emotions. It makes you approach people in a sympathetic way.

Appreciation is not an art. It only needs signs or characteristics by which you can assign a value to a person. Every person has these characteristics. If you think optimistically, you will find them most easily. Just as these rules apply to your behavior toward other people, they also apply to your thinking about yourself.

Exercise

Now it's time for you to show appreciation for yourself. If you have not been doing well so far, this exercise is of utmost importance. If you have been giving yourself appreciation so far, this exercise will help you to give yourself even more appreciation.

Write down all of your personal characteristics – both positive and negative: external features, physical abilities (including those used in work or sports), mental abilities, character traits, your resume (from birth to now), and other things you can think of. Go into great detail. Write down one personal characteristic on each line. Leave space for more text next to these characteristics on the right side of the list.

Next step, write down everything positive that is connected with the respective characteristic on the right side. If there is nothing positive, leave it alone. But don't give up too soon if you can't think of anything. For example: You don't tend to finish anything, instead you are always starting new things. This superficially negative characteristic has the positive accompanying factor that you like to try new things. Being open to new things is by no means an attribute that everyone has. It can open up more scope for you because you come into contact with new things, impressions and experiences. So, congratulate yourself for this!

Lastly, try to find ways to use the positive sides of the negative thing to your profit. It will help you find out your strengths by focusing on your positive traits, and may even directly create solutions to problems that have been bothering you for a long time.

The consequences of appreciation

How does appreciation lead to mental strength?

It should be noted that appreciation makes you consider yourself or others to be more important. Being important strengthens people, because it provides a reason to live. If you were not important, a large part of your motivation would disappear. This can be related to the whole of life, or individual parts it. Someone who is not wanted in a family because of a quarrel, or a misunderstanding may be made to feel unimportant. That person loses a significant amount of support in life. The same scenario is conceivable at work. Imagine a person helps build a company for 30 years and then suddenly gets fired in exchange for severance pay on the grounds that he or she can no longer lead the digital transformation and align the company in a modern way. Such a scenario is not unlikely. Being sidelined and deemed unimportant hurts one's own esteem. This steals your motivation; perhaps even the general motivation to live. With esteem, the exact opposite results:

You are important!
You are needed!
Your qualities are known and recognized!

These words are balm for your soul. You gain more self-confidence. With more self-confidence comes courage. Because when others need you and count on you, your skills are special. You're more likely to dare to take a risk and you increase your chances of success because success requires a certain amount of risk-taking.

If you use the knowledge you have gained to make the connection to the last chapter, then you will notice that appreciation will give you a better present. This happens in several ways:

➢ You recognize your value and abilities, which reduces the amount of distracting negative thoughts. This makes it easier for you to focus on the moment.
➢ Self-awareness and confidence will make you more confident in your skills, which will help you with current performances.

> ➤ You are generally freer in your mind. Because where there are no worries and negative emotions, there is more room for absolute freedom of thought.

The more appreciation you show people, the better they feel. They begin to like your company. They may adapt your point of view so that you build each other up and keep each other happy. Appreciation based on reciprocity is a wonderful breeding ground for building pleasant interpersonal relationships. You gain in the form of contacts who value you, or interlocutors who are a support for you in difficult phases. In this way, mental strength also comes to you from the outside.

Interim summary

When you value yourself and others, you gain confidence, courage, self-esteem, and uplifting social contacts. All these resources strengthen you mentally and help you to build a mentally strengthening environment. This environment not only helps you, but you also help the people in it.

Tell yourself and it will be!

Up to this point, you have recognized the positive things about yourself and your fellow human beings. That is already enough to encourage appreciation towards your fellow human beings. But it is not yet enough for appreciation towards yourself. In simpler words: If you express appreciation in some way to your fellow human beings in conversations or chats, you have already done your best to get along well with them. Your job is not to play therapist and keep telling them how important they are. In the long run, that can seem too pushy. If a person asks you for help or expresses self-doubt, you are welcome to talk to them more often and encourage them. But otherwise, the appreciation you suggest in passing conversations is perfectly sufficient. You suggest this appreciation by smiling, showing interest in the topics the person is addressing, and generally keeping an open attitude with a bit of praise in between. It's different with yourself, though. Since you are reading this, you've probably identified some mental improvement needs in yourself. If you realize that your problems lie in low self-esteem, the lessons in this chapter so far will be of some help to you, but only a little. The important thing is that you keep working through the lessons. If you have noticed – to use the previous example – that an open attitude towards new things is your strength, you should remind yourself of this regularly. If you don't, you will most likely remain at the same level as before, and instead of positive openness, you will see your lack of perseverance as a negative aspect. After all, you are used to a negative self-perception in your mindset. Negative must become positive! The best way to do this is to change your mindset.

Notice

Changing your thoughts from negative to positive, from failure to success, from pessimism to optimism is an essential part of my book *Habits of Winners*. In this title there are a dozen exercises to program your thoughts towards positivity and success. By reprogramming your thoughts, you work on your subconscious mind. The subconscious mind is a collection of automated processes of both thought and action. They run automatically because you have become accustomed to them. If you succeed in shaping the automatisms in such a way that you think positively and act accordingly, then you take a decisive step towards success. The reprogramming of thoughts also works in connection with appreciation.

A useful exercise to help you program your thoughts for self-esteem works through affirmations. Affirmations are positive beliefs. The trick is that you repeatedly remind yourself of your strengths. Again, following on from the example earlier, an appropriate affirmation would be, "I am open to new things." This belief system can be continued by pointing out the advantages of your openness: "I always tell people about my new experiences. In conversations, I'm an interesting grab bag. People like me for that." You convince yourself of your strengths, until you no longer think of yourself as someone who abandons tasks. The mental strength is inside you. You just have to bring it to the surface!

Exercise

Based on the previous explanations and examples presented, you should now have a number of strengths on your list which you have derived from your weaknesses. Just as a lack of staying power has become a commendable openness to new things, you can find something positive in all your weaknesses. You write these positive insights as beliefs on another sheet of paper. Use one sheet of paper per belief. In order to keep paper wastage low, you could divide an A4 sheet into 2 or 4 smaller sheets. Stick each sheet somewhere in your home with adhesive tape. One sheet could be hung opposite the toilet and the other on your refrigerator for example. While another could be great on the inside of your front door. Ideally, you should be confronted with these affirmations several times during the course of your day. Take your time to read the respective belief when you see it, even setting a specific time slot every day to read it aloud repeatedly for 10 minutes. You will get used to thinking of the strengths naturally over time.

Developing appreciation for yourself takes practice. Writing down and repeating positive beliefs is only a 1st step, comparable to a map or a navigational route. You see there is a path to becoming confident, but that path must be walked.

Interim summary

Formulate beliefs. Write them down on several pieces of paper. Hang the notes in your home in frequently visited corners and confront yourself with them. Repeat them over and over again, even as a ritual at fixed times of the day. Over time, you'll get used to making your thoughts positive.

Caution. When is it too much appreciation?

Can there be too much appreciation? It depends entirely on how appreciation is practiced. Basically, appreciation does not mean praising oneself or others to the skies. Appreciation in general is a positive, respectful and benevolent basic attitude. Praise and recognition are instruments that serve among a multitude of other instruments to express appreciation. But they are not necessary for expressing appreciation. If they are used too frequently and excessively, praise and recognition are even dangerous. They carry the risk that weaknesses are ignored and problems are not perceived. This is the answer to the question of when it is too much appreciation: when it is used in an overdose.

What the overdose is depends on the individual context. A good guiding formula for you is: If you notice that appreciation contributes to further development and an improvement of the situation, you are doing everything right. If appreciation prevents you from developing further because you look at every problem through rose-colored glasses, appreciation is too high a dosage. Because the example in the last few paragraphs was used frequently and followed step by step, it is worth going back to it again:

Is it dangerous if you notice a lack of staying power in yourself, but ignore this weakness by substituting an openness to newness as a strength?

Yes and No. Completely "ignoring" weaknesses is never good. You should always have your weaknesses on the screen and observe them carefully. The exercises in this chapter were not designed to eliminate weaknesses from your consciousness. They were designed to help you focus on your strengths *first and foremost*, to motivate you and make you optimistic. But you should still observe your weaknesses. In this sense, the answer to the above question is: If you ignore the weakness, such a form of appreciation is dangerous. But if you keep the weakness on your radar and critically examine it regularly to see if the positive mindset has improved anything, the appreciation is not dangerous.

If the meaning of the word "appreciation" is analyzed precisely, it is never dangerous. But for an adequate explanation of what appreciation means we would have to write a whole book on the topic. For now, just practice it and discover for yourself through experience.

Interim summary

Appreciation – despite all the focus on positive thoughts and strengths – does not mean disregarding one's weaknesses. The goal is to no longer let weaknesses dominate one's thoughts so that they shape one's mental state. A regular critical examination of personal deficits remains essential for further development.

Physical well-being for more appreciation

The calculation "Physical well-being + mental well-being = appreciation" rounds off this chapter. Because mental well-being exerts the greatest influence on appreciation, it had the largest share of attention. You are urged to continue the list exercises and affirmations. They are the most important component of expressing appreciation to yourself and also giving a sense of appreciation to others.

Physical well-being has an influence on self-esteem. It also makes pain, discomfort or lack of concentration less likely, enhancing your mood and performance. A particularly good physical condition (as you might have after a wellness weekend) has the potential to contribute extraordinarily to a sense of overall well-being. People achieve this through things like massages, sauna sessions, vacations etc. These special treats can be a great reward to offer yourself. But when are rewards appropriate? Mostly when one has accomplished something that deserves a reward. Rewards like this are often associated with appreciation in the subconscious mind. So, when you reach for a reward, it may automatically activate the feeling of appreciation in you. Accordingly, rewarding yourself with physical wellness measures is beneficial for self-esteem in more ways than one. Be careful not to go too far though. They should not noticeably harm your finances (massages, for example, are costly) nor discourage you from working on yourself. These types of measures should always have a special value, otherwise you will get used to them over time and the self-esteem gained will decrease. So, use these measures sparingly, but under no circumstances give up doing something good for your body once a week or once every 2 weeks for a few hours. Healthy nutrition, sports and moderate exercise as measures of physical well-being may of course be practiced more frequently than massages, because they are a permanently important contribution to human health.

Interim summary

Physical well-being influences self-esteem less than mental measures, but it is also an influence. Regular measures to increase physical well-being and a permanently healthy lifestyle promote your self-esteem.

MPS Step 2 in a nutshell

➤ Strengths and weaknesses are a matter of opinion. Every strength brings with it weaknesses. Likewise, every weakness brings strengths. The goal is to focus on positive personal characteristics.

➤ Positive thoughts about oneself and others lead to appreciation. Appreciation does not mean blindly praising and closing one's eyes to weaknesses. Instead, it is about adopting a respectful, benevolent and positive attitude.

➢ Those who adopt such an attitude while still working on their personal weaknesses, are charting an optimal course in life.

➢ Appreciation contributes to more self-confidence. One's own abilities are implemented confidently and offensively, which is an important factor in delivering the best performance and being successful.

➢ When there is appreciation towards other people, there is a high probability that one will be perceived as sympathetic, liked and also appreciated. Through reciprocity, positive human relationships and conversations occur, which strengthens one mentally.

→ Pay the most attention to your strengths while being aware of and working on your weaknesses. Meet people respectfully and benevolently. This is how the appreciation principle helps you gain mental strength!

MPS Step 3: What you really want, you will do!

Determination does not mean that you want something. Wanting is a possible initiator of determination, but it is far from a guarantee of it. For example, you may want to lose weight in order to reach your dream weight. But isn't that what many people want? Yet they fail because of the obstacles; because they are not determined – because determination means pushing through against resistance. You know the resistances beforehand and prepare yourself for them to achieve your objective anyway. Or unexpected resistance arises spontaneously, in this case, too, you know no ifs and buts, because you are determined.

Determination can do little with phrases such as "would like to have," or "should really have." Determination knows little to no compromise. If you make a resolution, you put the intention into action. If you live in the present, confidently make a plan, are self-assured, and block out all obstacles through determination, you will be mentally strong. In this chapter you will learn what it takes to be determined. By means of the insights and exercises, you will train your determination directly.

If you don't want or need to, don't!

A lack of determination can even have dangerous consequences. The best example of this is provided by Bernhard Moestl in his work *Shaolin – Du musst nicht kämpfen, um zu siegen* (2008). In it, he describes the preparations travelers make for trips to dangerous parts of the world: they would plan to carry a firearm with them to defend themselves in case of attack. But those who had never pointed a gun at a person before would not consider that pulling the trigger requires determination; after all, you are taking a person's life... Most people would still possibly draw the gun, but few would pull the trigger. The attacker, on the other hand, might become aggressive at the sight of the gun. At worst, he would seize the weapon and use it against you.

This example, which uses a life-threatening situation to demonstrate how important determination is, can also be applied to more banal circumstances:

> ➤ A degree graduate has received a brilliant job offer. In addition, he has recently obtained his driver's license. Since he is not a "normal" novice driver, but a driver with very good earnings in his new job, he decides to finance a sports car via leasing. The only reason for him to get this car and not a good mid-range car is the approximately 400 hp. He just wants to "let his hair down" on the weekends and race along the roads. As a novice driver however, he doesn't even begin to take advantage of the vehicle's power and speed. He lacks the courage to fully press the gas pedal. Now he has leased a car that is too expensive and to which he is tied for 2 years.

Lack of determination has the potential to make purchases of luxury and equally ordinary items redundant. It should be considered beforehand whether one will be determined to wear the eye-catching garment, to fully exploit the potential of the sports car and to perceive other margins.

➤ You have a very good friend. You both get along great. There is a whiff of love in the air. The catch is that the person ended a relationship a few months ago and is mourning the former partner. The person is attracted to you but is not really ready to start something new. However, you convince them to try anyway. In the end, the relationship that has developed is partly forced. You both knew deep down that your friend's openness to a new relationship was not (yet) complete. From now on, everything you do, as well as the relationship itself, is accompanied by indecision: the sexual interaction, the conversations, the activities, every single hug. The relationship is breaking down, and the negative experiences have put rocks in the friendship's path. Nothing is the same anymore.

People should be honest and trustworthy in their relationships. The relationship – in whatever form – should be completely voluntary. Only in this way does each person feel comfortable in their role. Accordingly, the distribution of roles should be precisely communicated and considered in order to interact together with determination and full dedication.

My experience

I had a very good friend who I was in a relationship with many years ago. The subsequent friendship lasted for 5 years. In the meantime, the woman was with another man. She was young and it was only her 2nd relationship after me. The man was what in colloquial language is probably called a "bad boy": criminal record, aggression, insults towards other people. However, she gave herself to him completely. After the relationship ended, she was never the same. I noticed in our conversations that she was still mourning him because he had always been good to her. She was not over him I could tell. Nevertheless, a few months after their breakup, I suggested that we try getting back together again. I hardly had to convince her because she remembered our previous relationship and our good friendship. The relationship broke up after a few months though, because she was still thinking about her ex. She wouldn't let me touch her; we couldn't talk to each other as openly as we had in our friendship. She had entered into a relationship she was not ready for – and I myself had known it deep down. In the end, it was no wonder that we separated quickly. The determination had been lacking; especially on her part because she longed for her ex. My pity, which drove me to want to be with her, was also not a good driver for determination. It was extremely questionable of me to burden the friendship in this way in the first place. To this day, we have hardly exchanged a word since the breakup.

Buying things, interpersonal relationships, making decisions in life, organizing one's free time; ideally, everything is done with determination. The examples show why: determination leads to consistency. Consistent actions, in turn, favor the realization of one's qualities. This is where the uplifting connection to the last 2 chapters comes in: You are at this moment pursuing a task; your focus is optimal, and you are fully in the moment. Because of your self-esteem, you feel good and confident in your abilities. Because you are pursuing realistic goals and are fully confident that they are in line with your desires, you are determined. This determination leads to more enthusiastic actions. The stronger your determination, the less you pay attention to even the most stubborn obstacles (e.g., fear, negative coaxing from others, past failure etc.).

There are 2 factors that favor determination: Wanting and needing. *Ideally*, you do what you have to do in life. Taking children to school, going to work, studying, caring for sick parents or friends etc., are usually things you have to do. If you notice anything about these examples, it's that they're usually linked to "wanting" too. Don't you want your children to go to school because you want them to learn and grow up educated? Don't you want to study in order to have a financially secure life later on? Don't you want to take care of your parents because you love them, and they have always taken care of you?

The fact is that we have to do these things. But "have to" alone is not sustainable. Imagine if you only imposed duties on yourself in your life and consequently only did what you had to do. Man is not a machine. A purely compulsory program risks burnout, depression, and other mental and – depending on the type of activity – physical illnesses. Some things have to be done, but important in life are the things that are a combination of "must and want" or pure "want". In the case of "having to and wanting to", there are more and more attractive incentives to pursue a thing because of your will. The stronger the will and the greater the incentives, the stronger the determination.

Wanting has one challenge: You have to decide. While with "must and want" or pure "must" you are usually relieved of the decision by external factors, it is different with pure "want".

Example

What is certain is that you *have to* work. Only a few people, because of their wealth or age do not have to work. The majority of adults do. However, what job you do is decided before you go to college, university, or generally when you choose a job. You may have limited choices, but when choosing, you ideally still decide what you *want*. The challenge is freedom of choice.

So, for all decisions where you have complete or partial free will and multiple decision options, you are literally spoiled for choice. This problem is greater today than it was several decades or even centuries ago. In the past, one's career or life path was to some extent pre-defined. For example, it was not unusual for young men to continue their father's profession. Young women were not infrequently – in the English aristocracy of the 19th century, for example – forced into marriage. Marriages were supposed to have benefits and, ideally, to create new wealth. In the past, there were fewer options. This was rarely good, because life was to a large extent determined by others.

Nowadays, at least in Central Europe, the opposite is the rule: you are faced with an abundance options. In the digitalized world, which is rich in perspectives thanks to networking, people tend to find it more difficult to choose. While there is financial and educational inequality in Germany, there is no denying that numerous support programs offer a wealth of prospects on a silver platter to young people from a wide range of social classes. Study abroad with Bafög as financial aid? Voluntary social year? Taking a sabbatical year after school, earning decent money and then traveling the world? This is how the wheel of seemingly endless possibilities turns for many people. Somehow, some people then prefer to have it all; namely...

➢ ...become an influencer on social media and make a living with a few posts.
➢ ...manage life with a family of 4 on the side.
➢ ...follow the main profession, because as an Influencer they don't yet earn enough.
➢ ...but a degree program would also be exciting, which after all can be planned flexibly as a distance learning program and doesn't even require a high school diploma.
➢ ...in addition, there is the diet, for which you would prefer to cook fresh every day for 3 hours.

All at once? Impossible. But even those who have fewer options and enjoy few privileges in their lives still have more options than people in the same situation several decades ago.

Now it becomes important to remember the first step – namely the present principle. Because as you know, the present shows you what is realistic in your current life situation. The list you just made of things you would like to do all at once is an example of what can be possible. The things individually are not unrealistic. But to do everything at once *is* unrealistic. Due to an overload, the individual goals gradually break away because they cannot all be pursued consistently with your time capacities. Overload and lack of prioritization are often a reason for lack of determination. In this sense, we create the connection to the 1st step; that is, the 2nd chapter: You remember the exercise from the 1st step, which was about realism and fairy tale castles? Pull out the list again. You set realistic goals in the exercise based on your time capacities as well as resources. These, because they are realistic, are achievable for you. But are you really determined to achieve them? **Check it!**

While "wanting" something (a goal) promotes determination, it does not equate to more determination. If you simply want but are not determined to put in the necessary effort (e.g., physical work, mental work, money, patience), "wanting" is more of a burden to you than a help. Wanting without determination – it's like working without full dedication. You are not realizing your potential. You are also more likely to get distracted. Now is the time for you to continue working with the list from the Realism Fairy Tale exercise in which you formulated your goals. You need to identify the goals that you are really determined to achieve.

Exercise

Think about which of the goals you wrote down you could have achieved long ago. For which goal have you already made several attempts, but never followed through consistently? Consider whether it was due to a lack of determination or the wrong approach. If you can't think of an alternative approach and you have doubts about achieving your goal, you are most likely not determined. You probably lack the last bit of motivation to follow the goal. Therefore, put it aside, if possible, and examine all other goals. Ideally, the end result is that the list includes your realistic goals, measured against your desires and dreams. You are determined to achieve those goals. Determination is characterized by the fact that you don't put things off and you follow through consistently. If there is a lack of execution, you are at least creative and find different approaches to try. This is how determination shows itself – not through perfection, but consistent and creative work on your own plans.

Interim summary

Wanting and needing, as well as the mixture of both, are beneficial for your determination. But they do not guarantee decisive action. Therefore, shorten your plans around those things that you are not willing to overcome all obstacles to achieve.

With determination comes mental strength

Determination is directly related to mental strength. For one thing, it gives you confidence. When you're determined to do something, you're sure you'll see it through. This security prevents you from questioning yourself unnecessarily. The questioning is over – you have already done that with the previous exercises and now you have realistic goals on your list, which you will actually carry out! Internalize this thought: *"Everything that is on my note with goals, I will really carry out!"*

This unshakable thought means determination. In addition to certainty, determination gives you consistency in action. You can no longer be dissuaded from an action during its execution. The present principle learned from the 1st step is better put into action.

Example

Maybe you know a little bit about tackling in soccer. Imagine 2 players running towards a ball and trying to win it. One player is from a team in the champion's league while the other is from a team that was relegated. The champion has a pure winning mentality. He knows what he wants, and based on last season's titles, he knows he can do it. The player from the relegation team is intimidated just by the look on his opponent's face. The 2 players get closer and closer to the ball, accelerate and slide in. The champion is fully determined and follows through. While there is a hint of doubt in the other player's mind, just enough to take away his speed and strength for a split second and prevent him from getting to the ball first.

Determination is evident in you. It's the expression you have on your face at work while presenting a project in front of several people and arguing for its implementation. You stand in front of the audience with bright eyes and verve that your solution/concept is the best. People see your determination and trust you. Determination also means attraction. It makes you attractive and opens up opportunities for you to build a following or at least a social environment.

Closely related to your determination are discipline and motivation. Discipline, in particular, is a factor more closely associated with mental strength than probably any other. Discipline promotes your determination. It ensures – as you may remember from the definitions in the 1st chapter – that you are able to follow self-imposed and externally dictated rules. Following self-imposed rules is called self-discipline. If you don't feel like doing something, but you remember the rule and as a result you do the activity, you are disciplined. The more pronounced the discipline, the more unshakable your determination. Discipline is the protective wall around your determination. It leads to you holding on to your goals in the face of adversity. By regularly repeating your motives, you call your dreams to mind. Visualizing or aiming for realistic dreams strengthens your motivation. The more motivated you are, the more determined you are. It seems to make sense to strengthen these 2 components together. Three exercises for each will show you how.

Increase discipline with 3 exercises

Exercise 1

So far you have worked on plans with the help of this book, but not yet on rewards. If you allow yourself rewards in your stage goals – the extent of the reward must match the level of difficulty of the stage goal – then you will increase your willpower. You know that a reward is waiting for you while you are working on one of the milestones so it pays to be disciplined and stay disciplined. Assign appropriate rewards to your milestones now. Again, use the present as a benchmark and do it in a realistic way.

Exercise 2

Go after tasks that you don't like. Think of 5 things that can be practiced regularly, but you don't like. Of course, these tasks should make sense and move you forward in some way. An ideal example would be dusting. Start with 1 of the 5 actions and practice it for a duration that seems reasonable. Over time, increase the duration and gradually add the other tasks too. Through this exercise, you will condition yourself to have a higher "pain tolerance" to unwanted tasks.

Exercise 3

Get into the habit of keeping order in your home, your workplace, and any other place you visit. Order in the outside world rubs off positively on your inside. By keeping your surroundings tidy, you lay the foundation for discipline. Because if you keep seeing before your eyes in black and white that you live tidily, it will be easier for you to believe that you can do other things consistently as well. *As on the outside – so on the inside!*

Increase motivation with 3 exercises

Exercise 1

Think as if you have already achieved your goal. When you think about a milestone or a big goal, always say to yourself, "I have... accomplished." Be careful not to get sloppy and think you don't have to do anything. Use this exercise sparingly, e.g., as an addition to the beliefs. Say the sentences to yourself a few times a day in your mind or out loud.

Exercise 2

Keep a diary of your successes. Diary keeping has celebrated a resurgence under the Anglicism "journaling" anyway. More and more people are open to journaling and no longer label it as an activity for romantics. Be one of them and keep a journal of your progress! If you like, you can keep it in bullet points and concise.

Crucially, if you experience a drop in determination, have a book-let you can look into to remind yourself, *"I've made it this far and I'm going to keep making it!"* This sounds simplistic, but it definitely works. Therefore, just do it and be amazed!

Exercise 3

The 45/15 rule is that you do a task for 45 minutes and then take a break for 15 minutes. During this break, you can do your mindfulness exercises or anything else that is dear to you. All that matters is that you take the break. The fact that you only have to do a task for a limited period of time increases your motivation. For tasks that you don't like but are shorter in duration, you can of course shorten the 45/15 rule. For a 15-minute task that you absolutely hate, working for 5 minutes and taking a 3-minute break might have a good effect. Just try chunking the task and working towards your goal in a relaxed manner. Unfortunately, this rule will not be feasible for a professional job with prescribed working hours. Understand that it is not universally applicable.

Interim summary

Determination makes you mentally strong. Outsiders notice this strength in you. You develop your maximum potential. Work regularly on your motivation and discipline to keep it that way.

Accept obstacles and gently remove them from the way

You may encounter obstacles on your way to becoming more determined. Depending on the area in which you want to be determined, you may be confronted with various resistances. As Dr. Thomas Späth and Shi Yan Bao recognize in their guidebook

Shaolin – The Secret of Inner Strength (2011), accepting the obstacles is important. By accepting them, you become aware of them in the first place and can work on clearing them out of the way. If you ignore them, on the other hand, you run the risk of failure due to head-in-the-wall tactics. When faced with obstacles, the authors recommend focusing first on the reason for their occurrence. Every obstacle has a positive intention: fear, for example, serves to protect people. Convenience prevents people from consuming too much energy.

You have the choice to fight the obstacles rigorously: Possibly you acquire an additional guidebook for overcoming fear in order to fight the obstacle from all sides. But is this the right way? At the very least, it is not the path that is most likely to lead you to success. After all, a lack of compromise and a rigorous approach carry the risk that you'll overextend yourself. What about compromise?

> ➢ If you feel fear, meet it halfway by first accepting its protective function and then looking for ways to gradually free yourself from it.
>
> ➢ If you consider yourself lazy, admit to being lazy, but gradually reduce it. Also, try alternatives to laziness, such as massages. Again, you're relaxing and just lying around; but with the difference that you're doing something good for your body and – there you go again after the last chapter – showing yourself appreciation.
>
> ➢ If you see your environment as a hurdle, reduce contact with people who you think are counterproductive for the development of mental strength. Or tell them directly that

you hope for more understanding or respect from them, depending on where you see the deficits.

Dealing with obstacles is about acceptance and in finding creative solutions. Surely you understand that when 2 people share a journey, a problem, or a task, they must coordinate in order to act in unity. An association of 2 people where each person acts as they please would be indecisive. So, it is with you: Several different versions of "you" live through your thoughts, i.e., the inner critic, the optimist etc. They express themselves in your characteristics, strengths and weaknesses. Sometimes one person dominates, sometimes the other. Developing mental strength and determination means finding a consensus between your different inner voices. When you succeed in this, you concentrate all your strength on the task you are performing and go about it with determination.

Finding compromises between your desires and obstacles is the best way. How do you find the compromise between fear and performing in front of an audience, laziness and an upcoming task, nervousness and ambitions for a successful exam, habit of snacking and targeted diet?

Exercise

Behind an obstacle there is not only the bare negative blockage, but also the positive intention. The exception is your personal environment, because you can't know why others put obstacles in your way. There can also be a positive intention behind it, but this is not certain. With your environment it helps to take things with a touch of distance *or* to address problems openly. But with the obstacles that arise from within yourself – your individual mental weaknesses – positive intentions are also hidden. Write down your obstacles and also note what positive intention could be hidden behind each one.

In the next step, think about compromises: For example, consider how you can tackle the fear gradually without setting yourself mammoth tasks. For arachnophobia, 1 option would be to get close to spiders, by a meter or smaller increments at a time. For claustrophobia, you would have the option of starting in a larger room first and then moving to an increasingly small one. Laziness is your weakness? In this case, you could put together a program where you only have to get up to do 1 thing for 1 minute on the first day. Over time, you increase the duration.

Taking small steps, being careful, responding to obstacles and incorporating them into your planning – that's your path to determination. Each step away from the obstacle strengthens your overall mental fortitude and makes you more determined. It is helpful to enlist the help of trusted people.

Finally, it should be noted that compromises require dynamism: For example, if you notice that overcoming an obstacle is much easier than you planned, increase the pace. If you've bitten off more than you can chew: It's no big deal – just take a step back and approach the whole thing more cautiously. What is important in all these points is a basic measure of patience. No obstacle disappears through thoughtless actions. As in the 1st exercises and in your life in general, you should look at yourself in the present and always question how you can best eliminate obstacles step by step with the current means at your disposal and your present attitude towards the obstacle.

Interim summary

Obstacles are accepted. They are not an unconditional enemy but have at least a small positive background. Compromise and adjust step by step with this positive background and your goals until you have eliminated the obstacle. If other people are the obstacle, then have a clarifying conversation or distance yourself from these people.

MPS Step 3 in brief

> ➢ Being determined means wanting or needing to do a thing while having the willingness, means and methods to remove all obstacles.

> ➢ The important initiator of determination is the "want" or "need" or a hybrid of both. The "want" should dominate in your life and activities so that you feel joy and fun.

> ➢ In your list of realistic goals, commit to the things you are really determined to do. Set your priorities so that you pursue these things first and foremost.

> ➢ Through determination, you pull other people along and win them over – whether as friends or in some other role. In addition, you carry out your actions with the maximum use of your potential.

> ➢ Motivation and discipline strengthen your determination. Do special exercises regularly, such as journaling, and bring order into your life to strengthen your determination.

> ➢ Accept obstacles and compromise on their removal. In this way, you will gradually and gently get rid of them without overextending yourself.

→ Acquire the determination to make the most of the present! Through determination you live more consistently in the moment and can thus let go of negative emotions and focus on the positive in the present.

MPS Step 4: Reduce your concerns!

Reducing concerns, like determination, is a result of living in the present while at the same time being an important support for remaining in the present. When you are more serene, you make sure that the personal problems of life do not dominate you. Attention: Although in the following we will talk about serenity; it isn't the same thing as doing nothing. It is simply about letting problems get to you less. This does not mean ignoring your problems, but instead tackling them at the appropriate times. Working on your solutions at the times you can, want to, and need to. Otherwise, you concentrate on other things.

The connection with this and the rest of the content in this book is that serenity acts as a calm antithesis to decisiveness and guards against actionist tendencies. It ensures a balance in your plans as well as your actions.

Dealing with minor concerns: Are they the laughs of tomorrow?

In life, there are both major and minor worries. In this chapter, we will start with minor worries – because the burden on the mind is the lowest and the worries themselves are sometimes even completely unfounded: In science, the distinction between major and minor worries is made on the basis of the thesis that major worries have the property of assuming pathological proportions. They permanently restrict attention, lead to higher alertness in phases of relaxation and literally torture the mind: they are transferred to other situations, which in many cases can lead to a generalized anxiety disorder.

Minor worries, on the other hand, are trains of thought that do not permanently haunt you but do bother you in certain situations. Possible examples of such minor worries are:

➢ Failed date with a person from work: the next time you meet this person, you will probably sink into shame – such is your worry.

➢ Stress with the boss: your boss was raging about your performance one day. He yelled at you about something or other seemingly every half hour. You're worried about how to deal with him next time and what consequences there might be.

➢ You got a bad grade, and you have to confess it to your parents, who are always very strict in such cases.

➢ You have to give a presentation in front of a large audience, but you have put on slightly transparent clothing. You are not aware of this before the presentation, but only realize it shortly before the end. You rock the rest of the presentation confidently across the stage and disappear afterwards. My goodness, that was embarrassing! You are still concerned about it, days later.

All these little worries, if you read it that way, are mostly temporary; "mostly" because there are exceptions. But we won't dwell on that now. As a rule, these worries are unfounded. The confession of your bad grade, the stress with the boss, the lecture, and the date are over – what reason is there to worry anymore? There could possibly be consequences, but if we think about it, these things are so trivial that they have happened to every person: For example, if the person from work complains about the date, the audience might agree with him, but just as well know that not every date goes well.

If you think about it, all these worries could have a positive ending: What if another person from work, hearing about the failed date, would learn more about you and think that you are an interesting person. Soon, the person approaches you, you set up a date and it goes well. What if your supervisor complained about you to the CEO of the company, but the CEO couldn't understand the criticism and would transfer you to a better department?

These positive consequences are not probable, but they are certainly possible. What is definitely not possible, however, is for these small worries to result in a serious negative consequence for your life. They are mostly irrational worries. Accordingly, it is hardly surprising that, with time, they even become laughs among family and friends.

Exercise

Find such small worries in yourself. Preferably, look for worries that are coming up in you at the moment; perhaps something embarrassing happened to you a few days ago that is causing you worry. You may also dig around in the past and recall embarrassing situations or minor disputes in order to learn for your future with the help of this exercise. Write down all the minor worries you can think of. Now write down at least 3 reasons why these worries are unfounded or even ridiculous. Common reasons are that you will never see the person again anyway or that they are normal mishaps that happen to everyone. Then imagine how you will later laugh with other people about exactly these worries.

My experience

In my life, I have often been thwarted more by small worries than by big ones, which is extremely paradoxical. I was able to deal quite well with big worries like high debts that I couldn't pay off in the meantime. I just dealt with it as long as it was necessary and worked to find solutions. But minor concerns where my livelihood and health were not threatened came up regularly in my memories. I think it was because the stage was set early in my childhood for such reactions: Time and again, the embarrassment of minor mishaps had been emphasized by my mother, so I had acquired that mindset. As life progressed, experience gave me the realization that minor embarrassments are perfectly normal. They are normal and often show in a funny way how imperfect we humans are. This imperfection in minor situations is what makes human charm.

Dealing with major concerns that threaten life, livelihood and future

All types of major concerns require impulse control and acceptance. This is evident even in the most extreme emergencies. For example, when a person has a heart attack, he usually feels it keenly. The severity of this stabbing pain is usually such that a person fears for his or her life. In first aid, it is recommended to calm the person down. Paramedics on the scene do the same. Calming creates control. Breathing is then slower, so there is even a direct medical effect.

However, in emergencies and in the case of particularly great worries (e.g., financial existential worries, worries about the health of a loved one), there is no need to deceive yourself. With previous exercises for control and regular practice, the effect is usually manageable. Emotions and impulses that cause emotions are best controlled when you train specifically for them. For this it is indispensable to prepare yourself with exercises.

By the way, you should never underestimate the effects of human emotions. Because the human brain usually reacts emotionally. The very way the brain works means that the first thing to switch on is the limbic system, which controls the emotional part of the brain, among other things. If you don't develop control over emotions, you risk the emotions controlling you. Where this leads depends entirely on the situation. There have been people who have hurt or even killed others because of a strong emotional reaction. Apart from these extreme cases, there are numerous other situations in which a lack of control over your emotions can harm you: this can be the case when you worry.

Worry is a deep emotion. If you are afraid of a spider, you are *afraid*. If you are afraid for someone dear to you, you are *worried* about him. *Worries are characterized by their long-term nature.* They enter your consciousness regularly and roam your thoughts. Worries can result from single embarrassing events, where they are small and irrational worries. You learned this in the last subsection. These worries are usually tomorrow's laughingstock. It is different with worries that result from deeper concerns, such as:

> ➢ Poor health with unpredictable consequences for one's life.

> ➤ Financial problems and lack of clarity regarding one's live-lihood.

> ➤ Problems at school, college or work and not knowing if they can be solved.

These 3 examples are united by uncertainty: you don't know how they will turn out. This poses a problem for you; namely, the fact that you cannot react decisively. You are caught between hope and realism. Uncertainty interferes with much of what you have learned in the past steps of this guide.

Let's take a situation as a counterexample in which the outcome is clear: In this example, you are aware that someone dear to you has only 3 months to live. The uncertainty is gone. Slowly, the worry about what will happen to the person also fades. Other worries take their place, such as how the person will cope with the situation and how you will manage life without them. However, you have the time to cognitively process these things slowly with the person and find solutions. The fact is that uncertainty is intrinsic to the existence of worry. You can rarely eliminate this uncertainty. Often it disappears by itself, in the sense of "time that heals all wounds".

Or you accept the uncertainty. This is exactly the point that always helps with major worries: to accept the existing uncertainty because it cannot be influenced. Based on this acceptance, you rethink your current situation (step 1) and determine how to react to it decisively (step 3). In order not to let your emotions overtake you despite the uncertainty, it is necessary that you control them and the impulses that lead to emotions. Max Janson, in her work *Training Resilience (2020), states* that a high degree of self-discipline is required to control impulses. Otherwise, you'll let yourself get out of control.

If worries occur for the first time, then a new assessment of the current situation is necessary. The 1st step in this book will help you to do this. Afterwards, it is important to decide to take a certain path despite the worry and to follow it. Self-discipline helps you to do this. You motivate yourself by demonstrating why you should continue to live and give your best despite the great worry. One possible motive would be to keep going to make the loved one on the bedside proud. In order to accept the new life situation with determination during periods of great worry, the impulse control and acceptance exercises described below are useful.

Three exercises to develop acceptance

Exercise 1

Because the death of a loved one is something that causes great worry and comes to every person sooner or later, Exercise 1 is specifically dedicated to this case. The worry of losing a loved one can be alleviated by making the most of the time with that person. If the person is willing, spend as much fulfilling time with them as possible. By the way, this also applies to yourself: Should you receive bad news regarding your own health, it helps to make the most of the time you have. In the book *Resilienz trainieren* (2020), Max Janson appropriately refers to an interview with Ottfried Fischer, who suffers from Parkinson's disease: Fischer does not want to despair about his illness. Instead, he set himself the goal of only doing what he enjoys. Making the most of remaining time and resources – that is the motto of this exercise. Time well spent also distracts you from the worries that plague you and/or your loved one.

What if it's already too late and you can't spend any more time with your loved one because, for example, they're already dead? In this case, memories help: Remember every moment you spent with the person. Remember your pleasure with other people. You will realize that the beautiful memories will calm you down.

Although intended primarily for coping with grief, this exercise is also useful for other types of loss. For example, if you fail with a major professional project, you can cling to the excellent experience afterwards. From this you gain courage and confidence for the present. Your exercise, then, is either to spend more time with people dear to you or to use memories to show yourself that you took full advantage of the time without worry.

Exercise 2

It is difficult to see the sense in it when one is plagued by great worries. But there have been numerous people who have found strength in difficult phases of life. They developed a way of looking at things that explained to them the reason for the problems. Explanations are the basic building block of acceptance. When you receive explanations and develop understanding, you will find things easier to accept over time. So, start looking for explanations: Is it possible that life wants to test your strength in this way? Is it possible that someone wants to make you aware that you have made big mistakes and need to change something in your life? Should you spend more time with that person from now on?

Whatever explanations you find: Try to convince yourself and derive an action from it, so that you accept the problems and gradually free yourself from your worries.

Exercise 3

There are good times and bad times. At the moment, bad times may prevail – but that will not always be the case. On the one hand, think about your own life: What crises have you successfully survived so far? How did you feel afterwards? On the other hand, look at other people, whether on television or in reality. People will be an example to you of how to act in your situation. By learning from past experiences and learning from the model – that is, learning from other people – you may find your way to accept.

Three exercises to control impulses

Exercise 1

Great worries can lead you to rash actions. You have no patience to wait for a result. You have to do something. Patience is therefore a 1st helpful means of gaining impulse control. It is not uncommon for individuals to resort to complete irrationality when they are worried. The student who can't keep up swallows Ritalin. The grieving family man flies his sick son to a faith healer in Honduras and spends a 5-figure sum. In both cases, there is probably no improvement. The risks, on the other hand, are quite high. So, learn to take a little time out in situations where worry overtakes you. Allow yourself 10 seconds to let the worry enter your thoughts. Worry and count down the 10 seconds. Afterwards, sit down and write a pros and cons list to find out which actions are really worthwhile in this situation. This is how you learn how to make rational decisions.

Exercise 2

Find a release valve. During difficult periods in your life that cause you anxiety, find an activity where you can let out all your emotions. Classic examples are the punching bag at home, the gym and jogging. In all 3 sports, you can let off steam while varying the intensity: running faster, punching harder, lifting more weights. Professional dancers and musicians are able to use dancing or playing music as a release valve. Some people, on the other hand, swear by doing household chores as a good emotional release valve. Your release valve is unique – so find the right one for you and use it. By shifting your emotions into an activity, you power yourself down and lower the risk of being overwhelmed by worry. You're more likely to deal with your worries in a rational way.

Exercise 3

Talk. Your environment is important. Talk to people – especially those who share your concerns –about what is bothering you. This way you will all gain support and understanding. Several people together also find more ways than a single person to identify a way to deal with worry. Difficult situations usually bring physical closeness: a hug here and there, maybe a little cuddling. This stimulates the release of happy hormones, which soothes one's aggrieved soul. Openness also promotes interpersonal relationships. Opening up to a familiar person encourages that person to open up as well.

Interim summary

Great worry brings with it the essential problem of uncertainty. Uncertainty causes you to be divided between the possibility of a positive or a negative outcome. Learn to accept this and control your impulses to act thoughtfully and rationally.

Slowness beats haste

"Slowness beats haste" – this does not apply to all areas of life. In a sprint, for example, only the person who is the fastest wins. Haste is indispensable in this case. But already in a marathon over a distance of more than 50 kilometers, things look different: If you hurry at the beginning to be 1st for as long as possible, you are not dosing your forces properly. However, dosage of forces is the be-all and end-all when it comes to long distances! Intimidating the other runners over an impressive 10 kilometers will do you little good if you run out of breath in the remaining part of the race. The principle of slowness can therefore even be applied to sports. Consequently, it is important to think around a corner or two: Essentially, the principle is about taking your time with certain things. That's the way it is with worries in particular.

As you learned from one of the exercises earlier, actionism is a risk of making the wrong decisions due to lack of patience and deliberation. Especially with deep problems, a slow approach to finding a solution is beneficial. How slow should it be? As slow as your individual situation allows. The challenge with difficult life phases or profound problems is that they are often a comprehensive construct. Multiple factors need to be considered:

➢ If the person dies, who will take care of the children?

> ➢ What happens to the person's estate?
> ➢ Who pays for the costs of the funeral?

As inappropriate as these trains of thought may seem, where the passing of a loved one is concerned, they often play an essential role in the subconscious of people close to the sick person. Those who write down the individual accompanying problems and prepare in time are most likely to be mentally strong. Imagine that you not only take care of the sick person before his or her passing, but that you create a schedule that tells you when to take care of which bureaucratic and organizational aspects: in this case, you will not be overwhelmed by the duties after the person's death but will have organized everything in advance step by step and will be able to deal with the grief after the death in peace. You can slowly work through everything and slowly process the grief without being rushed by bureaucratic aspects and the like.

The goal should be to eliminate major problems and worries in your life. For this purpose, you put other goals on the back burner for the time being and develop a plan to solve the new challenges. Through the plan you prevent actionism and solve the problems thoughtfully, because you take time for their solution. Despite worries, simply continuing your life as before is like a suicide mission. You will be overwhelmed.

Another advantage of slowness is that a phenomenon known as serendipity may occur. Serendipity means finding solutions without looking for them. Life is dynamic, as you have learned. Something is constantly happening that can affect your life against all expectations. If you act rashly and make rash decisions in your desperation, it is possible that when solutions fall into your lap, because of your previously rash actions, the problems will have piled up and it will bring you less.

Bernhard Moestl also expresses the benefits of slowness and composure in his bestseller *Shaolin – Du musst nicht kämpfen, um zu siegen* (2008). Both factors would help to reduce mistakes and control emotions. As a result, problems or worries would not grow, but solutions would be most likely to emerge.

Interim summary

Get into the habit of looking for solutions slowly, especially in the case of big worries. Hasty, impatient actions usually increase the problems or overwhelm you. By thinking before you act, you determine a sustainable and promising course of action.

MPS Step 4 in brief

- ➢ There are small worries and big worries. The small worries are often the little mishaps and embarrassments that befall us in life and sometimes occupy us for a surprisingly long time.
- ➢ Get into the habit of seeing events that lead to small worries as a normal part of human imperfection and put them to rest. Often you can laugh about these worries with a little time distance.
- ➢ It becomes more serious with major worries that threaten existence, health, happiness and other elementary components of life. These worries must be taken seriously.

➤ The best way to deal with the problem of uncertainty in big worries is to train your acceptance and optimize your impulse control with the exercises described.

➤ When you look slowly for solutions to big concerns, finding sustainable and optimal solutions is more likely.

MPS Step 5: Work on your skills!

The 5th and final step of mental strength work is based on developing your individual skills. In the 6th step, a slightly different program awaits you. It is no longer about building mental strength, but about how to handle it optimally. This chapter is, in a way, the last step on the way to mental strength. So, mobilize your full attention once again to continue the consistent work on yourself. Up to this point you have worked with mental factors, now you switch to practice: By promoting your individual practical skills, your mental strength will also benefit. *How does this work?*

Let's say you play an instrument: you've practiced several pieces and play most of them flawlessly. There is already a problem here that you can work on: *most of them*. Playing the piece *mostly flawlessly is* not enough for 100 percent confidence. Because when you have your performance, you can't be sure that there will be no mistakes. This fosters stage fright and anxiety. It complicates your focus on the present moment, calls to your attention the stern and expectant looks of the crowd, and deprives you of 100 percent determination in individual movements of the fingers on the piano or breaths on the trumpet.

Your program so far has helped you to optimize these aspects in particular:

➢ Living in the present helps you block out the audience and their expectations to better focus on performing correctly.

➢ Appreciating yourself will help you feel more confident about your abilities and how to deal with mistakes. If you become unsure or make mistakes during the game, you will probably be able to handle them better.

➢ Through determination, you perform your music game with more confidence and trust in your abilities, so the likelihood of making mistakes decreases.

➢ Composure helps you pay less attention to the watching crowd and not put the audience on some kind of pedestal. They are human beings who also make mistakes. With this mindset, you feel less pressured.

All of that helps. But what about being able to play the instrument and the pieces so well that you don't have to concentrate on them at all? Imagine if you had such a strong ability that you could wink at the audience and talk to them while playing – all at the same time, without thinking, worrying, fearing, doubting, lacking confidence or any other hindrance. The reason for this is your abilities, which are so trained that they cannot be shaken. You know no failure because you have mastered things by heart.

About the benefits of skills

The most comprehensive skills possible are an advantage in different contexts. Even if you are disrespected and bullied by people, it can help you to work successively on improving your skills. Suppose you are being bullied by other people and you have a desire to develop more mental strength against it: Bullying in today's times is no longer a classic student or employee problem, if it was ever limited to those groups of people at all. Nowadays, even teachers and supervisors are no longer immune to bullying.

Everything you've learned so far in this book will help you deal with bullying better. The skills you practice in this step will leave their own mark: they will enhance your reputation in the eyes of others by improving your skills and giving people less reason to bully you. Please don't think at this point that you would be guilty for bullying – not at all! Also, it should not be your goal to change yourself to please other people. But if there is a chance to improve yourself and thus to completely overcome the few mean arguments for bullying, and – this is the most important thing now – this is in line with your interests and goals at the same time, then take the chance!

Basically, training your skills is a potential cure for anything:

➤ You can silence critics and bullies by convincing them with new or expanded qualities.
➤ Doubts, fears, stage fright and other kinds of worries give way to the certainty that you have things fully under control through your skills.
➤ The more skills you perfect, the more transfer and linking you can do, so you learn other things faster.
➤ You gain more confidence in your strengths and are more likely to achieve your goals.
➤ Stress levels drop because you overcome challenges more easily, saving time for other things.

There are various models of the human being. These models are regularly used in psychology and business. One model that in my opinion represents today's times well is the human resource model, which sees the human being as a pool of different abilities and skills. First and foremost, in business this model plays a major role. It has led to the emergence of a lot of motivational models, such as Maslow's pyramid of needs, which was already introduced at the beginning of this book. The goal in the human resource model is to promote and develop a person's individual abilities and skills. Maslow's pyramid of needs explains why:

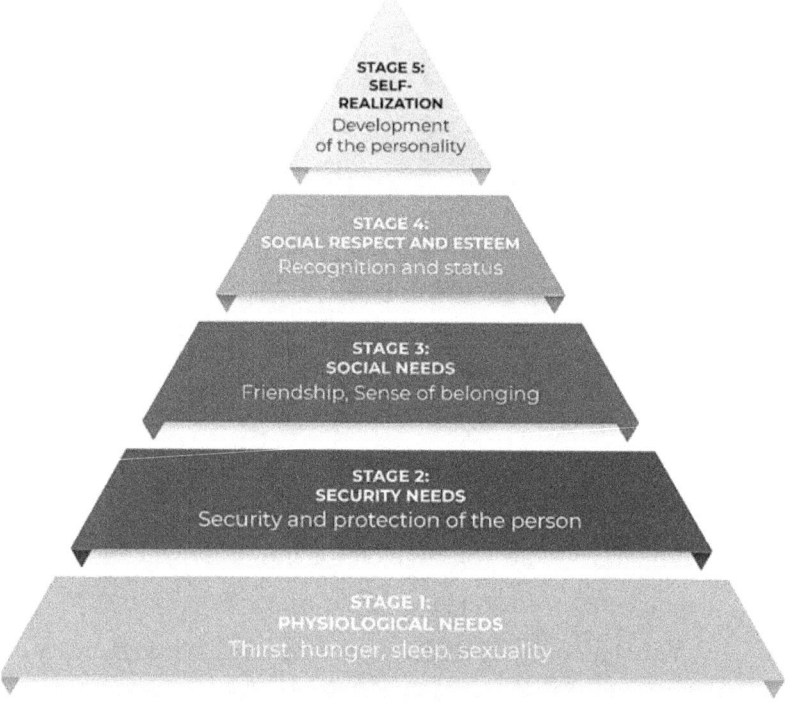

Need satisfaction takes place in order from bottom to top. First the physiological needs are satisfied, then the safety needs, then the social needs and esteem. Last but not least comes the need you are dealing with in this chapter: the development of your abilities, the unfolding of your personality and thus self-actualization. The importance of working on your own abilities is also clear from the closer classification of needs: the first 4 levels are considered deficiency needs. This means that the desire decreases with the degree of satisfaction. Only when the needs have not been satisfied for a certain period of time do they return. But it is different with the 5th stage and the development of one's abilities: These are the growth needs. According to the assumption, these are not satisfied with the extent of satisfaction, but increase. In this, the model reflects the human urge for constant further development.

So, you're not just working on mental strength in this chapter. This chapter is a kind of link to your whole life. It links mental strength with self-realization and also links self-realization with the human striving for more. Striving for more in turn leads to more meaning to life: no matter in which situation, no matter at which age and no matter in which context – your life will never be boring this way!

Interim summary

Continuously practicing your skills and acquiring new ones contributes to a better mental state and more resistance to bullying as well as other negative influencing factors by strengthening your competencies. Moreover, working on your skills favors self-actualization in the long run.

What skills and resources do you need?

The list of your goals serves as a very detailed template for this subchapter, which you have worked through precisely in the previous 4 chapters. You have formulated your personal goals precisely, subdivided them, prioritized them and checked them for feasibility according to your possibilities. With this list of goals, you now check which skills and resources you need. You train the skills or acquire them in the first place. Resources, on the other hand, you acquire. They are means that you buy, produce or otherwise bring into your possession. Sometimes even mundane resources can make quite a difference.

My experience

When I was a child at school, I was bullied. In fact, the blame did not lie with me. Because bullying is the fault of those who practice it. But I gave these people several reasons to bully: My hair was long and since it had no volume and I didn't care about my styling otherwise, it hung over my eyes. In addition, I had a mustache, which seemed rather out of place in the overall picture. My clothes were loose and partially hanging off my body. It was thrown together fashion. Every person has the right to maintain this style! I myself would not mob a person because of it. But what distinguishes a mentally strong person is, even when wronged, to think in several directions. Personally, at the time, I considered that a change in my style might do me good. Secretly, I admired my "cool styled" classmates. The injustice I suffered from bullying animated me to rethink: I had the ability to change visually. But the willingness was missing. The willingness changed somewhat when even my few friends told me to change my appearance. In essence, the "bullying mob" seems to have been right somewhere... This is exactly the important point you can take away for yourself: Sometimes people who do us wrong make us understand the right thing, just in an incorrect way. If, after consulting with people and our own reflections, we realize that right is hidden in wrong, we should definitely have the ability to change.

Through the good coaxing of my friends, I gained the willingness to change. They helped me with the implementation. One good friend in particular knew a lot about fashion. My parents gave me money for 2 outfits; it was early pocket money. Now I also had the resources to transform. When I came to school the next day, the bullying gave way to speechless amazement and the first "human" tones I'd received. People developed interest in my transformation. What I needed was, in the end, banal: An environment that initially brought me enlightenment – albeit in an inappropriate way – consultation with my friends, plus a friend with fashion skills and finally styling as well as clothing as resources to put an end to the bullying.

All this does not say that my actions were correct. What made me realize that it was correct to "give in" to the mobbing crowd was how I felt afterwards. I felt more comfortable with the new style; the way I really was. I had turned my inner self inside out. Therefore, think carefully about whether the unjust harshness of others in your case does not have a justified core now and then.

If the money is there, it should sometimes be used to acquire resources, as long as they offer a realistic chance of achieving your personal goals. Your advantage in using resources to achieve goals is that they are there quickly: As soon as you make the consideration or payment, you have the resources you want.

Exercise 1

In your list, write down which resources, that will be available within a few days at the latest, can help you achieve your goals. Write down 5 resources for each goal, such as clothing for improved reputation, cars and/or bicycles for improved transportation, magazines and books for increased general knowledge or expertise, etc. After noting the resources that are plausible to you, check which ones are realistic in a timely manner and align with your beliefs. Anything that is not financially feasible for you, or that you feel would have little likelihood of helping you achieve your goal, you can safely cross off the list.

It gets more complex with the capabilities. Unlike resources, these are not available immediately. Here you are called upon to practice for a longer period of time and to work consistently. Some skills require more time and training to optimize, others less. If you are familiar with the respective skills because you have been practicing them for a long time, then you will be able to estimate well how much time and practice it will take you until the next increase. If you plan to learn new skills, be generous in estimating the time and practice required. Since you are not yet too familiar with the skill in question, you should leave yourself time cushions. To help you understand the message in this paragraph, here are 2 examples:

I.   You've been doing a job or hobby for several years. With that comes certain skills that you use every day – whether it's skills in programming software, fingers hovering over the piano, or your deft hand in drawing. You know these skills well and know what the next step is to increase. Consequently, you can estimate the time and practice required to successfully increase. These are familiar skills where you consequently plan very carefully.

II.   You want to acquire a new skill that you have not practiced before. Perhaps the reason is that you have realized that what you have done so far is not for you. Now you want to do it all over again and are determined to succeed. Or you may want to acquire the ability to expand your existing skills. These and other scenarios confront you with the need to learn something completely new. Unlike a familiar skill, a new skill comes with more pitfalls because you have less knowledge about it and have a poor grasp of the processes required to improve it. For example, if you've never skated before, stumbling blocks could be that you buy the wrong equipment, lack talent and therefore need to practice more, and/or don't learn the technique optimally from the start, so all subsequent progress suffers. Therefore, be generous with the time you have available when learning new skills – rather a little more than too little.

Exercise 2

Now is the time for you, as a follow-up to Exercise 1 from this chapter and a continuation of your goals list from the previous chapters, identify the skills you could acquire to further your goals. The skills should always further your goals. Because you have formulated your goals in terms of your entire life – career, hobbies, family, etc. – having the appropriate skills ensures that you are furthering not only your professional life, but your life as a whole. Set priorities and time frames that fit your current situation. For example, if you have high ambitions in your career, it makes sense to develop new skills in this area first and only later devote yourself to skills that promote your hobbies.

Interim summary

Acquire resources and work on your skills to get closer to your desires and goals. In all of this, keep in mind that people who treat you unfairly can give you important clues to change. Sometimes it is beneficial to listen to people who are perceived to be unfair, as long as their incentives align with your own desires and goals.

3 tips to improve your skills

Training skills requires organization and regularity. Organization allows you to fit training into your daily routine and set the right priorities. Thanks to regularity you can always start at the level of the last training and build on it. In this way, you can follow the planned path step by step. The following 3 tips will help you with the 2 aspects of organization and regularity, but also make clear the importance of precise and patient practice.

Practice patiently and accurately from the beginning

This is a tip that comes first and to which many things should be subordinated. Learn 1 thing absolutely right from the beginning! What is meant by this? Don't be generous with technical or other types of errors in the 1st steps. Give mistakes the attention they deserve. Every mistake deserves absolute attention because it can negatively affect the other elements.

My experience

I often had this problem because I used to be impatient. Quick progress was more important to me than a solid foundation. That's how mistakes crept in later:

➢ When playing the piano, I always wanted to play fast and impress people with my speed. But since I never learned patiently at a slow tempo, especially the difficult passages of a piece became imprecise and unrhythmic.

➢ In weight training, I wanted to quickly increase my strength, which is why I only attached limited importance to technique. And so, it came to pass as it had to: when I was doing bench presses, my wrists were slightly over-bent, and when I did squats, my back was never absolutely straight. The result was regular injuries, after which I had to start again with lower weights.

➢ When I wrote my first book, I did it hastily and with the aim of publishing it as quickly as possible. The result was that it contained many spelling errors and colloquialisms. In addition, paragraphs devoid of content were the norm. I had to rewrite it completely.

This is real life. While on Instagram you have the ability to erase the mistakes from the piano piece or present a good excerpt from a weak book and charm people, none of that is feasible in real life. Keep that in mind, because some people are also blinded by the encouragement they receive on social media.

Ideally, you do things slowly and accurately from the start. That's exactly why it's also important to time your goals and skill training – so you have the opportunity to train slowly and pa-tiently! All of the people who trained slower and more patiently than I did are much further along in their respective skills today.

Use 1-2-3 method

The 1-2-3 method is not only an aid for training your skills, but also for planning goals in general. In their book *Richtig priorisieren* (2014), the authors Proske et al. explain how tasks can be divided into 3 priority classes using this method.

- ➤ Prio 1 tasks
  - o Main tasks with the highest priority, aligned with your most important objectives.
  - o Should be scheduled regularly, tackled in good time (i.e., without time pressure), and addressed with high quality standards.
- ➤ Prio 2 tasks
  - o Are not among your most important goals and are of secondary importance, but failure to complete them would still have negative consequences for you.
  - o Should be specifically scheduled into the daily routine, possibly with the help of other people, and should be carried out with a much smaller amount of time (20:80 %) compared to the Prio 1 tasks.
- ➤ Prio 3 tasks
  - o Unimportant tasks, which can possibly be postponed and whose non-completion would have no or only minor negative consequences for you.
  - o Should not be worked through during the time of greatest concentration and should be completed as quickly as possible.

Source: Prioritize correctly (2014)

Create your own curriculum

The syllabus is used to visualize and record your plans in writing. You probably remember the lesson plans from school: 6 columns and several rows. In each row was a time slot in which you were taught a subject. In the columns of the top row, the days of the week Monday to Friday were entered, and in the rows below, in each column, the subjects matching the day and the respective time slot. You can now do the same for your skills training by writing down the 7 days of the week. Below that are the skills you want to train, and the time slots you want to schedule for it.

Time	Mo	Tue	Mi	Do	Fri	Sa	So
10-12 h							
12-14 h							
14-16 h							
...							

This table is only an approximate suggestion. Certainly, a time structure with time windows of less than 2 hours makes more sense. The advantage of such a plan is that you can plan and enter your whole life into it. If you make an individual schedule every week, you can even include variable activities, such as your wedding day or taking the kids to an event. This way you won't neglect any part of your life.

MPS Step 5 in brief

➤ Strengthening your own abilities provides a solid basis for your mental strength. Because the better you can do an activity, the less reason there is for negative emotions.

➤ You can also stop or mitigate external factors, such as bullying, by improving your skills – and sometimes even just by buying new resources, such as clothes. The important thing here is to only look to external factors as an impetus for change if you see a sense in them that appeals to you and aligns with your goals and desires.

➤ Training and improving your skills are also important in terms of human needs. You not only support your mental strength, but also work to a certain extent on your self-realization.

➤ Patience and accuracy are key when it comes to training. The more precisely you learn something, the less you have to touch it up afterwards.

➤ The 1-2-3 method, visualized lesson plans and daily schedules help you organize your training and keep it regular.

MPS Step 6: Keep going!

This book is designed to bring you change with its 5 steps. Change can take place in several directions. A positive direction is always desirable. You may think that the previous steps to mental strength can only lead you in a positive direction. But this is wrong: because the more you create and the stronger you become, the more realistic a significant side effect becomes: arrogance; arrogance, ignorance, gloating and other attitudes can become established in you the stronger and more superior you become. Please do not take this as a personal attack. The risk of arrogance is a factor that can affect all people.

My experience

I, too, have already had the opportunity to experience what it is like to become arrogant. As announced in the introduction, my path to mental strength played out exactly as in this book: First, I acquired mental strength roughly on the basis of the first 5 steps. Then I was happy and strong. Unfortunately, I became arrogant. I mocked people who did not achieve individual goals. Moreover, I only respected the strong person who was able to overcome his emotions. Nothing could stop my arrogance. People stuck by me despite my character; possibly because they still saw the former good in me. Only when I was confronted with a power that was new and unattainable to me did my thinking change. This power was health. I suffered an illness that, frankly, wasn't that bad. But it was troublesome, and the doctors didn't know what it was. In part, it made me frantic. As I lay in bed at night or sat on my sofa,

I thought. I decided to change things. Eventually, my illness – or rather, the ominous complaint – was gone again. I had learned from that phase. There is always a way down again...

To make this downward path as unlikely as possible for you, it is important that you remain down to earth. Sharing successes with other people, working together and living together peacefully is important balm for the soul. This chapter will give you some theories and lessons to keep in mind, especially as your success increases, to always understand that strength and success are not a permanent gift but are fleeting. This is the last important lesson in mental strength: to be able to deal with the newfound success.

Lesson 1: Be kind and respectful to your enemies

What is an enemy anyway? Every person has his or her own opinion because it is largely a question of one's own attitude. While some see a person as an enemy who constantly says negative things about them behind their back, others see this as something that is normal in life. Because there will always be people who are not well-disposed towards you.

This first lesson is about such enemies: As long as a person does not take active steps against you that endanger your professional life, family or health, there is no reason to consider them a serious enemy. Most of the time, they are people who have problems in their own lives or are weak and are trying to mask that so they go on the attack. Especially with increasing mental strength and increasing success in the various areas of your life, you will encounter people who are not well-disposed towards you. As long as they do not harm you in an acutely dangerous way but limit their actions to negative talk and small pranks, it is best to position yourself as well-disposed towards these people. This way you have a chance to change your enemies. For these persons, who may have experienced little kindness in their lives, could be moved to rethink by your well-meaning behavior.

It is important to position yourself respectfully and sympathetically towards your enemy, especially in order not to get into the line of fire through bad luck. What if your opponent's hostility at work went unnoticed, but your counterattacks did not? Then you would risk warnings and a deteriorated reputation. Moreover, a hostile attitude may have a negative effect on your subconscious: You feel bad deep down because you are lowering yourself to the level of your enemy. This negatively affects your actions and creates a psychological burden.

Do not be reserved and do not make yourself a victim, but refrain from unnecessary actions and words against your enemies. You have the mental strength for this thanks to the learned impulse control and the principle of the present.

Lesson 2: Never forget where you came from

Where you come from – this means your former (more difficult) situation without mental strength. Before this book and its activities, teachings, and experiences, you were in a different situation than you are now. There is hope that you have become stronger. Strength leads to new possibilities and perspectives. If you take advantage of these, then your success is most likely to increase. With this comes a danger: You could take off.

Success has the ability to dazzle. This ability does not come from success itself, but from deep within you. If you do not regularly put yourself back in the position you were in before, it is quite possible that you will become arrogant over time. Therefore, practice humility and accept that you can do some things and not others at the same time. Remember that there are still some things about you that you can work on. And above all, *remember that there will always be things that you cannot change*. Always see your abilities as needing improvement and recognize your limitations. Then you will move closer to humility and modesty, which is essential for you to stay grounded and not take off. Also, avoid judging others because they have their own problems and challenges to deal with. Think back to yourself and realize that basically any person can become successful. Build up the people around you rather than putting them down – this way you won't be confronted with your own past and the hard road to success.

Lesson 3: Give and take are both necessary

What is wealth worth if it is only stashed away? Whether you are *successful*, rich in money or rich in love, wealth that is not used has little or no value. Let's imagine that you are a person with strong social skills, and you also have all the qualities for a committed relationship or marriage. You are faithful, have plenty of time, remember wedding anniversaries and birthdays, love children. You are rich in love. But you lock yourself up at home because you have suffered a loss, or you are afraid of not experiencing the same love from other people. Dramatic is such a scenario where you are rich in love but do not share that love. The same goes for money, success and other components of life: if you don't share, it's hard for you to enjoy it. This leads to the re-alization that you should spend money now and then – wisely, of course – if you want to feel your wealth. You should show love to others in order to experience it. Success is inspiring for yourself, but only under the encouragement and appreciation of others do you realize how successful you really are.

Life is a give and take. You give something – even something immaterial, such as your affection or your understanding – and receive something else in return. So, giving doesn't necessarily have to take place on a material level, but can also be intangible. You have several chances to give people what they need. Listen to people's wants and needs and give what seems possible and appropriate to you. Approach people with your "riches" and let them share. This is the best way to establish a position from which people will be grateful and well-disposed toward you.

Lesson 4: Use power to achieve goals with others

When you achieve mental strength, you also gain the competence to lead other people. "Leading" is a broad concept: On the one hand, you can advance professionally and become a department head or managing director. On the other hand, it is conceivable that you do not achieve any particular goals professionally, but instead build up an environment with people who perceive you as a leader. A leader is not necessarily characterized by a professional position or a special career. Nor does he have to have achieved a great deal in his private life. What distinguishes a leader is his charisma. This charisma is based on the fact that you have faith in yourself and in your plans. It gives you unassailability, which makes an impression on other people.

Charisma is an important keyword here. If you leave people with an aura of mental strength, you have the chance to achieve goals together with them. They will gladly follow you if your goals coincide with theirs. This gives you the opportunity to deepen relationships with those around you and move forward faster. Together you reach your goals faster.

Example

You have a fascinating idea for a business and start a company. Over time, you want it to grow. In the 1st case, you find it difficult to part with tasks and delegate them to other people. Because you do everything on your own, you don't have time to take care of the growth of your business. In the 2nd case, you enlist the help of other people and manage them wisely as a leader, giving them the opportunity to contribute their own ideas and merge them with yours. After you have made the final decision, people are happy to put your wishes into practice because they are allowed to act independently, and you do not interfere with them. In this case, nothing stands in the way of your company's growth.

Closing words

Developing and expanding mental strength is beneficial for any person in any situation in life. Especially MPS Step 6 has shown that mental strength is not only about having it. It is equally necessary to be able to handle it. Otherwise, there is the threat of arrogance, and with time, as a logical consequence, the loss of what you have worked for. Therefore, this book is a perfect permanent reading in life. Read it regularly – perhaps every year, every 2 years, or every 5 years. There will always be things, with time, that you can still work on with the help of the steps and teachings in this book.

I have read many books and had many experiences on my way to a mentally stronger personality. In the process, I have made use of 1 thing that, unfortunately, no author has directly recommended: I read each book several times and still do. Why? Quite simply: because I want to avoid *experiencing* bad things and because I want to learn them or remember them again. Therefore, it is best to handle it the same way. My father was once in Thailand and told me about his trip. I remembered 1 thing in particular. I don't know why, but the story of his visit to a temple left a lasting impression on me. Perhaps a part of me knew even then that they would be important words for my life. He told me that it was the custom there to kneel down and say several times in one's mind what one would like to become or do. One should tell oneself what should become better. Several hundred times one should do it regularly to remember it later.

What my father told me and what I did with the repeated reading of several books is another difference between mentally strong and mentally weak people: the ability to learn through narratives, affirmations, and from the lives of others. You have a choice to learn from the mistakes of others or from your own. It lends itself better to learning from the mistakes of others. So read this and other helpful books several times to internalize and remember the content. Listen to other people when they tell you things and warn you. Think about whether it might be better to rein yourself in. This will reduce the likelihood of gross mistakes on your part in the long run and maintain the mental strength you have gained with the help of this book.

Work constantly to deepen and retain what you have gained with the help of this guidebook. Because mental strength is like many other things in life: building it up is difficult and tedious work. Losing it can often happen in a very short time. All it takes is 1 wrong decision in which you violate the principles you have learned. Or you set 1 goal too many, which throws your objectives and priorities into chaos.

Therefore, cherish your mental strength and do everything you can to preserve it!

References

Heller, J.: *Resilienz – 7 Schlüssel für mehr innere Stärke.* München: Gräfe und Unzer Verlag GmbH, 2013.

Janson, M.: *Resilienz trainieren – Wie Sie innere Blockaden lösen, Ihre psychische Widerstandskraft stärken und stressfrei alle Krisen überstehen!.* 2020.

Lorenz, S.: *Resilienz entwickeln: „Ich schaffe das!“ – Wie du deine innere Stärke entfaltest, um an Stress, Krisen und Schicksalsschlägen nicht zu zerbrechen.* 2020.

Moestl, B.: *Shaolin – Du musst nicht kämpfen, um zu siegen.* München: Droemer Knaur. 2008.

Proske, H.: Reichert, J. F.; Reiff, E.: *Richtig priorisieren.* Freiburg: Haufe-Lexware GmbH & Co. KG, 2014.

Späth, Dr. T.; Bao, S. Y.: *Shaolin – Das Geheimnis der inneren Stärke.* München: Gräfe und UNZER Verlag GmbH, 2011.

Stangl, W.: Online Lexikon für Psychologie und Pädagogik, 2020.

Webb, R.; Pedersen, C.; Mok, P.: *Adverse Outcomes to Early Middle Age Linked With Childhood Residential Mobility.* American Journal of Preventive Medicine, 2016.

INSTANTLY STOP PROCRASTINATION

4 Powerful Concepts That Will Help You Effectively
Complete the Tasks You Keep Avoiding

by

Patrick Drechsler

Table of Contents

Introduction

You have a task to perform, but everything in you goes on strike at the thought of doing it; even though you know that if you don't do it, there will be negative consequences. Sound familiar?

Is it your term paper at university perhaps?

Or rather that project at work that has been bugging you for ages?

You already know how putting it off ends – with numerous cups of coffee and some extremely late nights. And yet, you still you do it – You procrastinate!

But what exactly is procrastination?

The word procrastination has its roots in Latin and originally described a *positive quality*. This would suggest that procrastinating isn't necessarily a fault on your part but could just as well be an indication that the task itself is redundant. Procrastination doesn't need to be branded as *negative* without first looking more closely at it. And that's what this guidebook aims to do. The methods highlighted in this book will show you how to prevent procrastination, and eventually how to completely remove the tendency altogether.

But how is it possible to prevent procrastination, when some tasks are such a nuisance that everything in your being refuses to complete them?

Personal transformation sometimes occurs from one day to the next when people have drastic experiences; like the death of a loved one, the end of a relationship, or a big fall after previous success – these types of situations can cause people to have the much-cited *now-first-right attitude*, where a loved one's character is fundamentally changed in order to save his relationship; or when every ounce of someone's strength is mobilized to find a way back to success. The brain researcher Gerhard Roth calls these events *teachable moments*.

Teachable moments usually release previously unimagined forces. The problem though, is that people can end up handling themselves destructively. The associated, *tunnel vision* can lead people to neglect their own well-being in order to achieve their goal. This occurs with most forms of rapid change, that tend not to be sustainable in the long run. But what can still be learned from them, is that if certain events can transform a person quickly, then change *is* indeed possible.

The path laid out in this book is not a *teachable moment* and does not claim to be a *quick cure*. Instead, it offers you methods that lead to a *sustainable* way out of procrastination, acting *without* tunnel vision and *with* consideration for your health.

In chapter 1, we explore different ways to assess procrastination, as well as the most common causes for it. Once these causes are known, there are several self-tests and methods that are tailored to your unique tendencies. Think of it like a customer service site, where you can scroll through numerous options and find the ones most helpful to you.

If you tend to struggle with motivation for example, the second chapter provides useful insights to help you deal with it. While chapters 3, 4, and 5, go into a deeper analysis of the causes of procrastination, with practical exercises that will help you to deal with it effectively. Including showing you how to develop more self-conviction and greater self-control; how to set priorities, and how to slow down, in today's fast-paced, digital world.

You *can* change. You have already taken the first big step by selecting this book – it is an excellent place to start! The next step will be to read it thoroughly and put into practice what you learn. You don't have to change anything big overnight or throw your worldviews out of the window. Everything we will show you, will always be just a small and manageable step, that leads you to a sustainable path that will be your long-awaited key to success, in the fight against procrastination.

On the trail of procrastination

As we have already learned, procrastination can actually be helpful as an indication that you could benefit from rearranging some aspects of your life. It can help you to understand when to let go of things, relationships, and tasks that no longer add value to you.

There are different interpretations for the cause of procrastination. For example, you may be a very disciplined and consistent person who has simply imposed too many tasks on himself. In this case, either prioritizing, or even abandoning certain tasks altogether, could be the right solution for you.

If you are a person who is easily distracted by impulses, due to the fast pace of life associated with digital media, Concepts 3 and 4 will offer you concrete approaches to solve this problem.

First though, we will look at the different, scientifically defined, types of procrastination that led us to create the concepts and tasks in this book. The goal being, to show you how procrastination can be used as an important decision-making tool. A tool that has become increasingly established in recent decades through digitization.

In search of causes - latest findings and old theories

Recent findings have shown that some of the general tendencies that cause procrastination, are perfectionism, rebellious behavior, and a pronounced interest in new things. With perfectionism, the cause is the desire to perform a task to the highest standard while at the same time lacking the knowledge to do so, leading instead to postponement. Rebellious behavior and a strong interest in new things are equally easy to understand. But these findings don't go into the same depth as we will in the upcoming pages, beginning with the 4 causes of procrastination described below.

Cause 1: Aversion to the task

Task aversion is a classic cause of procrastination according to numerous studies. Aversion can often result from a lack of ability. If a person is unable to perform a task well, procrastination may occur. In addition to lack of skills, matching with personal interests is also a relevant factor: A person has the ability to perform a task, but still doesn't, because it doesn't interest him. This can result in underachievement, which leads to procrastination.

Aversion is often determined by a person's individual character and corresponding tendencies towards motivation. Some people are able to motivate themselves right away even to the tasks they feel a great aversion to. Other people need time to motivate themselves or they just do not succeed at all. *How* and to what extent you can motivate yourself varies with each person. But developing motivation is a skill that can be learned through training. After all, motivation means nothing more than finding motives.

According to Steel (2012), researchers have determined that rewards for performing unwanted tasks are good motivational factors. The closer the reward, the more the willingness to pursue the task increases. There are several other methods too, that we will highlight in the further chapters of this book.

Self-test questions to help you find the right concept for you:

- ➢ Having a hard time getting started with the task in the first place? Concept 1 offers the appropriate ways to tackle this problem.
- ➢ Don't know where to start because there are too many tasks? It's worth taking a look at both Concepts 1 and 4.
- ➢ Feeling overwhelmed by the task and therefore reject it? All of the concepts offer you potential solutions, but especially 1, 2 and 4.

Cause 2: Lack of conviction that you can succeed

Success, in one form or another, is a component of life that every person strives for. To achieve it, challenges must be met effectively. In some cases, great effort is required, and in other cases, less so. The less the effort and the greater the success, the less the tendency to procrastinate. The greater the effort and the less the success, the greater the tendency to procrastinate. Great effort often requires even greater motivation.

People who have confidence in themselves are likely to cope better than a person who is not convinced that he or she will succeed. Lack of conviction is also referred to as low self-efficacy.

The term self-efficacy refers to a person's ability to successfully overcome challenges.

Who has high self-efficacy? As a general rule, people who have already mastered several crises can be said to have high self-efficacy. In addition to this general form of self-efficacy, there is also specific self-efficacy, where individuals are convinced of their success in specific areas.

Example

You're sure to have fond memories of your favorite subjects when you were at school. In those subjects, in which you got good grades, or which you enjoyed more, you were more likely to succeed. This probably meant that you were convinced of your success, right?

You understand the basic principle: conviction is a great motivator. Not surprisingly, the keyword *motivation* comes up again. Conviction can be compared to an insurance policy or a binding contract. You are absolutely convinced in your mind that you will succeed in performing a task, so you feel a bit like you have signed a contract that assures you of success. Would you perform the task if success were certain? Perhaps not if the success did not justify the effort, but otherwise, certainty increases motivation. Even though there is no such thing as 100 percent certainty, the added value of great conviction cannot be denied, because it suggests certainty to your subconscious.

Self-test questions to help you find the right concept:

➤ You doubt it is possible for you to accomplish the task well? Concept 2 and partly Concept 3 are tailored for you!

➤ Your determination is not great because you don't really care about the task? In this case, you should deal with Concept 4 first and foremost.

➤ You prefer to devote yourself to other things because they are more promising or fulfilling? Look especially into Concept 3!

Cause 3: Low self-control, high impulsivity

Impulsivity and lack of self-control are often associated with outbursts of anger, acts of violence, or other highly conspicuous acts. However, drastic reactions aren't always the result of these traits.

In the case of procrastination, people who cannot control themselves well tend to procrastinate. Lack of self-control has several possible causes:

➤ Habit: Habits are automated behavioral patterns programmed into the human brain. The inclination is stored in the subconscious, making it difficult to resist acting in the same way. As a result, people regularly give in to their habits. The more pronounced the habit, the more difficult it is to control oneself and resist the temptation.

➤ Character: People all have their own specific character traits, including impulsivity. Impulsivity can develop at any stage in life for various reasons. For example, growing up with parents who tend to use a loud tone, bad career choices, meddling life partners and drastic experiences can all be potential triggers for impulsivity, as they become ingrained in a person's character. Affected individuals find it difficult to distance themselves emotionally from an issue, often giving free rein to their emotions.

➤ Disease: Individuals with certain mental illnesses, either congenital or developed over the course of life, often tend to be impulsive. Impulsivity due to lack of emotional control is a borderline mental illness. An example of a mental illness in which impulsivity may result not from emotions but from the very nature of the disorder is ADHD.

These 3 triggers are frequent causes of behavioral patterns that develop into a tendency to procrastinate. A lack of self-control alone is not usually enough. But combined with a general dislike of the task and low self-efficacy, you have all the ingredients for procrastination. Then counterproductive emotions arise that encourage giving in and prevent the task from being performed.

An interesting insight: Motivation beats emotion! Should you associate more with low self-control, then you may feel consoled by the fact that you can usually beat this by treating the first 2 causes. Because if you positively influence your motivation levels to such an extent that you believe you will succeed in the exercise and feel motivated to perform the task, you will be better able to defy the impulses that encourage you to procrastinate.

Self-test questions to help you find the right concept:

➤ You give in to various impulses that distract you while performing the task? Concept 3 is tailor-made for you. While concept 2 also offers indirect good advice and methods too.

➤ You often get distracted by other things which affects your consistency in performing a task? Concept 4 helps you to weigh between several perspectives to deal with this issue.

➢ You are generally always full of energy and switch back and forth between different things? In this case, we recommend studying Concepts 3 and 4.

Cause 4: Long time horizon

Imagine a task that you are facing that you keep putting off. Maybe you currently have such a task that you are working on... if not, then just think of one. Now imagine that you have to do it for only 5 minutes for it to be completely finished, with the success safely in your pocket. Would you say no to this deal? Probably not.

Now imagine you had to do the same task for 5 minutes every day for 3 weeks. Here it already becomes more difficult. Then think that you have to do it for several hours a week for several years. An unpleasant shiver is likely to run down your spine at the thought of it in this case.

The longer the time horizon associated with a task, the higher the risk that the task will be postponed. This is doubly treacherous. Because in addition to the problems caused by the postponement itself, unforeseeable events in the future are also a potential cause for postponement.

Self-test questions to help you find the right Concept:

➢ You always devote yourself to your tasks in a relaxed and leisurely manner?

Take a look at Concept 1 and see if it wouldn't be better with a little more consistency and determination.

➤ Other people distract you from the task at hand and you always refer to the long time-horizon you still have?
Learn more about this in Concepts 2 and 3.

➤ Because of the long time-horizon, would you rather perform the many other tasks that are in front of you that are more urgent?
In Concept 4, learn whether it would not be better to think about fixed prioritizations and a reduction of tasks.

Determining the usefulness of a task - is procrastination appropriate?

Apart from the causes, there are other forces at work that lead to procrastination. According to Dr. Steel (2007), the following influencing factors are also present: Expectations of the task, value of the task, and delay. Using these influencing factors, Dr. Steel created the Temporal Motivation Theory to determine the utility of a task.

$$Usefulness = \frac{E \times V}{D}$$

As interesting as it may be to have a concrete formula for calculating the probability of procrastination, it should be just as clear at the same time that no concrete numbers can be used for all the influencing factors, which is why the result cannot be concrete either. Certainly, models could be created according to which the numbers for expectations, appreciation, procrastination and finally benefit could be derived by a question-answer game with fixed values for each answer. But the model would hardly be suitable for general use.

What you take from this formula in the ideal case is only the connections between these influencing factors. Now it is possible for you to anticipate the possible extent of your procrastination in order to use the measures described in the concepts of this book to improve over time.

But what exactly are the relationships that this model describes?

> Expectations: Expectations represent the probability you expect to get a certain result. Negative expectations are basically nothing more than low self-efficacy (see causes). If expectations are low, a low number would be put into the formula.

> Value: The value of a task or your appreciation of it is measured by your perception of how rewarding the performance of the task is. A high learning factor that would be valued would result in a high propensity to perform the task. The number in the formula would be high. If the value placed on the task was low (see aversion to the task under causes), the number entered in the formula would be low.

> Delay: How much you delay a task also affects its usefulness. It makes sense to include this value in the fraction of the formula in the denominator, because otherwise the formula would not make sense; examples will follow shortly.

> ➤ <u>Benefit:</u> The usefulness of the task is representative of the likelihood of procrastination. This is based on the idea that useful tasks are not postponed. If procrastination does occur, it is only for valid reasons. In general, tasks with a high utility do not have a tendency to procrastination. A low benefit, on the other hand, leads to an increased probability of procrastination.

Three examples are used to calculate the benefit. For the formula, it is assumed that scales from 1 to 10 are used. This is practical in that the results are then percentages and allow a quick overall assessment of the task. The numbers in the examples are subjective estimates. You would also calculate with such estimates if you want to use the formula.

Example 1

Hannes F. has very low expectations about the output of a task, but a high appreciation towards the execution, because it makes him repeat and consolidate existing knowledge. He pursues the task without delay. The formula could look like this:

$$Usefulness = \frac{2 \times 8}{1}$$

$$Usefulness = \frac{16}{1}$$

$$Usefulness = 16 \ (16\ \%)$$

Example 2

Ina L. expects the greatest profit from the task and likes to do it because she enjoys it. She does not delay the task, but always performs it at the scheduled time. This is how the potential formula is created:

$$Usefulness = \frac{10 \times 9}{1}$$

$$Usefulness = \frac{90}{1}$$

$$Usefulness = 90 \ (90\,\%)$$

Example 3

Thomas G. has devastatingly low expectations and no appreciation for the task. Discipline is also non-existent in Thomas, which is why he delays the task as long as possible. The formula in this extreme case would be as follows:

$$Usefulness = \frac{E \times V}{D}$$

$$Uselfulness = \frac{1 \times 1}{10}$$

$$Usefulness = \frac{1}{10} \ (0{,}1\,\%!)$$

As we can see, the formula is very well thought out. The delay in the denominator of the fraction ensures that high or low delays have the desired effects on the result. A high delay minimizes the overall result and invalidates good intermediate results from the numerator at the top of the fraction (E x V), a low delay does just the opposite. The benefit, when calculating on a scale of 1 to 10 for the 3 influencing factors that present themselves, takes 100 as the highest value and 1/10 as the lowest value. Thus, the result can simply be represented as a percentage.

Low benefit encourages questioning

Even without calculating in this form using concrete numbers from a scale, it is helpful to keep the formula in mind. This is because it shows how different influencing factors are interrelated. If you take into account several components that define the value of an influencing factor, this formula provides you with a good decision-making aid to know whether you should pursue the task or activity at all.

Let's assume that the benefit would be so low that it would be less than 10 percent. This would be an almost damning verdict for the task in question. The best example is an obligation in an asso-ciation, which you pursue: After some time, you notice that this association is rather disorganized. The work does not reach the planned effect by far. Moreover, it is not unlikely that the goals will be missed year after year. You understandably have lower and lower expectations of the task, and feel no appreciation during the execution, because the association hardly lives up to its purpose, so you procrastinate longer and longer on your tasks as a result. In this case, the situation is clear: resign from the association. Find a better club elsewhere, where you can better develop motivation. In this example, procrastination is not a negative thing, but an im-portant decision-making tool. Even the most disciplined people would break with the club in a case like this; unless they had the chance to turn the club around themselves and push it forward according to their own ideas. But these are rare exceptions.

The formula for calculating the benefit can also be applied to interpersonal relationships and professions. Basically, it can be applied to all areas in which you have to make a decision, and then fulfill obligations.

Explanation based on interpersonal relationships

Now, when it comes to interpersonal relationships, *usefulness* isn't necessarily appropriate. After all, friends, life partners or even acquaintances are not there to be of use to you. In fact, it is a term that seems out of place given the emotional connection we have to these people. Feel free to replace the term with *attachment* if you like. Probably you have experienced two people drifting apart. They may develop conflicting interests or pursue different careers. The mutual benefits of the relationship to each other or the bond between them starts to diminish.

➢ Expectations: Expectations can also be reduced between two people. Initially, partner A still has the hope that partner B will someday remember his birthday or their wedding anniversary. In the beginning, girlfriend C has the hope that she will be able to help boyfriend D out of a drug quagmire. When these hopes give way to disappointments, expectations fall. As expectations fall, the added value of a relationship falls too.

➢ Appreciation: In the beginning, many things are new in a relationship. Almost everything that the significant other has to offer is fascinating – from playing the piano beautifully to having an attractive body to having money in the bank account (people have different incentives to feel appreciation). The special value of these things is often reduced over the course of the relationship and the appreciation may be lost.

➢ Procrastination: In relationships, when the delay in performing favors or duties for the other person increases, this type of procrastination suggests a diminished sense of care has developed. It starts with the simplest things, such as when a partner complies with his or her partner's request to wash the dishes or take out the trash less and less often...

Procrastination is also noticeable in interpersonal relationships. It is one of the factors that provides insight into the value of a relationship. Nevertheless, it must be taken into account that, in addition to the 3 influencing factors from the formula, emotions are at work. These emotions make you think back to the past or develop optimism for the future. The recommendation is therefore that you use this formula in relationships as a decision-making aid by taking into account the strength of the emotions. If you feel emotionally attached, do not break with the person, but look for ways to raise expectations, appreciation and benefits, while reducing the delays.

In the case of negative emotions, combined with a low calculated benefit from the formula, it is indeed worth considering whether the relationship should not be paused or ended. What reasons do you think there could be for friends to go their separate ways, for married couples to split up, and for newcomers to get tired of talking to their neighbors after just 2 weeks? The formula offers some sound solutions.

Example based on profession

Talking about a low amount of benefit for your profession is a sensitive topic. Because it could make you realize that it's time to change professions altogether. But who can simply afford to change professions?

Expectations of and appreciation for a profession are largely derived from previous experience, prospects in the industry, and the careers of one's colleagues. The better all these factors are, the higher the expectations. Esteem is a very important factor because it is largely what tends to keep most employees, and self-employed people in their jobs. A large proportion of people have no prospect of changing jobs just like that. It would often involve too much effort because retraining would have to be done in addition to the current job. This effort can often be enough that it makes people feel like changing jobs is virtually impossible. Therefore, most people have a distinct appreciation towards their jobs. After all, it brings them money, which they need to live. So, it is hardly surprising that even people who haven't completely liked their job for decades, do not change it. With regards to career, delays are a very important signal. Because even a person who has despised his job for decades will, if he has no alternative to earn money, usually complete tasks without delay. This is because automatisms and routines take hold that are stronger than low motivation levels. In turn, people who procrastinate with work usually do so because they are not completely dependent on the job. After all, who would take the risk of not adequately fulfilling their duty, of being fired, and of being left without an income? As a rule, only a person who has alternative jobs available. Of course, there are even exceptions to this as well...

The example of profession illustrates how closely lack of appreciation and procrastination are linked. There is no denying that procrastination in this case should always be the trigger for serious reflection: Am I still right in this job? What prospects do I have to change the job? And above all: What are the existing problems, and can they be resolved within the profession or with the respective employer? In the most extreme case, it is indeed advisable to think about quitting. After all, low esteem and postponement of duties lead to deteriorated work performance, which in the long run will most likely lead to consequences initiated by the employer anyway.

Honesty with yourself

Now for some general hints about the thematized *Temporal Motivation Theory*. The whole formula can only be of help if you are honest with yourself. A common mistake people tend make is to reject personal responsibility. If you have agreed with your partner to improve on a certain point and do not do so, you will not be able to say that the relationship is failing because of your partner.

Example

If the garbage is left lying around everywhere and the willingness to clean up decreases with the duration of the relationship, then the relationship will most likely fail because of you. Meanwhile, the likelihood of finding a new partner with a penchant for clutter and mess is slim. Here it is necessary to take a look at your own behavior.

When discussing whether procrastination is a long overdue sign of a necessary change or a personal weakness that you need to work on, being honest with yourself is an incredibly important component. Impulsive people in particular don't find it easy to blame themselves. They let emotions and impulses control them and often disregard rational judgments. With some distance from the event, however, even impulsive people will succeed in putting their emotions aside and being honest with themselves.

But how do I become honest with myself? How do I manage to make an objective judgment about whether procrastination is a sign of necessary change or a mistake on my part?

Self-reflection is the key. This requires that you take time in the evenings for reviewing your days, so you can deal with how you felt and decide whether you did everything right. Evenings are perfect for this, once everything has settled down and the day is over, it is optimal for self-reflection. Ideally, you would write down your feelings so that you can still understand them several days later and do not forget them again. Self-reflection should be done without emotional attachment, if possible. Take a differentiated look at the facts from several perspectives to decide whether you did the right thing.

Task 1

Take some time each evening for a week to think deeply about your procrastination. As you do so, consider whether you might have overlooked several positive aspects of the task at hand. Write down all the positive and negative aspects. Collect it over several evenings and then see if anything has changed in your expectations, appreciation, usefulness, and urge to procrastinate. You may be more motivated to pursue the activity because you see a greater benefit in it.

Self-reflection sometimes works more, sometimes less well. Practice makes perfect. Here are some useful further methods to help you find out the reason for your procrastination:

> Use personal examples: Personal examples are especially advantageous in a professional context. If you suspect low career prospects, it makes sense to find out about people in your company or in the industry in general. If it turns out that, with a lot of effort and dedication, a considerable climb up the career ladder is possible after all, you will gain greater expectations of the profession and a higher appreciation for it. You will realize that the problem was not a lack of prospects, but your lack of knowledge. Personal examples can be used in all types of tasks to develop motivation. You can even use them in sports by looking at pictures or YouTube videos of role models. Surely you can find one or the other person who started an activity under the same (adverse) circumstances as you and still became successful.

> Have conversations: As soon as you have conversations about your situation, you will gain additional perspectives. You are probably familiar with the recommendation that certain changes or challenges should be tackled in pairs, because then you can motivate each other. Conversations have the same intention. If you present your problem, you will get helpful information from other people, which will give you new perspectives on your prospects and increase your appreciation. You'll also get tips against procrastination here and there from other people. Conversations are worthwhile. A little tip, if you're uncomfortable admitting

that the problem affects you: talk about the problem as if someone else had it. If you tell them that a friend is in the same situation, it will be easier for you to talk openly about the issue.

➢ Turn the tables: Turn the tables by imagining what it would take for you to always follow through on the task in a timely manner. What would have to happen for your expectations and appreciation of the task to be so high that you would no longer put it off? Even imagine absurd scenarios, but stay within a realistic framework. You may end up realizing that what should be possible is already there, but you have ignored it so far. And maybe, in addition, much of what you want is possible, provided you put a little effort into the task. In extreme cases, you may realize that no prerequisites in the world could increase your affection towards the task. If it gets to that point, then it's a sign that the procrastination is just a logical consequence of your profound dislike for a task, and you should abandon the task as soon as possible and find something new.

Task 2

Now devote yourself to the methods described. During the day, before you do the self-reflection, do one of the 3 methods. Take one day for each of them. Of course, it doesn't have to be the entire day. Methods like turning the tables may only require 30 minutes of time, while conversations require finding several people first and then having the conversations. The fact is that the 3 methods presented will enrich your self-reflection and you will gain new insights through the methods themselves.

Sometimes the causes lie with yourself. In particular, if you look at your past experiences in life, you will discover clues as to whether the task is generally bad or if you just need to work on yourself. Honesty is the basis for a reasonable analysis. **Remember**: No relationship will end, no job will be quit, and no task will be simply discarded, without a completely honest analysis of what the reason for procrastination is, whether it is justified and how you can defuse it, if necessary, by changing your perspective!

"Procrastinare!" – Procrastination through the ages

The negative stigma associated with the word *procrastination* today did not exist in the past. Although it was a long time ago, the original view proves helpful as a support for you to determine in which situations procrastination is beneficial for you.

Did you know?

The word *procrastination* has its origin in Latin, namely in the verb *procrastinare*. Surprisingly, the original meaning of this word is not negative. In the past, putting something off and thus waiting until the next day was considered a sign of wisdom, and testified to good thinking. It is not known how the word came to have the negative meaning it has today.

Procrastination used to be seen as a positive approach. Today, on the other hand, it is perceived negatively. How could it come to this? Possible answers are provided by the documentary *Zeit ist Geld* (2016), which was shown on the German TV channel *arte*. As the title suggests, the plot focuses on time. Although procrastination is not the main topic of the documentary, it does come up. In fact, there is a close connection between procrastination, time and – in a more distant sense, which will be explained in a moment – money. Time defines procrastination. If there were no time, nothing could be put off. As a deepening aspect, you have learned that a long time-horizon for unwanted tasks increases the probability of procrastination.

How does money fit into this context? What does money stand for anyway?

Acceleration in today's world causes problems

The scope for interpretation is wide, but in the documentary it is mainly attributed to capitalism and globalization. In addition, digitization as an influencing factor must not be disregarded. Anyone who follows the history of time, especially since capitalism's inception, learns that the first punch clocks came in during the course of industrialization. Work has been measurable since that time at the earliest. Words like *productivity* and *optimization* crept into factory jargon, that of companies and even private individuals. In the early 20th century, universal time was established in Paris. Time was measurable everywhere. Looking further into the future, we notice its influence with digitalization that was supposed to create more simplicity and freedom. But that's still not the case in the reality of companies today. Instead of digital possibilities loosening the lines for employees, expectations are increased. Digitalization is not bypassing private households either. In general, the new possibilities serve only to tempt people to be more productive. It is becoming increasingly out of fashion to slow down. The documentary asks the question:

"Where do you find the time for relaxation and idleness when any time outside of work is considered a lost minute?"

Career. Prospects. Optimization through digitization. Social trends. All these things tempt people to take on many obligations. Maybe there are even so many obligations that it can only go well for a limited period of time in the first place? This is a question you can ask yourself: Are you allowing yourself enough time off or are you overwhelming yourself with the amount of tasks? If the latter were the case, then procrastination wouldn't even begin to be surprising. It would be a logical consequence of being over-whelmed.

Most people have a guilty conscience when they put some-thing off until the next day. Whether this guilty conscience is jus-tified must be judged in relation to the overall burden. In today's times, it seems more important than ever to set priorities. Not being able to say *no* to individual tasks or activities can become a huge problem over time. Concept 4 will help you with these things with a wealth of exercises and the ultimate guide to prioritization.

Deceleration counteracts procrastination

Surprisingly, over the last few decades, as technological pro-gress has been at its highest, the amount of mental illness has also been increasing. An interesting change within the German popu-lation can be observed compared to the early 2000s: Back then, it was the unemployed who had a disproportionate incidence of mental illness. Today, it is the employed. Sick leave due to mental illness has risen steadily in this country since 2006. Cases of inca-pacity to work increased by 50% from 2006 to 2016, and the amount of days of incapacity to work has increased by 80% over the same period. A deeper look at the statistics reveals that the following mental illnesses led to incapacity to work among employees in 2013:

> Affective disorders (including burnout, gloom, dejection, elevated or irritable mood, persistent mild depressed mood, decreased drive): 46,2 %
> Neurotic, stress and somatoform disorders (including anxiety disorder, panic disorder, obsessive-compulsive disorder, panic attacks): 44.9%.
> Disorders due to the use of substances that affect the psyche: 3.9%.
> Schizophrenia and delusional ideation: 2.2%.
> Personality and behavioral disorders: 1 %
> Other: 1.9 %

Source: Statista

According to information from the *Ärzteblatt,* the proportion of early retirements in 2010 was 36%. More than one third of German pensioners thus retired earlier than actually planned! The BKK Health Report of 2018 also identifies drastic increases in mental illnesses within the past 40 years.

Did you know?

In Japan, burnout affected 40% of the population in the 1980s. As a major global power at the time, the country slid into an economic crisis because – almost unbelievably – the population worked too much without taking vacations. As a result, there was hardly any consumption among the population, which is why a recession occurred.

What do mental illnesses have to do with procrastination?

Many things. First of all, it should be noted that mental illness promotes procrastination. Those who are listless, depressed, or in otherwise poor mental health will have a greater tendency to put off tasks. In these cases, the cause of procrastination is usually the same as the cause of mental illness. You'd be surprised to know how many of the mental illnesses go undetected for a long time or slowly develop. In some circumstances, overwork and increasing procrastination lead to the discovery of the mental illness in the first place. In any case, you need to ask yourself if the procrastination is not caused by an excess of tasks. If you have so many tasks in front of you that you can hardly cope with them and only with the greatest of efforts, you must make changes to your daily routine. Otherwise – and this is absolutely serious – sooner or later you may develop a mental illness.

However, mental illnesses do not only promote procrastination. It is the same the other way around. Imagine that you put off one or more very important things every day. You would then eventually get into a predicament of having to catch up on everything. However, this does not necessarily cause mental illness, which becomes apparent over a longer period of time. It often becomes problematic if you regularly put things off. It can cause you to start doubting yourself at some point. In the worst case, you feel inferior, even though you are not. In addition, other people may put pressure on you and constantly remind you that you have things to do. They may even make fun of you. One domino sets the other one in motion, and so initially simple procrastination turns into a deeper psychological problem.

These explanations are in no way intended to frighten you. They are only meant to illustrate that procrastination is becoming more and more common in today's world. Almost analogous to the increase in mental illness, an increase in the number of things that are put off by different people in different contexts is becoming noticeable. There may or may not be a connection to mental illness. Most people who seek help for procrastination are not affected by mental illness. But life is long. To ensure that everything runs smoothly psychologically and in terms of life plans in the many years to come, it is reasonable to consider whether procrastination might not be the natural consequence of unnecessarily excessive demands. Again, we refer you to Concept 4, which will also help you with this concern.

The most important things in a nutshell

➤ Procrastination usually arises from dissatisfaction or excessive demands.

➤ Dissatisfaction may arise from a general dislike of an activity, certain impulses related to the activity, a lack of appreciation, or low self-efficacy.

➤ Being overwhelmed is a classic consequence of taking on too many tasks. If possible, priorities should be set and rest breaks should be integrated into everyday life. Otherwise, in the worst case, it is even possible for mental illness to manifest itself.

➤ If a task, relationship or activity is of little benefit, then its maintenance should be questioned. In this sense, procrastination is a decision-making tool for changes in everyday life.

➤ Whenever a task is a must-do or related to something personally important, procrastination must be addressed.

➤ Likewise, measures against procrastination must be initiated when the smallest and most self-evident things of everyday life, such as hygienic or social norms, are postponed due to procrastination.

Concept 1 | Purely a matter of attitude: Finding the right start

Your attitude describes what opinion you have of something. It is the expectations you have towards a task, which you learned about as an important influence for or against procrastination in chapter 1. This chapter provides you with insights that increase your expectations and thus your motivation. In order for you to understand these insights, it is a good idea to carry out the corresponding tasks.

First of all, a small warning: The insights are a matter of opinion. You don't have to insist on rediscovering yourself in every insight. It is enough if you agree with the insight, the task helps you and you are motivated to fulfill the otherwise postponed duty. It is quite possible that the realizations are too simplistic for you. Some of the contents in one insight even contradict the contents in another insight from this chapter. But this is not a bad thing. Because the goal of the insights is to give you food for thought. How you use them is entirely up to you.

Insight #1: You'll never regret anything once you get it over with

This realization first encourages you to remember. Think back to the last time you did an important thing that you didn't feel like doing. Try to trace back the emotions and thoughts you had before doing the task. In some circumstances, it will have been acute unwillingness. You may have had low motivation. In addition, there were a thousand other thoughts that distracted you and tempted you to do something else.

But what did you do? You defied those odds and carried out the task. You demonstrated enormous willpower and a strong sense of duty to yourself and possibly even to others.

What was it like during and after performing this task? At first, it might not have been easy to do, but by the middle of the execution, you were in the flow.

Could it even have been easy? It was suddenly actually not so difficult to take on the task and perform it with appropriate quality.

How did you feel after it was done? All the barriers were gone at once: you were relieved, proud, happy; yes, even free!

Next, think of another situation where you did a task that you didn't feel like doing for any reason: What were your emotions before, during, and after doing it? Collect in your memory as many situations as possible in which you successfully beat your inner resistance.

My experience

This realization has helped me massively. For me, it was probably the most effective measure against procrastination. I used to envy people who pursued their private goals in a highly disciplined manner, who turned their hobbies into their profession or consistently followed through with their diet. When, in rare situations, I followed through on otherwise postponed tasks, I noticed how well it made me feel. It was then that I realized that before performing an unwanted task, I might even feel unwillingness for the rest of my life. But one thing was also certain: after performing it, the pride would be all the greater! After forcing myself to perform postponed tasks for one week, I managed to feel this moment again and again, the feeling of pride after the task was completed kept increasing. Eventually I had a smile on my face even before starting to perform the task – today I will successfully prove it to myself again! It became easier for me to motivate myself each time.

With the first realization, you are made aware that overcoming is only temporary. Pride and satisfaction in completing the task, on the other hand, are long-term. Unfortunately, the same is true for the negative: if you decide not to perform your unwanted duty, stress about the pending completion and other negative emotions will also be long-term. To help you understand the simplicity of it, here are some choices for the situation:

1. You have the choice to struggle with yourself and decide against performing the task. The result is that you feel relieved for a short time and pursue a preferred activity. However, you will not develop maximum pleasure in this

preferred activity because you will still be preoccupied in your subconscious mind with the task that needs to be accomplished. If you don't do the task at all, you will be unhappy in the long run.

2. Likewise, you are free to struggle with yourself, to try to perform the task and to stop at the beginning because the task does not suit you. This is, after all, a step in the right direction. Try to take away lessons from the attempt and stick with the task a few minutes longer each time.

3. The third option is that you are aware of the challenge, but think back to the many times you have already overcome and successfully pursued an unloved task. You realize that you will be happy and relieved after completing the task. So, you generously allow plenty of time to complete the task, create the most inviting atmosphere possible for completing it, and persevere with it. In between there are breaks every now and then. Don't let anyone or anything rush you. You struggle with yourself for a brief moment to get over yourself. After that, you complete the task and feel proud over the long run.

Task 1

Imagine the third scenario in relation to the tasks you have been putting off. Sitting down in a quiet environment with your eyes closed, visualize for several minutes how you successfully overcame the resistance, and gratefully receive all the positive emotions after the task is done. The important thing is to feel these emotions properly! Make every effort to feel the freedom and bliss after the performed task. Do this exercise several times a week or several times a day. Don't you want to finally tackle this task; to take the credit and prove to yourself what a strong-willed and consistent person you are? It's all up to you...

The advantage of insight #1 is that it is universal in nature. It is applicable to any type of task and any type of interpersonal relationship. Visualizations, as described in Task 1, are a powerful way to motivate yourself using your imagination. You see yourself at the goal and feel the success before it is achieved. By doing so, you make completing the task more attractive to yourself and increase the benefits you generate from the task.

Insight #2: The goal is progress, not perfection

Perfectionism often masks a fear of not living up to an impression of oneself or one's work. Students often face this problem, according to the *University of North Carolina at Chapel Hill*. Procrastination, which results from striving for perfection, is unfortunately based on the wrong thought processes. For one thing, perfection is not attainable by waiting and procrastinating on one's duty. For another, perfection itself is a term that leaves much room for interpretation and usually describes an impossible goal.

The focus is only on the first aspect, namely the counterproductive waiting time. Obviously, a person has the goal of delivering a perfect performance due to his or her previous performance or for other similar reasons. The delivery of this performance is postponed due to doubts about one's own competence. Think about it logically: you want to deliver perfectly, but you doubt your competence. The only solution in this situation is to acquire the competencies. This only works if you take on the task as soon as possible. The other things you are *always perfect* at, you are doing very well anyway, right? So why do you prefer these *kids' games* to big challenges? Perfection – and this is a segue to interpretive latitude – is hardly admirable if all the time you're only mastering challenges you're comfortable with, isn't it? Prove true perfection to yourself by acquiring new skills and delivering an unexpectedly strong performance!

Now to the second aspect mentioned: the scope of interpretation of the term *perfection*. Perfectionists usually overlook the fact that there is not just one interpretation of perfection. What is perfect for you may not be for other people. Moreover, when you work, study, or otherwise perform in a way that is judged by others, you are subject to the mood swings of those individuals in their evaluation. General perfection does not exist. What is even more striking is the fact that people who are not perfect also enjoy prestige: They have stains on their clean slate, but usually enjoy more admiration than other people who appear perfect. This is because there were obviously obstacles that did not pass by these persons without leaving a trace. But still, these individuals have mastered their way. Isn't that worthy of admiration? Isn't it perfect, in a sense, when a person successfully manages not only the things that are like child's play for him or her, but also the distinct challenges that are noticeable in hindsight?

Task 2

Think about what the term *perfection* means to you. As you do so, think about how weaknesses might play a critical role in the recognition of achievement. Is it possible that you would receive more recognition if you completed a task that everyone knew you were not good at? And wouldn't it be absolutely impressive if you mastered this task with a very positive result?

Changing your attitude is not easy. It is especially difficult if you have only known one view of perfection in your life up to now. But it is worth turning your own way of thinking around. You will discover that perfection – if it exists – does not automatically mean faultlessness. In the end, small mistakes even make you likeable, because they testify to humanity. Mistakes and weaknesses help you to stay grounded. Because if someone takes off, he can lose his perfection by underestimating challenges and making careless mistakes.

Insight #3: Not by hook or by crook, but with breaks and stages.

Behavioral and brain research shows that setting stages is helpful in achieving goals. A stage is an intermediate goal that can be checked off as *done*. The world-renowned behavioral scientist Gerhard Roth has put forward a number of theses regarding habits that can be seamlessly applied to other circumstances. Gerhard Roth cites the division of the major overarching goal into stages as an important step. It is important to make the individual stages more attractive with rewards. The rewards should be varied and beneficial. *Varied* means that the rewards should not lose their attractiveness, and thus their usefulness, at some point because they are used too frequently. *Conducive* provides that the rewards should not conflict with other goals or frustrate progress in performing the task.

Task 3

It is not possible for every task, but if it is feasible in your case, then divide your previously postponed task into several stages. These stages should be such that you feel more motivated to pursue the task. At the same time, the stages should be large enough to make progress. For example, there is no benefit to setting a task for 30 minutes a day if you need 15 minutes to work your way in. So determine meaningful stages. Set rewards for when you reach the stage. Make sure that the duration of the stages gets a little longer each time. This way you will get used to performing the task for a longer period of time.

If you are working on the task for a long period of time, it pays to build breaks into the completion of the task. Working for 2 hours at a stretch is generally not beneficial. Breaks in between are helpful for productivity and to prevent distraction. If you have an impulsive nature with little self-control, as you learned about as a possible cause of procrastination in the first chapter, you will best understand that distraction carries a high risk of stopping task completion. How about allowing yourself this distraction, but only during certain periods of time? Wouldn't this be an excellent compromise, thanks to which you could give in to impulses, but at the same time be highly focused on your duty?

A top technique for balancing work on the unwanted task and breaks is the *Pomodoro Technique*. It works as follows:

1. Formulate task (e.g., your daily stage).
2. Set first work stage and set alarm clock (e.g., 25 minutes).
3. In the time slot consciously pursue only this task.

4. Point out the status of the work and the progress made in carrying out the task. Possibly address a few motivating words to yourself: "I have mastered the first part great!"
5. Take a 5-minute break and set an alarm clock. During this break, it is allowed to give in to distractions or practice other preferred activities.
6. After the break, start again from the beginning.
7. Perform 4 of these time-break blocks and then take longer breaks.

The important element here is the alarm clock. Without the alarm clock you would tend to deviate in time. Through the alarm clock you have a clear signal that immediately calls you to the next step of the Pomodoro Technique.

Insight #4: Start with the most unpleasant task

If you have a choice, it is recommended to start the day with the hardest task. At the beginning of the day, you still have many hours ahead of you. Accordingly, the confidence to successfully master an unpleasant task is greater. In addition, productivity is highest in the morning. Well rested and more in front of you than behind you, the drive tends to be great. The prospect of having completed the unpleasant duty early in the day and then being able to spare the entire day for pleasure usually has an inspiring effect.

Task 4

Try to get at least some of your unpleasant and previously postponed tasks done first. This doesn't necessarily have to be at the beginning of the day, although in terms of productivity it is of course a good idea. Should you be putting off tasks at work and the work doesn't start until 2 p.m., as a rule, of course, you can't do the task in the morning. It's simply a matter of doing the unpleasant duties first at the beginning of each task section. How does that make you feel? Are you inspired, because you have done the most unpleasant things at the beginning and now you have all the freedom for the pleasant things?

You automatically avoid a feeling of pressure and melancholy during the day by doing the task right at the beginning. In addition, concentration is higher in the morning because the body is refreshed after sleep, due to improved release of the sleep hormone melatonin, if it takes place under optimal conditions (room temperature around 18 °C, fresh air, comfortable mattress, darkness, six to eight hours duration). A strengthening breakfast and morning coffee also have a beneficial effect. At breakfast, care should be taken to avoid sweet spreads and other sugary foods. Because yes: sugar is also detrimental to consistent task performance. First, sugar has a stimulating effect by shooting into the blood and providing instant energy. Then the blood sugar level drops rapidly and cravings set in. Nobody wants to start the day like this, let alone carry out unpleasant tasks! So, the ideal cornerstone is to successfully carry out the unpleasant things as quickly as possible with all the fresh energy in order to then make room for the pleasant tasks.

Insight #5: There is no beginning and no end, only doing

Some people approach an unpleasant task with vigor at first. They firmly resolve not to put it off. But then comes the question, "Where do I actually start?" This question often ruins all good intentions. A motivational film inspired by a true story called *The*

Peaceful Warrior – Path of the Peaceful Warrior highlights this when the gymnast in the film has everything one could want at his age; until fate takes a turn for the worst... and all the doctors tell him that he will never be able to practice sports again with the knee injury he suffered in his life-threatening motorcycle accident. But he manages to do it thanks to the help of an old man who slowly leads him back to his old strength. The gymnast, when asked by the old man to resume gymnastics, thinks he is completely off his rocker. "But I don't even know where to start!?" He is plagued by fears, doubts, the huge road ahead, the neigh Sayers etc., so that he not only tends to procrastinate, but is completely at a loss as to whether to do it at all. The old man's words are "There is no beginning and no end, only doing."

In his song *Alles was ich hab,* artist Fynn Kliemann encourages people to, "just think about it. Problems become more comfortable later and don't matter afterwards." In this context, it's more about the general attitude to life. In his view, people don't have much time to live and tend to make too little of it. Possibly, many people feel that life is passing them by. Because yes: Procrastination can also take on such characteristics – precious life passes you by and many opportunities are not ceased because too many concerns prevail. It is always postponed!

Use this time to think back to the situations in which a supposedly difficult task became easier the longer you worked at it. There have already been such situations in your life, right? Either the big hoopla was over after only 2 minutes when you realized that it's possible, or you already got used to something after a few weeks or months, so that all the initial difficulties were relieved by the routine. Often the question of the right beginning is related to other problems, like insecurity, striving for perfection, lack of ideas due to a lack of motivation, and so on. In fact, it is confirmed that the longer you pursue something, the simpler it becomes. In this sense, you can have even the worst chaos in front of you, but you will make a good start, as long as you *do* just start. Grab one part of the task and get started! Everything else will come with time. Sure, you will have to rework and correct due to the lack of a plan in the beginning, but this will be easier in the end once you have the full overview of the entire task.

Task 5

Think of at least one of the tasks that you are not at all comfortable with. On a sheet of paper, write down all the subtasks that it involves. Now write down all the points that you have to accomplish in the subtasks, if a further subdivision is possible. At the end, look at your list and mark with a check mark the subtasks that give you an idea of how to get started right away. Maybe you even really feel like doing some of the subtasks? Do this exercise for as many tasks as you can that you would otherwise put off. Each task broken down into subtasks, or other smaller items, will give you more opportunities to find a good starting point.

The exercise is as simple as it is ingenious: On the one hand, you subdivide the task and set milestones. On the other hand, you show yourself the many individual steps. With an overview of the individual steps, you can even work through the subtasks crosswise without order if that helps you at first. Feel free to start at the end if you like this subtask. It is your free decision. In the course of this subdivision of the often postponed task, you may even find that the task has many aspects in its individual subtasks that you like.

Now to come to the last big trump card of this subdivision strategy: By successfully accomplishing many subtasks, a synergy effect occurs. What does a large whole, such as the task in front of you, consist of? It consists of several individual smaller parts! These parts have to be connected, which requires synergy. Now you are completely on the winning track because the more sub-tasks you complete, the more the synergies will have their effect. So, you will become better and better able to cope with the whole task. With this in mind, may I once again remind you of Fynn Kliemann's words, "Problems become more comfortable later and don't matter afterwards."

In the same way, later on the tasks become more comfortable for you, until they are unimportant afterwards, because you have all the necessary tricks up your sleeve and the whole task is no longer a problem. But to get this far, you need a smart start. Pick one of the many subtasks and just do it. Everything else will come by itself. Start with the subtask where you make fast progress.

The most important things in a nutshell

> ➤ If you visualize how happy you will be after completing your duty, your motivation will increase. Use your imagination. Focus on the positive emotions you will have after completing the task. Think back to the moments when you were relieved after completing an unpleasant task. **In retrospect, you will always be proud!**

➤ Perfectionism in its official definition of faultlessness and flawlessness is not attainable. Moreover, perfectionism that consists only of meeting easy challenges is less admirable. If instead you set progress as your goal, you will lose fear of the task and expand your competencies.

➤ Difficult tasks are best tackled with a clear plan. If rushed, the risk of poorly performing the task or failing altogether is great. A plan with breaks and stages for completing the task is better.

➤ When the day begins and productivity is at its highest, you ideally start with the unpleasant and deferred duty. Your resources are greatest at the beginning of the day and encourage discipline.

➤ It often turns out that if an unwanted task is done consistently for a while, it's not as hard as you thought after all. That's why it's helpful to start in the first place. If there is no plan yet, just start with the easiest part of the unpleasant task. Once the beginning is done, the more you do it, the more the other problems will fade away.

Concept 2 | Self-efficacy: Conviction of success

This chapter is useful for people who tend to put off tasks due to doubts about their capacity to succeed. You have to work on increasing your self-efficacy. In addition to being useful for people who suffer from generally low self-confidence, this chapter is also great for perfectionists. Those who don't tackle tasks, because they doubt, they can live up to their personal idea of perfection, need more confidence. But a lack of self-efficacy can also occur in even the most confident and competent individuals. Because confident individuals with expertise in the task have little doubt in themselves, the only possible causes of sudden lack of conviction are external, such as an environment that continually emphasizes the negative aspects of an activity. If the devil is painted on the wall, the risk arises that the task which is actually tailor-made will suddenly be postponed due to doubts.

Lack of self-confidence.

Lack of conviction.

Negative environment.

These and other hindrances must be dealt with in order to increase the likelihood of performing a task. However, this chapter is not only about execution. Your goal is to accomplish the task as convincingly as possible. But how is it possible to activate conviction of success and thus high self-efficacy in the face of several negative influences?

The easiest way is to have your own positive experiences. Clearly, if you've already seen that you were capable of something before, you'll have a greater conviction that you can do it again. The more often this happens, the more unshakable your conviction becomes. If you have successfully performed a task hundreds or thousands of times (by the way, these numbers are absolutely realistic with respect to some tasks) then no one will be able to take away your conviction in a hurry. Your belief in success will be huge. Your self-efficacy will eventually be at a high level.

But what happens when one's own experience is lacking? Especially new challenges present uncertainties to people with self-doubt or a negative personal environment. If you have to manage something new or lack positive experiences, then you need methods. This chapter contains 4 methods with corresponding exercises for you to do.

Method #1: Learn from the model

Model learning according to the psychologist Bandura is known under various names: Imitation learning, model learning, observation learning and more. In some cases, distinctions can be made between these terms, but they are not relevant for this guidebook.

In model learning, an existing model is used to learn from. The model does not have to be present. Videos, stories, news articles, newspaper articles and other sources are great for this purpose. You achieve the greatest effectiveness with the best learning process when you watch videos. Because videos show you moving pictures in which you gain processes, positive emotions and numerous other impressions that make it easier for you to become enthusiastic about the model. Model learning can take place in both positive and negative ways. If you look at it in the words of Karl Valentin, "We don't need to educate our children, they imitate everything we do anyway." It is clear that children especially learn through this medium. Copying parents has produced many a child who adopted the same inhibitions for example – this is model learning with a negative effect. Conversely, there were plenty of children who learned their parents' discipline partly through a strict upbringing and partly through their own observations.

Successful model learning works best when the tasks are simple. Learning to skate for example, without hands-on practice is impossible. On the other hand, there are less complex things like hammering nails into the wall and creating an outline for a term paper. All these things can be learned well using a model. It must be ensured that there are recordings of the model. Without video recordings or at least texts model learning it just doesn't work.

The great thing is that you can find plenty of video material to help you learn how to stop procrastination on YouTube – The most popular social network for videos doesn't miss a topic. There are two ways to find the right videos: Either you enter the search term "*stopping procrastination*" or other closely related search terms, or you directly enter the task you want to perform. In connection with this, it is important that you enter this task in such a way that YouTube suggests videos with instructions: So not "*stop early rising*", but rather "*early rising tips*" or "*early rising tutorial*" would be optimal. For some topics you will have to search longer, for others shorter. But you will definitely find models as you try. Also, use the power of feature films and series: If you have a popular series or movie character who can serve as a model against procrastination, watch him/her often!

We learned in the first chapter that lack of conviction about the occurrence of personal success is one of the main causes of procrastination. Perfectionists are also affected by this. This lack of conviction is called low self-efficacy. Self-efficacy can be developed by watching people accomplish a task. This works best when you have a positive or neutral attitude toward the person in question and the person is accomplishing the task under the same or worse conditions than you. An example of this I suppose would be to watch a video on social media of a person doing weight training without hands. So, what excuses are there now for not starting to exercise? Certainly not the excuse that you yourself cannot succeed. A great example that can be useful in any context is Stephen Hawking. Abundant video footage, documentary films, written records and various impressions of people around the world serve as models that show how a person confined to a wheelchair from his young adulthood, and increasingly limited in speech, became one of the most important scientists of our time; as well as rich and famous worldwide. After these examples, what excuse is there for you to put off doing anything at all? Ideally, look for models who start out in the worst possible conditions, but still accomplish the tasks you are resisting.

Phases of model learning

Model learning consists of 4 phases. An important part of it is the reinforcement and motivation processes, both during the execution and/or afterwards. In Bandura's view, learning is not a reaction to the environment (e.g., one observes an event and realizes that one needs to learn about it), but an active process of observation. This means that one observes a particular performance in others and decides to acquire it. Model learning can also be passive, in that observations are made without wanting to learn a thing. Then, a latent knowledge develops anyway; that is, a knowledge that is available but is not called up because one's own readiness for it is lacking. You should not lack readiness, after all it would be better to eliminate the postponement voluntarily and with a willingness to learn.

> ➤ Phase 1 – Acquisition phase: In this phase, you focus closely on the model. What it does, how it does it, and how it motivates itself is carefully observed. The greater your willingness to learn and the stronger your will to stop procrastination, the more attentive you will be.

> ➤ Phase 2 – Retention processes: Store the observed behavior as well as possible in your mind. The more of the behavior you retain and the more it is rooted in your mind, the more likely you are to recall what you have learned.

> ➤ Phase 3 – Reproduction processes: You imitate the behavior. Either you do it for practice or directly in the situation. Based on the retention processes, the behavior of the model is reproduced, whereby even small steps (e.g., the completion of a part of the postponed task) are purposeful.

➤ Phase 4 – Execution phase with reinforcement and motivation processes: Reinforcement and motivation to practice what has been learned (e.g., due to motivating words from other people or self-praise) creates an incentive to implement what has been learned on a regular or sustained basis.

Model learning is not the same as finding and observing a role model. It does include this step, but it consists of several other points. You notice in every detail that it is a psychological model. From this type of professional psychological model, you are very likely to achieve great results. Keep in mind the important points that model learning teaches you in addition to finding and observing a model: attention, memorization, reinforcement, motivation. These are all important parts of the big picture.

Task 1

With all the important clues, now for every single task you put off, find at least one model that does it better. If you only put off one task, you only need one model. If you have several different tasks, you will have more work to do because you will have to look for more models. Watch the model in as many videos as possible. Make sure it starts in about the exact same condition with the exact same challenges or in worse condition so the observations catch your attention. Write down all the things the model does correctly. By writing them down and reading them regularly, you will better remember the means by which the model, and presumably you, can fight internal resistance. Set small rewards to help motivate and reinforce the process. Dedicate yourself to working on the model for each postponed task every day for at least a week. Learn from the model, implement it, and see how it helps you.

Motivation is the key

Motivation determines whether model learning really moves you forward, or rather falls into the category of *latent knowledge*. Latent knowledge means that you've probably learned something, but it's not completely getting through to you. You lack the incentives to put the knowledge into action. For you, this would mean that the task would remain in procrastination and no improvement would occur. A reason for lack of motivation is given when the model starts under more favorable conditions. Model learning degenerates into a joke when you learn from a model who has mastered a task perfectly anyway. For a person who was in the armed forces for 20 years, had to get up at 5 a.m. every day and do morning sports, getting up early is a cinch. Often the problem with such models is that your inhibitions cannot be understood and the advice has no effect.

> ➢ **Lesson 1 for more motivation on the model**: Great motivation is ensured through identification. The better you can identify with a model, the easier it is for you to develop the motivation to implement what you have learned in the model.

Further information about the model is an influence on motivation that should not be underestimated. If, for example, you find out that the career person you chose as your model achieved all his professional goals, but was lonely and had a failed family life, your conviction and motivation will crumble. Such models are not helpful for model learning, but there is another use for them: Using these models, who subordinated their family life to their career or prioritized it in a different context to the detriment of other desires, you learn better how to decide whether your goals are right: How big is the benefit of the task? Is procrastination appropriate, or logical; should I abandon the task? (See: Chapter 1)

On to the actual text: What should be expressed is the importance of the model's other career. If the model became satisfied by performing the task and had a fulfilling life or a good reward for performing it, you will gain a greater conviction and motivation to do the same.

> **Lesson 2 for more motivation on the model**: Prefer models that, in addition to the successful execution of a duty, have also been able to profit from the execution in the long term. In this way, you will promote the reinforcement process in the execution.

Notice

Model learning can also be done the other way around. By using a model to see how much something is hurting you, you do everything you can to make it better. For example, the children of alcoholics experience it in an extreme way when they suddenly step into their parent's urine on the way to the toilet because the parent *couldn't hit*. Violence as a result of alcohol consumption, accidents and other radical experiences also leave such an impression that the negative model leads to positive behavior. Therefore, in conversations with the children of alcoholics, it can often be seen that they have not touched a drop of alcohol until later adulthood because of the negative model in the parental home. In this sense, it proves to be an interesting approach to choose a negative model. If you're tough, you'll choose an extreme model to show you exactly how serious the situation is. Basically, positive models are more purposeful.

Either radicality works in model learning or it turns into the opposite. Therefore, it is best to always start with models that serve as a moderate example. If these examples do not show any effect, then you can gladly change to a more radical model. Each person is his or her own best teacher. Be brave in exploring the models and discover the right one for you. In the beginning, don't be intimidated by a model that is too strict.

> **Lesson 3 for more motivation from the model**: The discipline, consistency, and other skills that the model teaches you should not be discouraged by the fact that they are difficult for you to implement at first. Choose a model that you can keep up with.

Method #2: Trick your body

Albert Bandura's observation that physiological states are a source of self-efficacy expectancy leads us to the second method. Physiology describes functions and processes in the body. Physiological processes always take place in connection with the expectations of a task. Some are so deeply hidden in the human being that we cannot trick the body when they occur. An example of this is hormone releases that cause us to look at a task with strong dislike or feel stress at the thought of it. As a result, we may put it off. As mentioned, the body cannot be tricked in these situations – or can it?

In this method #2, processes are presented where we *can* trick the body after all. These include increased heart palpitations, tremors, weak knees, sweating (especially wet hands) and similar symptoms that you can feel and identify directly. So Method 2 is about obvious and usually outwardly recognizable signals from your body. Your body gives off these signals in response to something. It is likely that your body is giving off these signals because it is feeling discomfort in thinking about an upcoming unwanted task.

The above examples of physiological states, i.e. increased heart palpitations, etc., you have already experienced in your life in numerous situations. Certainly, these symptoms do not occur only at the thought of an unwanted task. They also manifest when you have something positive coming up. You realize that the same physical processes that occur when you think of an unwanted task can also manifest when you have positive things coming up. And another thing: How many uncertain, difficult or dicey situations in which you had sweaty palms beforehand have ended positively for you in the end?

So, you have at least 2 anchors with the help of which you can trick your body: On the one hand, you can occupy the physiological states with positive emotions based on your positive experiences; on the other hand, you can defuse the physiological states with positive experiences in negative situations. *Anchor* is the keyword here, which leads you directly to practice with another task.

In Neurolinguistic Programming (NLP) there is a method called anchoring. It was created to evoke positive resources in one's own body in negative or difficult situations, virtually at the push of a button. NLP itself is a collection of psychological strategies, methods, and procedures that were assembled in the 1970s by John Grinder and Richard Bandler through observing the most successful psychotherapists. Although some core theses have since been disproved, NLP is used in diverse fields for a wide variety of purposes. Whatever keeps you from performing a task – whether fear, striving for perfection, lack of attractiveness of the task, negative experiences in previous attempts etc. – NLP provides ways and means to overcome the challenge. One of the methods in NLP that can be used most flexibly to solve various problems is anchoring. The basic idea behind anchoring is that whenever you get into the situation where you don't feel like doing the task or are afraid of doing it and are putting it off, you set the anchor to evoke a different mood in you. This is because during your exercises you condition yourself to feel positive by using the anchor.

Task 2

Anchor. Choose the physiological state (trembling, increased palpitations, etc.) that you experience when confronted with the unwanted task. Think of the many instances with positive outcomes where you felt the same physiological state. Close your eyes and think carefully about each situation, focusing on the positive moments. *Feel* those moments. Now comes the important part: set an anchor before this exercise. An anchor should always be unobtrusive. You can discreetly and quietly snap your fingers, tighten your toes or briefly blink your eyes. The important thing is that the anchor does not attract attention. Because that way it can always be used. By setting the anchor you enter into your positive perception of the respective physiological state. Practice this anchor several times a day for a few minutes each time for several weeks.

Practice makes perfect because it produces the intended conditioning. When you get into the habit of thinking positively during each physiological state, an automatism develops in the brain. Automatisms are ingrained in the brain and simplify our daily routines. There are both positive and negative automatisms. A negative automatism is, at the upcoming thought of the task at hand, to hear a palpitation, to get anxious and to postpone the task. A positive automatism is to hear heart palpitations at the arising thought of the upcoming task, to anchor the positive feeling of anticipation based on positive experiences with heart palpitations in your life, to look at the task with more confidence and maybe even to completely accomplish it on the first try.

Finally, it should be noted that you can trick your body with many positive emotions. There is no physiological state that cannot be filled with positive emotions based on your past experiences. Here are some examples:

➢ Sweaty hands: Nervousness before the interview, but where you got the job absolutely convincingly and with ease.
➢ Shiver: Cold during the trip to Antarctica, which is a highlight of your life due to the company of family and/or best friends and many sights you saw.
➢ Weak knees: Insecurity before an important performance in front of an audience, for which there was an incredible amount of praise and admiration afterwards.

These ideas are just to inspire you. You will find plenty of positive emotions in your life that you can anchor. The more successfully you master anchoring, the stronger you will anchor the positive emotions, even in the most difficult situations when the respective physiological state occurs. This will subconsciously increase your expectation towards the task, strengthen your confidence, and thus, contribute to a higher self-efficacy.

Method #3: Let other people convince you

One more Bandura, then it's over. The psychologist cites social persuasion as a source of self-efficacy. According to Bandura, social persuasion leads to more confidence in one's own abilities. Further, the thesis put forth in this guidebook holds true, that contact with fellow human beings is helpful, even when confidence in one's own abilities is present, but drive is lacking. Other people can have a far-reaching effect on your actions.

Sympathies and trust: Did you already experience having sympathy for that one person you wanted to impress at all costs? If you did it wrong you pretended, but at least you overcame your mistake, which led to actions that you would otherwise not have performed. If you did it right, then the person served as an initiator for you to question yourself and get better. People you trust are most likely to have this effect because several years of intense relationship, leads to paying attention to each other's words. Consequently, these types of friends are able to cause great changes for the positive in oneself.

<u>Intelligence:</u> It doesn't always have to be years of relation-
ships. Sometimes just one intelligent person who sounds convincing and argues sensibly is enough to convince you of the need for
a change in action. These *bus stop acquaintances*, which sometimes
last no longer than 5 minutes, and after which there is never a
reunion, can give you numerous insights and make you believe in
yourself.

<u>Realism:</u> For persuasion by other people to work, it is also
important to be realistic. A person who promises you the blue of
heaven is not your key against procrastination. More effective are
people who have successfully helped you in life as often as possible. "*Never change a winning team*," as the saying goes – so why
shouldn't it work again with the same person who has helped you
get on a successful path before? Above all, seek out contact with
people who know how to build you up. A rock in the wall is often
your parents, partners or spouses, even children, if they are adult
enough. Good friends should not be ignored either.

People with real-life help records who have helped you more
than once are a good place to start. Realism and good success rates
in previous conversations, gives weight to the words, which is why
you will be all the more convinced. It is similar to the existence of
something: if the existence is uncertain and no one shows you it,
you are unlikely to be convinced of its existence. But if the person
puts the thing on the table for you, you will be fully convinced.
Think carefully about the people who have always presented your
strengths to you in black and white and never let you even begin
to doubt them. They motivate you the best.

Success and competence: Success and competence often prove a person right. People who have, themselves, been successful in the matter you are resisting, and/or have competencies to show in this regard, are more credible. If a man stands in front of your door and pretends to be a policeman, would you have him show you his badge, or grant entry at the drop of a hat? Let people show you their "*badge*" so that they can convince you best. Professionals in the subject areas that relate to your deferred task are helpful. Speaking of model learning: Real people from your environment that you can touch and talk to are also models. This is where you are most likely to get individually focused recommendations that will help you overcome your problem. You can hardly find better models!

The point of this third method is to put together an environment that helps you, not one that slows you down. A negative environment is a common cause of procrastination. If all you hear around you is that you shouldn't do something or that you're incapable of doing something, you'll eventually be forced to believe it yourself. You will now learn how to create a conducive environment in 3 simple steps. Keep in mind that a positive environment will help you in all aspects of life and not only in stopping procrastination.

Step 1: What is generally right, what is generally wrong?

Of course, no human being is inherently wrong. Everyone is made up of both positive and negative qualities. Also, people change. So, this first step is not meant to make you accuse or break up with certain people. It is only to point out which person is wrong company for you at a given moment. It is not meant to be disparaging. Imagine, for example, that you and your best friend share a number of common interests. However, your friend knows absolutely nothing about ice hockey and is not interested in it, whereas you are a passionate ice hockey fan and player. Because he is your best friend, he can be moved to visit your games every now and then, even though it wouldn't be a suitable permanent program. But you have other friends who are interested in field hockey. They like to talk about hockey generally, and they also like to watch your games. The bottom line is that we have to admit that your best friend is not the right person to talk to in the context of ice hockey and is not the right company in your hockey related goals. This does not devalue him at all, because after all he is competent in other things and invaluable for your general environment.

And here lies the important point, that you yourself carry a share of responsibility in keeping your environment positive: You cannot expect to receive approval and to enhance your abilities when you talk to others about the wrong things. It is true that you can sound out interests here and there and possibly inspire people to try something new, just as they are probably trying to do with you. But if, after a few attempts, your interests don't align, then it makes no sense in continuing to exchange views. You run the risk that even your best friends and family will not correctly assess your skills if they have no idea about the subject.

Task 3

Think about how it could be if you often seek advice from the wrong people in your circle of acquaintances. In this context, *wrong* means that they are unable to give you appropriate advice due to a lack of experience, lack of expertise, and/or lack of interest in the topic. If this is the case for you, which people should you turn to more regularly that have more expertise in the respective area?

The problem with people who are not knowledgeable in a field is that they will usually give you the wrong advice. Because they don't know the subject well, they may try to play it safe. *Playing it safe* usually means restraint. Restraint, in turn, leads to less activity. Less activity may go hand in hand with procrastination. So your goal in conversations should be to regularly choose topics that match your interviewees' skills and experience over the long term. Then you'll be more likely to get realistic and credible motivation that places your strengths in the right context and moves you forward. So, in general, the right thing to do always involves mutual competencies in the situation at hand.

Step 2: Which people do you need in your environment?

Again, a note at the outset: This step in no way dictates how you should compose your environment. It is not based on any stigmatization or one-sided characterization of people. Every person is more than his 1 or 2 competences. Every person is capable of disappointing even in his or her greatest field of expertise, or of surprising all along the line despite a supposed lack of competence. People's individualism knows hardly any limits, which is why every person in your environment – as well as yourself – deserves to be heard. But one thing cannot be denied: Somewhere in our subconscious, it plays out that some advice from certain people becomes particularly deeply ingrained, while certain advice from other people doesn't even make it into the top 100. The reason for this is that some people have certain qualities or preferences that make them particularly heard. Let's start from your deferred tasks: What you definitely need are people who can help you in terms of procrastination because they bring certain qualities to the table. This doesn't mean (!) that all other people in your environment are unimportant. So, at this point, the case is purely made for expanding your environment, not for shrinking it. Which companions do you need for your *"mission against procrastination"*?

> Connoisseur: This refers to the people who have always succeeded in boosting your confidence. Who has a high level of persuasiveness? Who has almost always been able to inspire you?

> Realists: Realism creates logic. Logic creates conviction. Conviction creates opportunity for success. Chance of success creates self-efficacy. If you have people around you who give you realistic arguments for good chances of success, you will develop more willingness to accomplish the task at hand.

> Experienced: These people have experience with the task you are resisting. They have performed the task themselves or have observed it several times in other people. You are guaranteed helpful tips on how to do it and how to stick with it from the experienced ones.

> Models: Basically, like the experienced ones, only with the advantage that they were in the same, a comparable or an even more adverse situation than you when performing

the task. The degree of identification with these people is high.

➤ Theorist: Unlike the *experienced* and *models*, these people have a theoretical knowledge of the task you are facing. Complications can arise, especially with tasks that have a high practical relevance. A lower credibility towards these people can creep into your own subconscious. Nevertheless, good tips are possible. For tasks with a theoretical reference, the theorists are ideal.

➤ Drill Sergeant: These people do not necessarily have to have theoretical or practical knowledge. They do not have to be experienced or good models in relation to the task. Realism is not necessarily their strong point. And most of the time they don't know you anyway. These are simply people who are highly disciplined in everything they do. Likewise, they always demand the maximum from their environment. They are doers who often lack interpersonal skills. But every now and then, a spark of their almost pathological obsession will jump out at you. Important: Too much companionship to these individuals can be counterproductive. At worst, it will cause you to overexert yourself. So, it's best to use drill sergeants when you're at risk of backsliding after initial consistency. Ideally, they will give you a powerful push in the right direction.

Task 4

You don't have to have each of these or similar types of people in your environment. It is enough if 3 of these types are present and have a certain effect on you. Try to find out how often you need contact with these people and which of these types of people are most important to you. Then it is likely that you will find the support you were hoping for in these people, who will put you in a positive mood and convince you of your qualities – or drill you from time to time so that you can convince yourself of your qualities.

Step 3: Negative environment – does such a thing even exist?

In the first step, we found out that it is partly due to your perceptions and decisions whether an environment is negative. By choosing the right topics, you can let the people around you give you a positive feeling and in turn motivate other people in the best possible way. The latter is also important, after all, relationships are based on mutual added value and mutual sympathy: not only should you be motivated, but you should also motivate others.

Another part of whether an environment is negative or not, however, is far beyond your control. There are people who primarily look negatively at things. For some, this almost degenerates into a disease: Almost everywhere disadvantages are seen, pessimism outshines any other thoughts. Sometimes the pessimism in these people is temporary, because they are going through a bad phase. If they are good friends, people important to you or good people in general, it is important not to turn away from them. Stand by them and be their pastor as long as it does not burden you. Because only if you help other people in their predicaments, can you expect the same from them. Especially if you know the negative thinkers from their positive side as well, it is worthwhile to remain loyal to these contacts and help them back on the right track. If you notice that negative thinking is affecting you too much, then the time is ripe to step back for a while. That being said, and this is not meant to sound macabre, these individuals lend themselves to negative model learning. You see how bad negative thinking can be, and you do better yourself. Even if their negative thoughts have nothing to do with your deferred duty, they can encourage you to pull yourself together in order to approach life more positively yourself.

Task 5

Do good, and good will happen to you! Look for people in your environment who are important to you or have helped you several times, but are currently in a bad shape. Stand by these people regularly for a while. Try to motivate each other. If you don't get any motivation, don't worry. After all, you are doing an important person a favor, which will improve the mood around you. Eventually, it will pay off.

But what about people who have been thinking negatively for years or decades and have made it their main task to consistently complain about life? If it is true that there are such people in your environment, then you should carefully consider whether the relationship in this form still makes sense. If these people are important to you, then try to help them. But their attitude must change. Because thinking only negatively for years or decades is not a strategy for life. These people are not suitable for negative model learning, because they could harm you. Especially in the case of people to whom you do not have a strong connection, it is advisable to break off contact as quickly as possible if only negative things are permanently conveyed.

Why does this guidebook advise these radical upheavals? Apart from the fact that you may have had to experience how stressful it is to deal with their problems and negative beliefs, there is a scientifically proven risk of contagion. The keyword here is the so-called mirror neurons in our brain. When in the frequent company of people who think negatively, we can unintentionally adapt their way of thinking.

My experience

Here I can report from the other perspective. I was not negatively influenced by merciless pessimists but was rather myself the merciless pessimist who negatively influenced the people around me. For a long time I did not understand this. So when, conspicuously, many people from my circle of friends stopped contacting me, I was astonished. Only over time, as I transformed myself into an optimist through reading books about success and increasing my own success, did I understand what a burden I must have been to other people. So, I know first-hand that pessimists are not beneficial to your environment.

The most important things in a nutshell

> ➤ A strong sense of self-efficacy gives you conviction, and confidence in your abilities. You can best strengthen your self-efficacy by learning from the model, tricking your body and a positive social environment.

> ➤ Learning from a model is nothing more than learning from role models. These role models can come from reading or video material or be people in your environment.

The important thing is that they are in a situation that is as comparable as possible to yours.

➢ You trick your body, by using anchoring techniques to change its negative reactions to the postponed task, with positive emotions, and memories. *"My heart was pounding so hard the last time I lifted the trophy at the Junior Championships and celebrated the greatest success of my youth!"* Program this mindset firmly into your thoughts through exercise, and more positive associations are likely to precede the unwanted task, encouraging you to perform it.

➢ An all-positive or all-negative environment does not exist. No person is simply bad or good. You should judge things depending on specific situations and topics of conversation. In connection with your task, set up an environment that encourages you.

Concept 3 | Self-control: Defying and focusing on impulses

Self-control can be defined in many ways. People are in control when they don't immediately flare up when someone criticizes them or upsets them in some way. When it comes to performing tasks, those who do not allow themselves to be distracted are considered to have good self-control or to be disciplined.

Discipline, self-control related to performing tasks, and self-control related to reactions are all about resisting emotions. External stimulus lead to emotional reactions, which are either automated, mentally controlled or a mixture of both. The goal of this chapter is to help you control your emotions. Longing to give in to distraction, aversion to the task, anger at a person who stands in the way of completing the task – all of these should become a thing of the past.

But how do you switch off or reduce your own emotions when humans are emotional beings? Brain research shows that the limbic system reacts first to external stimuli. Emotions form in the limbic system in the neocortex. This means that, no matter what we think, emotions always come first. Only subsequent activity in other regions of the brain makes it possible for us to weigh our actions.

Since you can't turn off your emotions, control becomes even more important. This chapter shows you how to create automatisms that will slow down the emotional effect when a negative impulse occurs. In the long term, this approach will help you to act and react in a more controlled, deliberate and goal-oriented manner, not only with regard to procrastination, but also to life in general.

Before you work on the long-term aspects of self-control in Step 3 of this chapter, you'll get some short-term *first aid* in the first 2 steps. These short-term steps, combined with long-term practice, will help you gain more over all self-control.

Step #1: Ideal conditions as a basis

Depending on which task you want to pursue, there are specific ideal conditions. Tasks that are theoretical in nature for example take place in a quiet environment which helps with concentration – less distraction means fewer impulses. Fewer impulses makes for easier self-control. But not all tasks take place in a quiet environment. For example, sports at the gym, where the environment tends to be noisy. Or family obligations where small children are present. Again, it can get noisy and hectic. A person who has little ability to cope with the high activity level of children will tend to react impulsively in one way or another.

Now ask yourself what is more likely: that you will learn to control the impulses, which are firmly anchored in your character, through methods, *or* that you will have greater self-control by creating ideal conditions that counteract impulses? The answer is more likely the latter. The reason for this is that in the first scenario, you have to fight against a part of your character, whereas in the second scenario you are simply preventing it from being triggered.

Think of it like a protective wall that wouldn't be able to withstand an onslaught, so you build an additional wall to reinforce it. Or maybe you know people who are sensitive to certain issues. It is just smarter not to bring up the subject that triggers them rather than triggering them and then trying to deal with their emotions. Another example, specifically related to procrastination. You know that the ringtone on your smartphone is preventing you from completing a task, so you simply turn off the smartphone.

To build a protective wall against impulses and potential distractions, you must first identify the attackers. Only by precisely naming them can you plan countermeasures. First, choose an ideal place. Taking into account the aesthetics. For example, if unwashed dishes dominate the landscape, this will have a distracting effect. Order and aesthetics are important in helping you combat procrastination, so choose a place that you find visually appealing. Also check if you feel comfortable in your seat, notice if smells are pleasing to you and so on. Listen to sounds; in sports for example, it could be that the music played at the gym doesn't appeal to you, but maybe you can bring your own headphones. When reading, quiet music is more conducive. Every person is different, some don't like studying in libraries or at home because it's too quiet for them. They prefer busier places where things are happening. How you get into your flow is up to you. Just make sure you're in a place that doesn't make you put off the task due to unwanted music, an uncomfortable seat, or other such factors – conjure up a place that you really like.

Conclusion: Choose a place that ideally combines suitability for the task and your well-being. By choosing an appropriate place, you do not even have to identify the triggers of procrastination in the first step, because the probability of their occurrence is reduced by your choice.

My experience

How individual each person is evident in my preferences: When I sit at home in silence and comfort, I can hardly focus. I prefer to work in places where there is movement. Cafés are ideal for me. I also enjoy working in the waiting area of the gym from time to time. Basically, I have no problems with noise at work. When something is going on, it increases my creativity. So have the courage to choose your place with a certain stubbornness and really listen to what helps you perform the task; even if it seems absurd to others.

Step #2: Identify triggers for procrastination and determine countermeasures

Here we focus on the small triggers that could occur despite having chosen the optimal place to do the task in. Digital devices play a big role in distracting us. The problem is that they have become a habit. Even when we set the goal of not using them while performing our task, reaching for the smartphone is automatic. It is the automatisms that take hold.

Other smaller triggers to consider besides digital devices are dietary related. For example, people who use sweets as a kind of *compensation*, but end up with belly aches and downers, or certain people in the environment can be distracting, like work colleagues who pull you away from a task all the time.

Conclusion: Triggers exist that are location-independent. Smartphones are the most common example. People can also take on the role of negative impulses, discouraging you from completing a task and causing procrastination. Spotting these subtle triggers helps determine countermeasures.

Task 1

Now it's time to practice. First, establish one or more environments that make you feel good and are conducive to focus. Then visualize what specific triggers might occur. Write down these triggers so that you can determine countermeasures for each one as you go along.

Now you'll learn how to determine countermeasures. What if you need the procrastination trigger to perform the task? This is exactly the problem with digital devices. Smartphone or laptop, which bring multiple distraction factors through popping messages, calls, media offers and other functions, are usually needed at work. The key question in finding a good solution here is what options are available to limit the range of functions or add features that mitigate the trigger characteristics. An example on the smartphone: WhatsApp is your temptation, but the smartphone is needed for the activity. How do you reconcile doing the activity on the smartphone with resisting the WhatsApp trigger? One solution is available in the smartphone itself, namely to turn off the ringtone. If this is not enough and the brightening screen distracts you when you receive messages, then you can disable the message notification so that the screen does not brighten. Nothing will happen until you check WhatsApp yourself. Also, programs or add-ons with features that minimize distractions can be downloaded for free or purchased for a small price.

Did you know?

There are special apps on the market that can help you with procrastination. They are either programmed with a focus on specific tasks or can be configured individually. *YellingMom* is one example. The app starts making noises as soon as you don't follow up on your task at the required time. The apps usually create impulses through a high "annoyance factor" that obliges you to perform the task.

The case where the source of negative impulses is at the same time necessary for work does not only apply to digital devices. People can also be a similar problem. You may have that one person in your environment who always has a way of keeping you from completing a task. Again, we come to the topic of negative and positive environment, which we already had: You were told why you should create a positive environment and how to do it. Let's say you can't avoid the disruptive person because they are necessary to perform the task. Such scenarios occur especially when good and bad students are put together in group work. In our example, the bad students distract the good ones. Simply excluding them is not an option. Similar cases can occur for adults. A solution is difficult to find. Radical countermeasures would be to blackmail or force a person to cooperate and stop interfering with the task. Less radical, but uncertain in terms of effectiveness, would be telling the teacher.

Countermeasures for triggers: Not always an easy thing to do that sometimes requires resourcefulness. The more important the task, the less scruples you should show. After all, being blocked from succeeding by a preventable negative influence is incredibly annoying.

Here is an overview of a few possible triggers of negative impulses and countermeasures that minimize the susceptibility to procrastination:

Disruptive factors	Countermeasures
• Loud music • Noise • Distraction through negative words	• Earplugs • Headphones and instrumental music
• People	• Spatial separation
• Animals • Insects	• Protective sprays • Spatial separation • Procurement of external assistance
• Bad odors • Tempting smells (e.g., sweets)	• Change of location • Nose clip • Remedy the cause • Airing

Task 2

As a continuation of Task 1, let's determine countermeasures for your personal triggers. Feel free to use the ideas from the table and previous text and add to them. In the end, you should have a sheet of paper on which your ideal measures are written, which you can use when you are confronted with your negative impulses.

Step #3: Develop long-term self-control

Steps 1 and 2 serve as short-term and situational measures for more self-control. Because this guide is intended to help you as quickly as possible, but the character traits are not quickly changeable, you have first dealt with the external measures. Now you come to the inner measures; that is, what happens inside you and occupies your thoughts when an impulse affects you. If you get the impulses under control like this, you don't even need the first 2 steps.

Now for the procedure, so that you can work on yourself in the best possible way:

> ➢ If you can already control yourself for a short moment without immediately giving in to an impulse. Start at the subchapter titled "*Third*".

> ➢ If you start the task and do it for at least a short time until you postpone it, even though you don't feel like it. In this case you overcome the impulse for a while. Start at the subchapter titled "*Fourth*".

> ➢ If you immediately give in without thinking about it or making an effort to suppress the impulse. Start at subchapter titled "*First*" right at the beginning.

No matter where you place yourself above, start at the recommended step and practice all the steps up to the fifth, and it will help you to develop long-term self-control. The advantage of long-term self-control is that you minimize or even eliminate the effect triggers have on you so that you will rely less on the short-term actions from the first two steps in this chapter. This reduces the overall effort required of you.

First, become aware

In order to work on the solution to a problem, you must first become aware of the problem. When you consider how many people carry around heavy stuff in their subconscious, it becomes clear that not every personal problem is known to the person concerned. Dishonesty towards oneself can be observed quite often. Hiding a problem start with a lie. As an example, we can mention an overweight person who keeps postponing her diet or gives in to the first impulses after a few days: She has heard that there are people who are overweight because of a disease. Since then, she persuades other people that this is the case with her. Others develop understanding and no longer judge her because of her weight. So, she feels secure with her excuse and eventually begins to believe it herself; not necessarily literally, but in a modified form, considering herself not responsible for her weight. This occurs with procrastination as well. If tasks are put off out of fear, but the person does not want to admit his fear, he might find other reasons for putting them off.

Becoming aware of your problems serves as an initiator for long-term changes by ensuring that no further negative impulses develop.

The best way to raise awareness is to look inside, while at the same time asking others how they assess your reasons for procrastinating. Remember the tips on creating a positive environment from the last chapter? The more of the recommended character types you have in your environment, the better they will contribute to a complete picture of your character. A realist who has been friends with you for many years will not mince words in naming the problems clearly. Ask them to give you their honest opinion without shying away from your reaction. Write down the problems that people see with you without judgment.

The other reliable method for identifying your problems is to search within yourself. Nowadays, people hear so much from friends, from superiors, in the media, from newspapers etc. etc. it is really beneficial to simply deal with ourselves more often. All of your unique truths lie within. Becoming *aware* of them is a long process.

The following task will help you even if you think you are aware of all your problems. It is not uncommon for people to live what they think is an ideal life, but there is something inside them that is oppressive. Feel free to use this task on a regular basis in order to be "up to date" with your mental state even after you have eliminated your procrastination.

Task 3

It will be difficult to get into the habit but do it at all costs — journal for at least 15 minutes every night. You don't have to write for the entire time, but you should at least spend that time thinking and getting something down on paper. Some days there will be more writing, others less. That's normal. What do you think about and *how* do you think? Think in a quiet environment and don't let anything distract you that would cloud your concentration. An ideal place is an armchair at the table. You can also lie down on your bed and write while lying down.

Write down in your diary with regards to your day: 1. what happened, 2. what you thought and felt about it, and 3. what caused your feelings in the described situation(s). All 3 steps are necessary, because if you only write down what happened, but don't include your emotions, you will have a log, but not a helpful diary. Keep a diary for 2 weeks before taking stock of whether you are more aware of your problems. Then continue with the exercise for as long as necessary.

You will gain important insights through this inner dialogue as you practice every evening. Be careful that you don't invent "substitute impulses" for putting off the task. In the long run, you will not be able to hide from yourself or lie. You will become aware of your problems and be able to deal with them head on.

Second, use beliefs.

Beliefs are statements that you anchor deeply in your subconscious through repetition. It takes time for their effect to strengthen. It's all a matter of how quickly your brain develops the automatism to cultivate a different thought when confronted with the impulse. In the case of beliefs, you replace a previously negative impulse that encouraged you to abandon the task with a positive impulse that encourages you to get going and keep at it.

Let's first shed some light on what the subconscious is. To this end, think about processes that you know well. Whether it's cooking the same dish, driving a car, or doing your job – there are things you do well even without thinking. The reason that everything works automatically are automatisms. Science has located automatisms partly in the subconscious. Partly, because some scientists deny the existence of a subconscious. If by the term subconscious we mean a place in the brain, the deniers are correct. But if we think of the subconscious as a collection of automated processes and thoughts, as defined, for example, by the science site *Spektrum*, then the deniers are wrong.

The first person who dealt with the subconscious and called it "the unconscious" was Sigmund Freund. His trains of thought are still taken up today and reinterpreted again and again. Today, the unconscious mind stands for all thoughts, feelings, processes, and other things that occur in our brains without thoughtful effort. If you think about how strongly some behavioral tendencies are noticeable in some people, there must be a reason for it, right?

- ➤ If a person always reacts aggressively, it is in his nature.
- ➤ If a person always expresses pessimism, it is in his nature.
- ➤ If a person is incredibly disciplined, it is in his nature.

But these characteristics are not innate. Individuals either acquire them or choose not to. Model learning, which we have talked about, is one reason why people acquire certain behaviors. But behavior can also be acquired through persuasion. If a person has doubts about themselves because of negative experiences and keeps mentally repeating to themselves, "I'm a loser. I'm a loser." the probability increases that this depressing and discouraging thought will become firmly programmed in the subconscious.

Now the connection of all this with procrastination: if a negative reaction to an impulse is firmly anchored in you, which prevents you from performing a task, then reprogramming the subconscious is a key to solving the problem. This is nothing more than taking steps to help you replace existing automatisms in your brain with others. So, if up to now, when you had an impulse, you thought of abandoning the task, now you develop an opposite belief set, such as: "I am staying on the task because the task offers me... (name benefit)."

Task 4

Develop beliefs that make the stimulus unattractive. One or two sentences per belief should be enough. Important rule: do not use negations (e.g., not, none) because the subconscious mind does not perceive them. Clearly state the attractiveness of the task and make the stimulus unattractive. Repeat your belief regularly. It's best to say it in front of a mirror for 5 minutes every morning.

Automatisms are therefore the goal; beliefs are the way to get there. If you practice automatisms by saying beliefs out loud with focus and conviction, you will be better able to resist the initial temptation. After several days or a few weeks of practice, you should be able to suppress, at least temporarily, the impulse that tempts you to procrastinate. This will be the key to a little more self-control, because your first thought from then on will be, "Wait, this impulse is unattractive because the task gives me advantage XY." So, the first resistance is stirring, which is a start on the path to self-control.

Third, set stages, carry out increases

If you are able to defy the negative impulse for a while and perform the task, it is a success. Congratulations on that! Now you will work on increasing the amount of time you defy the impulse. This action helps to toughen you up. If you defy the impulse a little longer each time and do your task, you will be better able to resist the impulse in the long run. Self and impulse control are often mentioned in the same breath as self-discipline. This is because increasing discipline means being able to resist negative impulses more effectively over a longer period of time.

Now let's get practical: You increase your self-control by proceeding in stages. You set a stage up to which you want to persevere without giving in. Then you give in to the impulse. After giving in, you decide whether to resume the task or abandon it completely. Because it depends on the type of task, there are no guidelines here.

Some more information about the stage: If you manage to hold out until the stage you have determined, then a goal has been reached for the time being. After that, you move on to the next goal, namely a longer stage. In order not to overexert yourself, it makes sense to maintain a stage and to reach it a certain number of times.

Let's assume, for example, that you are dissuaded from your plan to drink less alcohol and study in the evening instead, because you are tempted by student life: Stage 1 could be to drink only on the weekends, if you have been doing it more often. After you've managed this for a month, drink only on a weekend day. After this has worked for two months, you increase the stage again to a level you want. The point is to keep increasing the requirements until you reach the level you are aiming for.

Task 5

Determine which stages are realistic and sustainable for you. Consider at what intervals you feel comfortable increasing the demands. Choose a pace that suits you and is encouraging.

You make each stage more attractive to you and increase your discipline when you set rewards. These rewards are given to you whenever you have done everything according to the plan. The rewards, however, should not be allowed to undo your progress. Everything should be coordinated in such a way that it moves you forward.

Another way to increase your discipline is to keep a record of your progress so that you can visualize it or write it down. For this purpose, you can use your diary from the first step. If you have decided to keep a diary for the long term, you will now benefit twice. As you can see from keeping a diary and recording your progress, all the steps in this book are interrelated and have the greatest effect when they are carried out together – ideally in the prescribed order. An alternative to the diary for documenting progress are checklists, visualizations with pictures, and conversations with other people in which you report on your progress. Here you include the environment as an important factor already presented.

Fourth, find the release valve for the pulse

The fourth point of your self-control cure pulls the pin on the effectiveness of the impulse. You have already learned to control the impulse for a time while performing your task. However, one problem that is likely to remain, is that as the task progresses, it continues to push you to give in to the impulse. The trigger of the impulse to procrastinate has its effectiveness: after spending some time on the task, you notice that you feel drawn to give in to the impulse. The initial belief that the impulse is unattractive weakens with the duration of the exercise, because it can no longer be denied that you actually don't want to do the task.

At this point, it is important that you stick with the first 3 steps presented in this chapter and do them regularly. Continue to practice the pronunciation of the beliefs every morning. But how do you manage to improve the effectiveness of your beliefs so that you consistently stick to your task and the impulse no longer feels so strong? The solution is a release valve: for every impulse there is at least one appropriate release valve, which has the advantage of reducing the effectiveness of the impulse because the impulse has already been yielded to by the release valve. An example from anger therapy is sport: the anger impulse is weaker if intensive sport has already been done the day before, because less energy is available. This insight is now to be applied to the procrastination impulses. Subsequently, the determination to perform the task is greater.

Task 6

Consider what valves might be useful for your case. Since release valves can vary widely, the frequency and duration of their use required may vary too. Do you need to use it for over an hour every day, or several times a week for 10 minutes each time? For 2 weeks, try out the release valves that come to mind and see how they best help you release your impulse so that you feel as little urge as possible to give in to the impulse during the task.

Exercise and diligence play a role in the release valves. Impulses that show up as too much energy (e.g., aggression, impatience, restlessness) are usually remedied by exercise. If you have exercised yourself physically and/or mentally properly, your urge to indulge will be less – after all, where is the energy supposed to come from?

Other impulses (e.g., doubts, discouragement) may occur during the course of the exercise when you realize that it is not going according to plan. In this case, it is worthwhile to use a tip from the previous chapters as a release valve: start with the easier part of the postponed task. Then you will see that you are capable of accomplishing the task. Your doubts will be removed.

If you tend to get distracted by electronic devices, the best way to counteract the impulse is to set aside time slots during the day when you allow yourself to use the devices with full abandon. But beyond that, use them only when necessary. In this way, you have used the impulse itself as a release valve, only at a more appropriate time.

Fifth, transfer positive trends

Once you've gotten to the point where you've increased the stages and reduced the effectiveness of the stimulus through dump valves, there are only 2 steps left for you to slowly but surely gain long-term self-control.

1. Keep the program from the first 4 steps: In a sense, what you have done so far in the 4 steps is an adjustment. Adjustments and withdrawals take time. When you think

you're out of the woods, the opposite may be true. In particular, changes made too quickly carry the risk of lack of strength. Therefore, maintain the previous program from steps 1 to 4. If you feel that you have had or are having severe problems, keep the first 4 steps for 6 months. If you have a mild case of procrastination, 3 months should be sufficient.

2. In addition, it is important that you transfer the positive trends. Transferring them means that you will also benefit from them in other areas of your life. Because the more situations you demonstrate self-control in, the more it becomes a new defining character trait. If it comes to the fact that you have changed your character fundamentally to a controlled one, then you do not have to follow the first steps anymore and radiate full control in any situation – an absolute character gain!

Let's assume that you would radiate self-control only with regard to the postponed task: true, this would correspond to your goal of being able to perform the task better without giving attention to the interfering impulses. But if self-control were lacking in all other areas of life, you would be at risk of relapsing. Because at some point you would no longer practice the first 4 steps (journaling, etc.) consistently, and gaps would gradually appear; gaps in which your previous character traits might show through. If, on the other hand, you completely change your character and transfer the self-control you have gained to as many areas of your life as possible, you will expand your new automatisms. The brain gets used to reacting in a controlled manner in more and more situations and to weighing up whether the respective impulses are worth it before giving in. Think about it: In which situation is it not advantageous to weigh things up before making a decision? Only in a few exceptional cases. So make it your trait to be able to defy impulses and temptations in order to be more successful everywhere in life, to stop giving in and to stick to your own goals and dreams.

How do you transfer the positive trends into other areas of your life?

1. Do all the exercises from First to Fourth for other areas of your life! When journaling, stop focusing only on how you deal with and feel about procrastination, and start focusing on other tasks, challenges, and joys of the day. Proceed in this way for all 4 of the previous steps.

2. Start with the simplest challenges! If you want to make your character more controlled beyond procrastination, you should develop goal-oriented beliefs to solve all problems. Preferably start with the items where you find it easier to exercise self-control.

3. Let yourself be tested! If possible, regularly put yourself in situations where your self-control is put to the test. This also means hard cases. Character is defined primarily by behavior in extreme situations; surely you remember the *Teachable Moments* from the introduction to this thesis... Make sure that you have absolute control and that even stronger impulses do not throw you off balance.

The most important things in a nutshell

➢ Before you train your character to be more self-controlled (long-term measures), you provide the ideal conditions to get immediate help against the negative impulses (short-term measures).

➢ Ideal conditions are created by a work location that offers as few distractions as possible. You should also identify the impulses and determine countermeasures that you will play out as soon as the impulses occur.

➢ In parallel, you begin to work on making self-control your trait in the long run.

   o To do this, first keep a diary to become aware of all negative impulses and the effect on your emotions.

   o Formulate and regularly repeat beliefs that are the first automatism to help you not immediately give in to the impulse.

   o Set stages to stay on task longer and longer without procrastination. Increase the stages over time.

   o Find release valves for the emotions that arouse the negative impulses in you, to rob the impulses of their effectiveness.

   o Transfer the benefits of acquired self-control to other areas of life to make self-control your new general trait, which becomes instant and automatic in all contexts.

Concept 4 | Prioritize, relax and decelerate

It is conceivable that you postpone 1 or more tasks because of too many duties. For this reason, it is important to show you another point of view. This view sees the fault not in you, but as a classic phenomenon of today. In this increasingly digitalized and fast-paced world, it can be hard to say "*no*" to the many prospects that present themselves. If you want to take advantage of all the opportunities that come your way as quickly as possible, you may be overextending yourself. Even the most disciplined and competent person would develop a long-term urge to procrastinate in this case.

This chapter provides guidance to help you determine if you have too many burdens. If so, it provides you with ways, means, and guidance to help you better prioritize. You will learn the importance of free spaces, which are a great benefit to your health. With free spaces you will be able relax and decelerate from this digital fast-paced world, in order to recharge your energy. Because one thing is clear: without replenished energy stores, you'll be putting things off more often anyway. A person is only human – an often-forgotten fact in a digitized world.

The more you practice and the better you manage to switch to relaxation mode even in high-stress situations, the busier your schedule will be able to be without having negative effects on your psyche and health. As you can see, if you do everything right, a large amount of duties and tasks is not necessarily bad. But step by step...

Science with a clear opinion

Thanks to the fact that digitization is on everyone's lips as is progresses, it is being well researched. With the effect on the psyche increasingly coming to the fore. *Springer Professional* quoted the following statement by Miriam Goos from the book *CSR and Digitization*:

"The digital age has a major impact on the perception and importance of health in humans. Mental illnesses caused by sensory overload of the brain and by the rapid changes of the digital and globalized world are clearly on the rise in recent years."

Depending on the company, up to 40 digital programs may be used on their work devices. In addition, areas are being digitized that were not previously. For older workers, but equally younger ones with little inclination for digital applications, new challenges are arising all the time. Companies boast about Big Data and a large variety of professional tools, while workers face higher demands as a result. And while the latest technologies such as Artificial Intelligence promise to simplify everyday life for employees, in most cases the time gained is not given to workers.

Digitization – caught between obligations and perspectives?

But digitization doesn't only have negative aspects that over-burden people. It also provides plenty of new opportunities. At which other point in history has it been possible to start your own business without even renting a store or paying for employees, but rather with just a website and some computer programs? The prospects are even more far-reaching. The economy is on an expansion course and digitization is playing a significant role in this, as technology stocks are shooting through the roof. Even companies outside the technology sector can develop business models that are easier to expand and market, thanks to digitization. All of these circumstances mean that more opportunities are open to more groups of people. These opportunities even make themselves felt at an early age, when children can better connect with friends through digital devices like social media. Even young people have the prospect of gaining notoriety and reach through digital means.

All these many opportunities for people of all ages are initially something positive. Because perspectives mean freedom of choice. Freedom of choice means a greater chance to live the life one desires. Pursuing one's desires means striving for happiness. Are these conclusions correct? Partly …

After all, access to many options leads to people being spoiled for choice. And because many things can be done at the same time in a digitalized world, people try to *do* many things at the same time. Yet each additional thing on the daily agenda can be over-whelming and lead to procrastination. With that, the core of the problem is clear and a possible cause for your procrastination comes to light: overemployment. Remember how you learned in the first chapter that procrastination can sometimes be the logical consequence of being overwhelmed and doesn't necessarily have anything to do with personal weakness at all? This is precisely the problem that is becoming increasingly prevalent in the digital age.

In addition to the high pressure that people are already under at work, due to constantly renewed work processes, there are also self-imposed challenges outside of the workplace. All of which adds up until at some point the mind no longer work and people procrastinate.

So, the trick is, in order not to lose oneself in the digitalized world, to choose the *right level* of activity and the *right* activities. The way to do this is through prioritization and the incorporation of breaks into your daily life.

Consequences of technostress

Technostress is a term introduced by psychologist Craig Brod in 1984. It describes the modern illness of not being able to deal correctly with ICT (information and communication technologies). Technological, cognitive and social overload due to ICT thus lead to technostress in affected individuals.

Causes of technostress include multitasking (multiple tasks at the same time), the need to be constantly available, blurring boundaries between work and private life, and being overwhelmed by the complexity of technology. The consequences of technostress are sometimes:

- ➢ Exhaustion
- ➢ Headache
- ➢ Concentration problems
- ➢ Burn-out
- ➢ Anxiety

Are not all these at the same time factors that promote procrastination? Certainly, they are!

Burnout often remains undetected in individuals for a long time. The persons wonder why they feel such a strong lack of drive. They are there, but feel mentally absent. Long periods of sleep and a lack of willpower to complete tasks steal precious time.

Notice

Burnout is one of the worst and most powerful causes of procrastination because it is a mental illness. If you have the symptoms of burnout around the clock and very pronounced, it is only right that you decelerate and go to a specialist. He will determine the reasons for your exhaustion and listlessness. Maybe it's not so bad and you only have a vitamin deficiency, but maybe it's depression.

Whenever the world no longer seems bright and motivating, but rather becomes dark and depressing, especially outside of your duties when performing your favorite activities, going to the doctor is the right thing to do.

The other problems mentioned in the list also raise awareness of how many disadvantages result from being overtaxed with digital technologies, preventing perseverance in our tasks. Despite all of this, there are certain competencies that allow people to cope better with it, one such being a high level of self-efficacy. Author Srivastava (2015) cites this as a criterion for coping better with technostress. A high level of self-efficacy is therefore not only helpful in avoiding procrastination, but also in reducing technostress.

So, if you follow all the advice in this book, you'll kill several birds with one stone. Greater self-efficacy reduces technostress, because you accomplish your tasks better and more effectively. Faster task completion, in turn, means you'll procrastinate less and experience less stress.

Step 1: Priorities come before deceleration

Before you actively contribute to deceleration, you should define your priorities. By setting priorities, you end up with a skillfully crafted task list. Then, wherever there are gaps, you have the essential free space for deceleration. How much free space you need is up to you. Most of the time, it's just a matter of trial and error. You test measures for deceleration and see which work best and when.

Getting priorities right requires answers to several questions:

1. What do you need to live?
2. What do you want in life beyond that?
3. How much freedom do you need?
4. What can/do you do without?
5. How do you decelerate and how does it work?

Question 1: What do you need to live?

First, make a list of things you need to live. Normally, the first things that come to mind are housing, money, food and oxygen. All of which are necessary. Apart from oxygen, everything normally requires money, whether it be a purchased or rented property to live in, electricity, water, or food. And you usually earn money by working.

As long as the money you earn is enough, enter only your job in the list. If you have been having money problems for a long time, you should write that you need your job and also another job *or a* higher salary — after all, you have money problems, and they don't go away by themselves. This is equivalent to the first priority you set for yourself.

Deep needs must also be considered. Companionship, friendship and support would be such needs. Only if you believe that you could live your whole life without family, friendship, companionship, and any kind of support, may you omit these things from the list. And if this is impossible, you should write them down.

Task 1

Proceed as described so far, writing down all the things you need on a piece of paper. Afterwards, check your list to see how the things are related. For example, work gives me money and a place to live, so work comes first and you can cross out the money and the place to live. In this way you shorten the list and have the primary things on it.

Question 2: What do you want beyond that in life?

Life also includes wishes, dreams, goals and other personal desires. It cannot be ruled out that there are people who are perfectly happy with what they already have. Individuals who have a job they love, and their family as a balance are sometimes already satisfied. Again, individuals exist who want to have more. In this regard, you should question yourself.

Do not deceive yourself when you answer this question. As you have already learned, human beings have a lot of potential for self-deception. That's why it's important to keep a diary, even for setting priorities. You keep track of, what otherwise, gets lost in the hustle and bustle of the day. Keeping a diary, combined with open dialogue with other people, will help you uncover what you really want in life. Even in a perfect marriage, the urge for variety can still be an important element for your future. Even in a perfect job, there may be a feeling inside that you want to achieve more, which isn't necessarily possible with your current employer.

What you really want in your life beyond fulfilling your existential needs is an important key to happiness. There is room here for dreams, self-realization, family happiness, the little kitschy moments of life, the "*thrill*", closeness to nature, the desire to travel. Your existential needs (answers to question 1) in combination with your desires and goals (answers to this question 2) define how much freedom you need.

Question 3: How much freedom do you need?

If one were to formulate in a mathematical formula how questions 1 to 3 are related, the formula would be as follows:

$$Day\ (24\ hours)$$
$$= daily\ time\ spent\ for\ existential\ needs\ (x)$$
$$+ daily\ time\ spent\ for\ goals\ and\ desires\ (y)$$
$$+ daily\ time\ spent\ on\ freetime\ (z)$$

So, you have a period of time (x) in which you pursue the activities that fulfill your existential needs. Then there is a period of time (y) that you spend on activities that are related to your desires and goals. Lastly, there would be a period of time (z) that you need for free time. A free time activity that every person needs time for is sleeping. Winged sayings like "You can sleep when you're dead." are sporadically admired by some people, but are by no means sustainable as a philosophy of life. It has been proven that lack of sleep can lead to cardiovascular disease and other serious health ailments. With this in mind, getting enough sleep is a serious matter. Adults are generally advised to get 6 to 8 hours of sleep per day. Follow this advice and you'll be doing your health a lot of good.

"But with 6 to 8 hours of sleep, that's already a third or a quarter of the day sacrificed for free space!" That may be so. But it is this generous period of time for sleep – as defined by nature – that makes it especially clear how important free time is. When it comes to free time, always plan generously. Because once you've accepted binding duties and tasks, it's not always easy to regain that time again later.

Task 2

As a continuation of Task 1, determine in your list the answers to Question 2 from the previous subchapter and Question 3 from this subchapter. Take into account your existential needs and the amount of time required to meet them from the first question. Since all 3 questions are closely related, you should complete the tasks simultaneously. Be honest with yourself. If you notice that the *formula* isn't working because you are imposing too many duties on yourself at once and have hardly any free time, this indicates that your procrastination is the result of excessive demand, rather than weakness of character, lack of discipline, or any other possible causes.

Question 4: What can you do without?

Are there too many tasks on your list and is there too little free time? This is the case if you don't have an hour or 2 during the day to sit back and just laze around. By the way, hobbies like sports don't count as free time if they are associated with pressure to perform. Hobbies must be things that you can enjoy doing leisurely in real free time. Of course, sometimes in life there can be little or no free space for a few weeks, or on certain days. But it must not be all the time, these periods of life should end with a nice break

During free time you shouldn't let yourself be distracted by digital devices. Free time that you spend typing messages, video chatting, or on social media will drain you. Your free time should be like a vacuum that you can use for relaxing activities that spontaneously come to mind.

If there is too little, or too much free time, make adjustments. You may have heard stories of top managers who had plenty of money and suddenly quit their jobs completely because they were dissatisfied with their personal lives. They had been deprived of so much, that in one fell swoop they had nothing, but free time left. This is not a balanced way to approach it. It is far better to work with small, simple adjustments to achieve a better work/life balance, such as:

- ➢ Watch less TV in the evening
- ➢ Consume less digital media
- ➢ Reduce time for social contacts
- ➢ Reduce your workload
- ➢ Work on fewer desires and goals at the same time (realize one first, then start on the other)
- ➢ Get up earlier in the morning (if sleeping beyond 6 to 8 hours)

Task 3

And what about you, what can you do without? Things from this list, or do you have other ideas to add? For your personal situation, write down at least 5 customized items with which you can create more free space.

Question 5: How do you decelerate?

After you have created the rooms, you should occupy them. How you occupy the spaces you made will be revealed to you in the next 2 steps of this chapter after you have completed question 5. We will discover several interesting methods, ranging from Far Eastern concepts to conventional European medicine.

But before we get to this step, it's worth noting that you should regularly evaluate the measures you are implementing: Have you gained more free time? Do you feel greater urge to perform tasks due to increased relaxation time and effectively recharged energy reserves? If this is the case, then everything is going according to plan. Maybe you even have too many free time now. You could consider reducing it slightly to see if you increase productivity and success in other areas.

What to do if you realize that your free time isn't enough, but you can't create more? In this case, we propose 2 useful solutions:

1. **Get help**. Create "assistance" for yourself. Either literally or figuratively. Literally, means hiring an assistant for example. People in positions of high responsibility are often reluctant to relinquish responsibility. They don't want to leave the well-being of their company, child or any other important things in their lives, in other people's hands. Yet there are plenty of examples where delegation was successful. If you choose people well, you have much less to worry about. Figurative assistance could be for example if cooking takes up too much of your time, you could arrange for other people in the household to take over one dish a day. Or you could order food every other day and save yourself time that way.

2. **Increase quality**. By increasing the quality of your free time, you improve its effectiveness. It's no secret that some people can only relax in certain situations. So don't expect all the exercises in the following steps to work for you. Just test what works.

My experience

A clear prioritization plan, similar to the one described here, helped me to realize that I had a combination of several causes for my procrastination. I had a hard time motivating myself and occasionally got distracted by impulses because I had imposed too many duties on myself. In some ways, it was obvious that there were too many duties. But I always said yes because I wanted to prove something to myself, which I still can't understand today. But now I know that it pays to think first and say yes later. These days, besides work, I have a personal project and a hobby too. I enjoy having time for socializing, cooking, and doing nothing too. These are all valuable components of life in my eyes, that I couldn't do without.

Step 2: Simple introduction to deceleration

You probably know a few simple ways to slow yourself down. Lazing around probably being the best example. However, lazing around only works as a method of deceleration as long as nothing is truthfully being done. Anyone who is lazing around, but at the same time is thinking oppressive thoughts is not decelerating at all. In fact, you would be under mental strain that can cause stress and anxiety on a subtle level. If you are thinking about the worries of the day or you are annoyed that a task has been postponed again, then you are not decelerating at all. Fortunately, there are methods that assist you in focusing properly on the moment.

Method 1: "Slow" trends for individual areas of life

The following "slow" trends will help you to properly decelerate. They are possibly inspired by Far Eastern philosophies but have their origin in Europe where they are on their way to becoming well established. One particularly well-known method is *slow food*.

Slow food stands in direct contrast to fast food. Unhealthy fast foods, that many people reach for when they need something in a hurry, are avoided. No time to eat? That's hardly conceivable for followers of slow food. The movement, which began in Italy in the 1980s, believes that enjoyment should be the focus. Enjoyment can only be guaranteed through quality, and quality entails a certain amount of effort and time in the production process. Ecological and regional dishes are in the foreground here. Taste is not invariably defined as a question of subjective taste, but rather, among other things, as a sociocultural issue that should be debated. In the eyes of the representatives of slow food, the trend toward fast food is because more and more people are losing attention to food and no longer taste it properly.

If you have an affinity for delicious food, you may find slow food an excellent option for deceleration. Here is a suggestion for the evening:

➢ Turn off the TV
➢ If you have a partner, cook together. Otherwise cook alone
➢ Make the evening an hour shorter without TV, but spend it together, talking, laughing and reminiscing with home-cooked food and a glass of red wine instead

Whether alone, with friends at a barbecue, or visiting a restaurant, slow food and slow cooking is a sensual way to relax, which can become a great hobby.

Another interesting trend is slow travel. With slow travel, you avoid hotels, airplanes, luxury events and the like, which are usually associated with the perception of deadlines, waiting times and large crowds. Instead, you opt for a form of vacation where you travel with little means. As a result, you're usually close to nature and local people, which at the same time, offers you more authentic insights into your destination. Considering that traveling and vacations are usually meant for recreation, but stress often becomes a big part of it, slow travel seems to be a good solution. If you have noticed so far in your exercises that vacations did not bring the desired relaxation, Slow Travel is made for you!

Feel free to read up on other slow trends on your own. The Internet will provide you with plenty of inspiration. If you want, you can even develop your own slow trends. If it works for you, just give it a try. Theoretically, if you have a lawn that helps you to relax and "let your soul dangle", there's nothing stopping you from "slow mowing" even.

Method 2: Sports, music, art – but without pressure to perform!

Earlier it was mentioned that sport only serves to slow down as long as it is not linked to performance pressure. Because having fun is an important factor in distracting yourself from the thoughts and worries of the day. The same applies to other forms of hobbies, like music or art for example.

If these activities are linked to performance pressure, they should be classified with your goals and desires instead of hobbies and free time, because it is not casual deceleration. This differentiation is important. You should internalize it so that you don't do sports for 5 hours a day and wonder why you still don't manage to relax.

Here are some examples to illustrate the point:

➤ You play soccer in a club. The training times are prescribed, you have to win the games. You have to worry about offside traps and tactical triangles.

➤ You play the piano. Soon you'll be performing at a concert. There are several concerts like this every year, and you always prepare meticulously for them. Performing in front of large crowds makes you uncomfortable.

➤ With your craft skills, you have the goal of being accepted into a gifted course to develop with others at your level. Although only a hobby, you must meet requirements for admission and perform well to remain part of the course after admission.

How are you supposed to be able to relax in these scenarios? The stress of work and everyday life is now followed by the stress of the hobby. If you were doing it just for you, it would be different. But under the pressure of having to deliver and meet standards, the activities are demanding.

When sports, music or art is really practiced for relaxation purposes, without performance pressure, then positive effects on the psyche are medically well documented.

A study by Sandra Klaperski and Reinhard Fuchs of the Albert Ludwigs University in Freiburg, using 149 inactive male test subjects, found that lower cortisol levels (cortisol is a stress hormone) and a reduced heart rate were the benefits related to regularly practicing sports.

Scientists from Taiwan studied the benefits of yoga in stress management. People were divided into groups so that one group practiced yoga and another control group remained inactive. The group with yoga practice showed a decrease in stress levels and improved autonomic nervous system function after 6 to 12 weeks.

If at this point you start to lose the connection to procrastination, consider the path you have taken in this step: You have decided for yourself that you procrastinate because you have too many obligations and too little free time. As a result, you have decided to build free time into your daily life for relaxation, and deceleration, as well as to improve your mental state. If you improve your condition, you will be able to perform your duties and tasks much better. So, the mental improvements from exercise are likely to give you an "anti-procrastination kick."

Did you know?

It has long been known that sport acts as a "panacea". An article in *SPIEGEL* tells the story of Joanna Zybon, a running therapist who works in a Berlin correctional facility. She helps those with problems ranging from drug withdrawal to depression to sleep disorders. Sport is used as a multifunctional means of thought therapy. Even to the point where it can have an anxiety-relieving effect.

So there's no doubt that sports are a great way to relax and fill in the gaps in your free time. But can the same findings be applied to music and art? In answer to this question, the *SAGE Institute for Mindfulness and Health,* Berlin, compiled findings on the effect of music from several studies with the following benefits noted:

➢ Influencing brain processes and functions

➢ Influencing breathing, blood pressure, body tension and heart rate

➢ Classical music pieces contribute to calm and relaxation, while favorite music promotes arousal

➢ Reduction of stress when listening to relaxation music (lower cortisol levels in the blood)

➢ Positive effects occur sporadically also with physical complaints when music is listened to

➢ Reduction of depression possible

When you play music, the effects are very likely to increase because you are no longer just listening, but completely immersed. You either have to consider certain breathing techniques while playing or concentrate on the music more closely than when just listening. Also, provided you have a good command of the particular instrument, you can release your emotions through it.

The practical thing about music is that you can combine it with other activities. Listening to music while participating in sports or art is something many people do. Which type of music isn't that important at first, but calm, classical music can add a certain neutrality factor. At once offering a calming effect, while not stimulating personal memories. If you were to listen to the song *Unchained Melody* and think of Patrick Swayze and Demi

Moore making pottery in the classic movie *Ghost*, for example, there would be a distraction. This is not the case with classical music. You can even listen to this music excellently while performing the task that you usually put off. You may find the task easier then.

Method 3: Far Eastern approaches at a glance

What the Far East teaches has absolutely nothing to do with esotericism. Occasionally, the breathing exercises, meditations and mindfulness exercises are done an injustice by being pigeon-holed in this way. People who are not very well informed subsequently doubt their effectiveness. But did you know that numerous Far Eastern methods for relaxation have been reviewed in studies and found to be effective? In the meantime, even European orthodox medicine is opening up to Far Eastern theories.

To prove the benefit of breathing exercises with an example: The *Munich Breathing Therapy Working Group* conducted a pilot project with patients in 2011. Professional breathing therapists did regular breathing exercises with their patients over a certain period of time. The patients' condition improved in terms of clearer psyche, increased sense of satisfaction and decreased anxiety.

Breathing exercises lead to relaxation. Various breathing techniques can be rehearsed, or breathing can be used to support meditation. In meditation, the goal is to focus on the moment. People who have difficulties with this and whose thoughts regularly wander off in the direction of the problems of everyday life can find success by concentrating on their breathing. This is because it creates an anchor that distracts them from their thoughts. Through consistent regular practice, meditation will work better over time, so that the breathing exercises can eventually be omitted.

Task 4

Speaking of the breathing exercises-meditation combo: practice it. Meet this method of relaxation with an open mind. We are not talking about esotericism, but exercises with proven effectiveness. Take a daily window of 10 to 15 minutes to meditate. Sit comfortably in a quiet place. Set an alarm so you don't need to look at the clock and get distracted. Then breathe slowly and concentrate on each breath.

Incidentally, energy drinks and caffeine tablets should rarely be used! Now and then it's okay, but in the context of procrastination, they are counterproductive. They get you so worked up that you tend to stick to the distraction rather than the task at hand. A round of meditation, on the other hand, often provides a focus that lasts for several hours afterwards. So, it makes sense to do the meditation immediately before the task you're putting off, or as close to it as possible. Then your focus is sharpened for the execution without the need for energy drinks.

Qigong, Tai-Chi and Shiatsu are also great relaxation exercise, that have become part of the official relaxation and activity programs in the executive suites of several large companies, as reported by *WirtschaftsWoche*. If you're open to these techniques, check out the numerous videos available on YouTube. Find one that you're comfortable with and try it.

Step 3: Permanently establish mindfulness and deceleration

This third step is the supreme discipline. If you master this step, you will be able to keep your mental and physical condition at a good level, even without much free time and with countless duties being accomplished. Of course, you can't do it completely without free time, but you learn to make the most of even the shortest spontaneous breaks.

First, imagine a fairly busy schedule, so full that you have to rush from one appointment to the next. In between, you only have a few minutes free. By establishing mindfulness on a permanent basis, you gain the ability to slow down even in those few minutes. This is not as easy as you might think. Because between two appointments, your thoughts are usually already on the next appointment. Psychiatrist Michael Huppertz sees a big problem here: *"People are always rushing into the future in their thoughts so as not to miss anything. In the process, they miss out on exactly what is really happening right then."*

What if you could at least overcome the tendency to rush? What if you could create distance whenever you wanted to? This would mean that in the 5 minutes between one appointment and the next, you would have no stressful thoughts. You would rather just be in the here and now, relaxing in the midst of the action.

Like much of what you have learned in the previous chapters, lasting mindfulness and relaxation is a long-term practice.

Task 5

The methods from step 2 have helped you learn to *shut down* at specific times. Now it's time to use your favorite techniques to learn to shut down at any time. Get into the habit of always making good use of the small breaks that occur between appointments or tasks. Here are a few examples:

➤ When you eat, eat slowly

➤ When you're not doing anything, breathe consciously

➤ If you're waiting, practice relaxation exercises while you wait

➤ If you relax with music, always have your headphones and a small music player with you. The older Shuffle ipods are great for this because they don't have functions (e.g. Email, SMS) that distract you

The more often you get used to filling the small vacuum in your daily routine with relaxation and focusing on the moment, the better you will succeed. It's all a matter of practice! As time goes on, you should be able to focus on the moment and fill every moment of the day with mindfulness even without the exercises. One useful method is to always pay attention to the little things that surround you. Waiting outside a building can be excellent to link with being close to nature by looking at the green spaces. Or you can simply pay close attention to passersby and how they go about their lives. To conclude, in the words of an actor in the movie *The Peaceful Warrior – Path of the Peaceful Warrior,* "There's always something going on." Every moment offers abundant wonder. You just have to pay attention to it. This provides relaxation and space, even during small windows of time. Allowing subsequent task to be approached with renewed energy.

The most important things in a nutshell

➢ Scientists, psychologists, psychotherapists and professional associations agree that digitalization is creating new opportunities, as well as new challenges. Among the challenges is a new form of stress, called *technostress*.

➢ Too many options exist, which makes it difficult to set priorities. In work, private life and leisure, this can lead to indecisiveness.

➢ Start to determine whether your procrastination is not a logical consequence of being overwhelmed by too many duties. Reduce the duties where possible to create free space for relaxation and deceleration.

➢ Integrate relaxation exercises into your everyday life. Reduce stress by purposefully decelerating with slowing down processes, such as slow food and slow cooking.

➢ Try to use relaxation exercises and other methods that you have practiced for stress reduction, even in random moments of everyday. If you manage to pay attention to your breathing in the waiting room between your work appointment and your doctor's appointment and concentrate your thoughts solely on the moment, you can end up always being relaxed!

Closing words

If this guidebook has taught you one thing, hopefully it is a fair amount of respect for procrastination. It has the potential to take on morbid proportions. It may spread unnoticed like an ulcer and gradually take over several areas of your life. If you take procrastination seriously as a problem, you have the potential for far-reaching improvement. This improvement will save you from chronic dissatisfaction, lack of success, and possibly even mental illness.

At the beginning, as with a doctor's examination and diagnosis, apply the methods in this book and try to find the causes. Then you can initiate the right "*therapy*" with the respective concepts that are right for you. Then the therapy becomes much more than that. Because the more things you implement from this book, the more you learn to set priorities, reduce stress, gain greater self-confidence, optimize your social environment and generally make the right decisions in life.

Probably the most amazing lesson from this book, which you may even have already found yourself, is to be able to say *no* to a task. In this sense, it's not completely far-fetched that procrastination is not your real problem. Possibly the problem is that you're not completely eliminating the task from your agenda. That's a great lesson for you as you continue on your journey.

Learn to relax, let go, and slow down. By and large, people today, enjoy many options that didn't exist but a few decades ago, due to modern economic and technological advancements. Which is great as it creates more opportunities for you to live the life you dream of. Test these options out! And after you have tested, make a decision about what you need in life, what you want beyond your existential needs, and how much freedom is necessary for your physical as well as mental health.

Set an agenda that is realistic and that makes you want to live life and do the tasks that come with it. Then the likelihood that you will postpone things will decrease. If you do find yourself putting things off, you know what you need to do: either the cause lies within you, which you discover through honest inner dialogue, or it is happening because you have imposed too many tasks on yourself. Apply the appropriate measures with the help of this guide: If you are honest with yourself, then sooner or later you will always find the right solution to lead you to your goal.

I wish you good luck and much success with it!

List of sources

Achtnich, Leonie (2012), Prokrastination: Zehn Tipps zum Anfangen, in ZEIT Campus Nr. 4/2012 von https://www.zeit.de/campus/2012/04/prokrastination-tipps

Ammerlande, Andrea (2019), Beschäftigte leiden unter digitalem Stress, von https://www.springerprofessional.de/gesundheitspraevention/stressmanagement/deutsche-erwerbstaetige-plagt-digitaler-stress/16282378

Bühring, Petra (2010), Psychische Erkrankungen: Dramatische Zunahme – Kein Konzept, von https://www.aerzteblatt.de/archiv/78018/Psychische-Erkrankungen-Dramatische-Zunahme-kein-Konzept

Canfield, J.; Hansen, M. V.; Hewitt, L.: The Power of Focus – So erreichen Sie Ihre persönlichen, finanziellen und beruflichen Ziele. München: Redline Verlag, 2013. 1. Auflage.

Dr. med. Nonnenbacher (2019), Großhirnrinde, in MedLexi.de, von https://medlexi.de/Gro%C3%9Fhirnrinde

Eultgen, Simon (o.D.): Pomodoro Technik, effektives lernen leicht gemacht, von https://www.fernstudium-check.de/ratgeber/pomodoro-technik-effektives-lernen-leicht-gemacht

Gimpel, Lanzl, Manner-Romberg, Nüske (2018), Digitaler Stress in Deutschland – Eine Befragung, von Erwerbstätigen zu Belastung und Beanspruchung durch Arbeit mit digitalen Technologien von https://www.boeckler.de/pdf/p_fo-foe_WP_101_2018.pdf

Hauschild, J (2013), Beobachten, fühlen, entschuldigen, in Spiegel Psychologie, von https://www.spiegel.de/gesundheit/psychologie/achtsamkeit-kleine-schritte-zur-entschleunigung-a-890285.html

Jakob, N.& Dämon K. (2017), Was Kampfkunst über das Führen lehrt, von https://www.wiwo.de/erfolg/management/management-auch-fernoestliche-entspannungstechniken-helfen/19553278-2.html

Klaperski S. & Fuchs R. (2013), Effekte eines 12-wöchigen Sport- oder Entspannungsprogramms auf subjektive und physiologische Stressreaktionen, von https://www.sportwissenschaft.de/fileadmin/pdf/tagungen2013/2013_Klaperski_Effekte12Sport-Entspannungsprogamm.pdf

Kucklick, Christopher (o.D.), „Es gibt keinen Hinweis, dass ein Unterbewusstsein existiert", von https://www.geo.de/wissen/gesundheit/22098-rtkl-psychologie-es-gibt-keinen-hinweis-dass-ein-unterbewusstsein-existiert

Leadership insiders (2019), Technostress – eine Schattenseite der Digitalisierung?, von https://www.leadership-insiders.de/technostress-eine-schattenseite-der-digitalisierung/

Lern-Psychologie.de (o.D.), Soziale Lerntheorie: Lernen am Modell nach Albert Bandura von http://www.lern-psychologie.de/skripte/modelllernen.pdf

Leubner D. & Hinterberger T. (2017), Reviewing the Effectiveness of Music Interventions in Treating Depression, von https://www.ncbi.nlm.nih.gov/pmc/articles/PMC5500733/

Lexikon der Biologie (1999), Unterbewusstsein, von https://www.spektrum.de/lexikon/biologie/unterbewusstsein/68591

Lin, Huang, Shiu, Yeh (2015), Effects of Yoga on Stress, Stress Adaption, and Heart Rate Variability Among Mental Health Professionals--A Randomized Controlled Trial, von https://pubmed.ncbi.nlm.nih.gov/26220020/

Mende, Annette (2017), Placebo Effekt: Wirkung ohne Wirkstoff von https://www.pharmazeutische-zeitung.de/ausgabe-462017/placebo-effekt-wirkung-ohne-wirkstoff/

Moestl, B.: Shaolin – Du musst nicht kämpfen, um zu siegen!. München: Knaur Verlag, 2008.

Nier, Hedda (2019), Erhöht digitaler Stress das Krankheitsrisiko?, von https://de.statista.com/infografik/19229/digitaler-stress-im-job-erhoeht-krankheitsrisiko/

PsyGA (2018): Die psychische Gesundheit in Zahlen, von
   https://www.psyga.info/psychische-gesundheit/daten-,
   abgerufen: 23.2.2021fakten#:~:text=Psychische%20Er-
   krankungen%20nehmen%20in%20ihrer,Pro-
   zent%20(%20BKK%20Gesundheitsreport%202018)

SAGE Institut für Achtsamkeit und Gesundheit Berlin (o.D.),
   Die Wirkung von Musik auf Mensch und Gesundheit,
   von https://www.sage-institut.de/wirkung-musik-ge-
   sundheit/

Stangl, W. (2021). Stichwort: '*Selbstwirksamkeit*'. Online Lexikon
   für Psychologie und Pädagogik. https://lexi-
   kon.stangl.eu/1535/selbstwirksamkeit-selbstwirksam-
   keitserwartung/

Stangl, Werner (o.D.), Lernen am Modell – Albert Bandura von
   https://arbeitsblaetter.stangl-taller.at/LERNEN/Mo-
   delllernen.shtml

Statista Research Department (2013): „Verteilung der AU-Tage
   aufgrund psychischer und Verhaltensstörungen (F00-
   F99) in Deutschland nach ausgewählten Diagnosegrup-
   pen im Jahr 2013" von https://de.statista.com/statis-
   tik/daten/studie/189551/umfrage/krankenhaustage-
   aufgrund-psychischer-stoerungen-nach-diagnoseunter-
   gruppen/

Statista Research Department (2019): „Statistiken zu psychischen
   Erkrankungen" von https://de.statista.com/the-
   men/1318/psychische-erkrankungen/

Steel, Dr. P.: The Procrastination Equation: How to Stop Putting Things Off and Start Getting Stuff Done. Toronto: Random House Canada, 2012.

Stollreiter, M.: Schluss mit dem Aufschieben – Endlich anfangen zu leben. München: mvgVerlag, 2014.

Thakkar, N. (2009). Why procrastinate: an investigation of the root causes behind procrastination.

University of North Carolina at Chapel Hill (o.D.), Procrastination gefunden unter https://writingcenter.unc.edu/tips-and-tools/procrastination/

Von der Tann, Marie (2017), Wie Sport der Psyche hilft, in Spiegel Psychologie, von https://www.spiegel.de/gesundheit/psychologie/sport-gegen-stress-wie-bewegung-der-psyche-hilft-a-1173661.html

Zeug, Katrin (2013): Mach es anders!, in ZEIT Wissen Nr. 2/2013

www.ingramcontent.com/pod-product-compliance
Lightning Source LLC
Chambersburg PA
CBHW061130120626
46546CB00005B/1726